MOVING ON

ANTHONY EDWARDS

MOVING ON

A MEMOIR OF LIFE AT SEA

With 29 illustrations

Published by Singing Stone

Dedication

For Marjie, my soul mate, who helped me so much with this book.

AUTHOR'S NOTE

Any sailor will be only too pleased to talk about their adventures on boats. The good times can be indescribable – they need to be experienced and the bad times can be terrifying and are better not experienced!

We sailors have great respect for the sea and the weather, which are beyond our control but sometimes it's the craft itself that causes headaches. One such craft was the 'Passing Fancy', which caused so many headaches that I was compelled to write a book about it! That book was 'Paid to Live the Dream', and a lot of readers were curious as to what happened next. So here it is – what happened next, described in full momentous detail in 'Moving On'.

It would seem that it isn't possible to step foot on a boat without getting yourself into hot water! There are always problems lurking around every corner. If it isn't the weather it's the boat, or it could even be self-inflicted! After all you can't always make the right decisions. The boats in this book also contribute to the anguish and the mishaps, sometimes with devastating results, but more from neglect and lack of maintenance than through faulty design; the end results are the same though – extra hassles, extra work and more worries.

I have called it 'Moving On' because there is quite a lot of moving on involved in one way or another!

CONTENTS

LIST OF ILLUSTRATIONS

I WOULD LIKE TO THANK:

MARJIE EDWARDS, for her understanding, her patience and her invaluable assistance in the preparation for this book's publication. Without her contribution the book may never have been published.

CHRISTINA TURISSINI, for her incredible forensic proof reading!

"I really don't know why it is that all of us are so committed to the sea, except I think it's because in addition to the fact that the sea changes, and the light changes, and ships change, it's because we all came from the sea. And it is an interesting biological fact that all of us have in our veins the exact same percentage of salt in our blood that exists in the ocean, and, therefore, we have salt in our blood, in our sweat, in our tears. We are tied to the ocean. And when we go back to the sea – whether it is to sail or to watch it – we are going back to whence we came." - John F. Kennedy

Previously

'Paid to Live the Dream' ends with me sailing off the coast of the Côte d'Azur with my wife Jill and Twinkle, the tortoiseshell and white cat that we'd acquired in France and who'd spent three years sailing with us. We'd been working on yachts in the Mediterranean as Captain/Engineer and Cook/Deckhand and Twinkle just tagged along not doing very much other than looking cute and demanding attention. We'd taken command of a 70ft ketch in the spring of 1971 and had been based in the attractive old harbour of Cannes until the yacht was sold in the early spring of 1972. It had been a dream come true, sailing around the Mediterranean in a magnificent old, traditional sailing boat with red sails and getting paid a generous salary plus a percentage of all the charter fees. I had achieved everything I'd set out to do five years previously and was unbelievably happy. Whatever was needed to maintain the boat, the annual drydocking and antifouling, engineering works, laundry, daily, weekly or monthly supplies and virtually everything else was paid for out of the funds I received from the owner, which included our food allowance. To make sure that we kept going back to the same suppliers, it was usual for them to give the yacht Captains a commission of 10% as an incentive for us to continue using their services and there could be substantial amounts of money involved. I'd resisted accepting these offers when I arrived in the South of France because I'd considered it to be dishonest but gradually the temptation became too great. The rewards could be considerable and I could see that the Captains of other yachts were raking in large amounts of extra cash to supplement their already excellent salaries. I suspected that it may have encouraged some of them to create more work than was genuinely needed. The owner of the ketch knew about the commissions, accepted the fact that it was happening and even suggested to me that I give him half of what I received. I didn't agree to that but did make every effort to get him discounts whenever I could. However, accepting the 10% never felt right and Jill who was particularly uneasy about it reprimanded me.

"You're becoming just like the rest of them," she said and I had to agree with her. I stopped taking the commissions, which in fact, were nothing more than bribes.

The owner was a generous man and when the yacht was sold he gave us a percentage of the sale price and a salary increase backdated to the beginning of the season. So, although we were about to become unemployed, we felt wealthy and as there were still a few weeks before the skiing season ended, we rented an apartment in Valberg for two weeks.

Valberg is a ski resort at an altitude of 1700 metres located on the sunny side of a valley in the Maritime Alps. It was where Jill and I had first learned to ski and we had been regular visitors since. We flew Jill's aunt and grandma out from Southampton to join us for the holiday. We met them at Nice Airport and took them to the yacht to spend a few days in Cannes before setting off to the apartment with Twinkle, the experienced Seacat accompanying us. The holiday was enjoyed by everybody, even Twinkle. She coped well in the ice and deep snow and wandered off to explore on her own each day. Jill and I had become accomplished skiers and as the season was coming to an end, the pistes were largely free of the usual crowds so we had a fantastic time. Her aunt, a state registered nurse, and her grandma served as live-in carers for an elderly, disabled lady in Shirley, a suburb on the western side of Southampton. They were on call 24 hours a day with just a half-day of freedom each week. Between them, they did everything - the cleaning, the cooking, the laundry, the gardening and the nursing. Their work was demanding so to be free to enjoy a relaxing holiday in the mountains must have been overwhelming for them. At the end of the two weeks holiday when auntie and grandma returned to the U.K. Jill and I went back on board the boat with Twinkle for the final few weeks before we handed over command to the new owner and Captain.

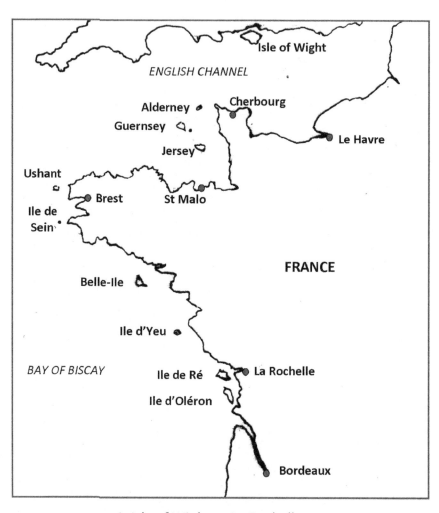

1. Isle of Wight to La Rochelle

CHAPTER 1
UPHEAVALS

We stood transfixed in horror as the angry crowd stormed down the hill towards us. We couldn't understand a word they were saying but their threatening behaviour, the uniforms and the pistols left us in no doubt that we were in trouble. My heart was racing as I realised that the buck stopped at me. They scrambled down the rocks and grabbed hold of our mooring ropes, pulled the boat towards them and leapt aboard onto the aft deck. Once they'd pocketed the wads of dollar bills that were offered them to go away and leave us alone, two of the policemen grabbed my arms, hauled me ashore and marched me up the hill to what I presumed would be the police station. How on earth did I get into this predicament? It really all began four years earlier.

The yacht in Paris

Before we left the ketch, we were offered the command of an 80ft motor yacht based on the River Seine at Choisy le Roi in the southeastern suburbs of Paris, ten kilometres from the city centre. We packed our belongings into our Citroën DS and drove there with Twinkle sitting on the back seat. The yacht was luxurious and it was great being back in the intoxicating city of Paris that I was already well familiar with. We drove into the city centre as often as possible and it was always a thrill to walk through the streets and stop off at a café for a drink. It didn't last long, however. We'd been sailing together since 1967 and Jill was tired of being constantly on the move with no permanence to our lives. She was from a very close family and longed to see more of them. Additionally, we discovered that we had been employed chiefly because the owner needed a qualified Captain to satisfy his insurance company. That in itself wasn't an issue; the problem was that he insisted on retaining his unqualified Captain as my crew member and it quickly became apparent that we were going to clash. So, it was after a great deal of reflection that we decided to leave the boat. We had been due to spend the summer season cruising Brittany and needed to depart before then. The decision was made easier for us because the previous Captain was still employed and on one of our previous visits to the U.K., we'd put down a deposit on a three bedroom detached house that was under construction and the completion date was only weeks away. We knew that in the meantime we would be able to stay with Jill's relatives whilst we waited to receive the keys, so three months after joining the yacht, we left and went back to the U.K.. That was when the heartaches began!

Whenever we'd visited England during our years away, we'd been annoyed at the officiousness of the British customs officers compared to those in other countries so I didn't want to take any chances when we returned with a cat. Before we left the yacht, I'd phoned the British Embassy to ask them to advise me on the correct procedure for taking a cat from France to the U.K.

"Oh, that won't be a problem," the woman at the embassy assured me, "If you just make sure that you declare it on arrival, the customs officer will tell you what needs to be done."

"Oh is it as simple as that?" I asked.

"Oh yes, they will tell you who to contact so that you can arrange to put the cat into quarantine."

"That all sounds straightforward enough," I said to Jill after I'd hung up. In our ignorance, we foolishly believed that the information we'd been given was correct. After all, isn't that one of the purposes of the embassy? When we arrived at the Southampton cross-channel ferry port with the Citroën loaded with our belongings, Twinkle was sitting innocently on the back seat. I drove up to the immigration control area and stopped at the "To Declare" spot.

"What do you have to declare?" we were asked.

"We have a cat that we understand will have to go into quarantine," I told him.

"Do you have the paperwork?"

"What paperwork? We were told that it would all be done here." I went into a full explanation of my conversation with the embassy employee. He stared at us and said,

"You'd better wait here." He disappeared. After a long wait, he returned and gave us a lecture on how we'd broken the law, before saying "So you haven't made any arrangements for putting the cat into quarantine?"

"No, we didn't know we had to do it beforehand."

"Well, you can't leave here with the cat," he said.

"What are you suggesting we do then? We've done exactly what we were told to do by the embassy," I told him with rising fear of what might happen. It seemed that we had been falsely advised by the very people who were supposed to know the rules.

"I'm going to have to make some calls. You pull over there and wait and keep the cat where it is," he replied. It was very early in the morning and we were tired, having driven from Paris to Le Havre the day before and hadn't slept much on the overnight ferry. It was also bitterly cold. Two hours later, a most unpleasant individual approached us and lectured us again on the law. He was a tall, well-built man wearing a scruffy tweed jacket and had unruly mousey-coloured hair atop a round, unshaven face. His watery blue eyes with bags under them conveyed his fury at having been called out so early in the morning. When he'd finished berating us, he told us the only option would be for us to find somewhere to put the cat into quarantine, explaining that it would be unlikely that we'd find a vacancy anywhere at such short notice. We hadn't a clue who to call or what to do and he didn't offer any suggestions, despite our obvious distress. He did make a reluctant gesture eventually and gave us a couple of phone numbers to call and he was correct in his assumption that we would be unsuccessful. By late morning with nothing resolved, I was getting worried and irritated.

"What are we supposed to do now? I did what I thought was the correct thing before coming here and did exactly what the person at the embassy told me to do," I said.

"We'll have to put the cat down," he told us. That was when I exploded! I'm not an aggressive person and I detest any sort of confrontation but to have been placed in that situation through no fault of my own and for him to tell Jill and me that he was going to put our cat down was the final straw.

3

"You bloody well won't, you're not getting anywhere near that cat." I glared at him menacingly. For a few silent moments, there was a tense standoff as we stared at each other. He couldn't fail to see the fierce determination and anger in my eyes. He turned and walked away, leaving us standing there in the cold. After about thirty minutes he came back and gave us another number to ring in Bracknell and we had success. Yes, we were assured, they could take the cat. After the arrangements had been finalised, Twinkle was taken from us and placed in a cage. Her little, furry face looked pleadingly at us through the bars and she was miaowing. It brought a lump to my throat. She didn't understand what was happening or why we'd abandoned her. Jill did not succeed in holding back her tears. Twinkle had been taken away from us to begin her six-month sentence in isolation and we were allowed to leave. What a welcome to the U.K!

We settled into the house we'd bought on one of our visits to the U.K.; it was in Midanbury, a suburb of Southampton, and was not too far from Port Hamble, where I found employment working for a well-known yacht agency. Initially, I maintained the new boats that were for sale and took prospective purchasers out on demonstration sails, putting the boats through their paces. The hope was that they would be so impressed that they would finalise a sale. I was also occasionally asked to go to Cherbourg or La Rochelle in France to sail the new boats back to Port Hamble so that we could display and demonstrate them. It was a far cry from being the Captain of a luxury yacht in the Mediterranean but it was what Jill wanted and at least I was out in the open air and messing about on boats. Jill saw an advertisement for a hostess in an upmarket hotel/restaurant in Southampton city centre but felt that she was too inexperienced and incapable of holding on to such a position. I convinced her to go for it. She got the job and made a success of it, but I paid a terrible price for encouraging her to do so.

Whilst Twinkle was serving her six months in quarantine, we made the 200-mile round trip almost every Saturday to visit her in Bracknell. We took her favourite biscuits and other treats and as we walked towards her cell, I'd whistle a sound that she knew and she'd be there to greet us with her tail up in the air, pacing backwards and forwards in her confined space, miaowing. We sat with her for as long as we possibly could, cuddling her so that she wouldn't forget us and feel forsaken until the painful parting happened all over again.

It wasn't long before I was summoned to appear in court to face charges of importing an animal illegally. I hired a lawyer even though it is not a profession that I look upon with much respect. In front of the magistrate, I pleaded my innocence. When I explained what I was told by the embassy staff, the prosecutor said: "That is only hearsay". I seethed at the injustice of it all. I was fined £60. I refused to pay it and eventually was threatened with a prison term if I didn't pay up.

"That's OK with me, they can do what they like but I'm not paying. I did what I thought was right because that's what I was told to do. If I have to go to prison so be it, but I'm not paying," I told Jill. I was adamant. Two days later, Jill had persuaded me that it would be better for everybody concerned if I paid. I deeply resented the fact that I'd been given false information and in effect been accused of lying and had been judged and sentenced by a magistrate, a volunteer with no formal legal training. I made several phone calls questioning the whole process to no avail. Martin Luther King said, *"Injustice anywhere is a threat to justice everywhere,"* and my experiences with the legal systems of both France and the U.K. have convinced me that there is no justice in the courts. It was a brutal introduction to the U.K.

How bad can it get?

I was asked by the yacht agency to go to Cherbourg and sail a new 27ft sailboat from there to Port Hamble where we would put it up for sale. I preferred not to sail single-handed so asked Jill to join me. She refused. She didn't want to set foot on a yacht again after our years sailing together. The following day, we drove to Southampton to do some shopping and were having a heated exchange about the forthcoming delivery trip.

A loud, sickening bang stunned us. Our bodies jerked sideways as our car spun around. Another car had crashed into us. The impact sent us reeling around at a 90" angle.

Because I'd concentrated more on our argument than on driving, I'd pulled out into the main road from our side road without looking. Dazed and shaking, Jill and I got out to meet the other driver. He left his car and walked over to us. He seemed unperturbed considering what had happened.

"Should we call the police?" I asked him.

"I am the police," he replied and then he went off, made a phone call and came back to wait for the arrival of his colleagues. After introductions, it turned out that he was a detective in the Southampton police force. He asked why we were driving a French car and I told him, then unburdened myself of all the misery we'd endured since we'd come back to the U.K. - the cat saga, the court case, the fine, the problems we'd had with the house and so on, with the accident we'd just had being the final straw - not realizing then that there were more final straws to come. When the police arrived they took details and advised him to press charges against me.

"No," he said, "I couldn't do that after all that he's just been telling me." His colleague insisted that charges be brought against me but thankfully he insisted equally that he wouldn't do so. Both his Rover and our Citroën were beyond repair. If he was upset, he didn't show it. We'd had a lucky escape considering that he'd had his Rover for many years and was very attached to it. I began to wonder if we'd done the right thing in returning to the U.K.

Two days later, I took the cross-channel ferry to Cherbourg with one of our friends, Ian, who had agreed to crew for me. I took a compass, a handheld, battery-operated direction finder, radar reflector, portable fog horn, oilskins, charts, navigation equipment, lifejackets, safety harnesses, sleeping bags, cooking utensils and anything else that I thought we would need. All of this was available from our chandlery and I kept the complete delivery kit in one of our stores when not in use so that it would always be ready for my next delivery. On arrival at Cherbourg, we located the yacht and installed ourselves, making it as comfortable as we could and spent the rest of the day, taking on fuel and water, shopping for food, stepping the mast and setting up the rigging ready to set sail the next day. In the evening, we rewarded ourselves with a huge *plateau de fruits de mer*, (seafood, generally shellfish, mostly raw) in one of the restaurants, accompanied by copious amounts of wine. One of the most enjoyable moments of my trips to France was always the seafood restaurants, made even more enjoyable knowing that the yacht agency was footing the bill - and Ian didn't complain either. The wind had been increasing in strength throughout the day and during the night had developed into a full gale. The next morning, after an unsettled night because of the noise of the wind howling and the rigging of the yachts clanging against the masts, I had doubts about setting off, especially as the forecast was for the wind to continue, but I was eager to get home to Jill so we cast off. It was a mistake.

As soon as we'd cleared the harbour entrance, I realised I'd been right to doubt the wisdom of attempting the voyage. We battled on, ploughing and crashing our way through the waves, which got more vicious the further out to sea we went. After having suffered a good battering by the wind and sea and getting soaked from the spray and the water crashing over the bows, we'd made such little progress that I decided to return to harbour and wait for better weather. I'd never forgotten a foolish decision, under duress from some American charterers, to leave the harbour of Cannes and head to Corsica in a Mistral. The subsequent twelve-hour journey was horrendous. It could so easily have ended badly and I'd vowed to be more cautious in future. So we did an about-turn and sailed or rather crashed our way back to Cherbourg. I was no stranger to sailing in gales; when the wind increases whilst you're out at sea you have no choice but it didn't make sense to me at that time to continue with the forecast of the gale to continue. At the approach to the harbour, I started the engine and Ian dropped and stowed the sails as I motored back to the mooring. That evening we forced ourselves to eat another *plateau de fruits de mer* in the same restaurant that we'd eaten in the night before and drank a bottle of Pouilly Fumé. Despite the howling wind, we slept well that night, snuggled up in our cosy sleeping bags.

The well-protected harbour of Cherbourg is located on the northern tip of the Cotentin Peninsula in Northwestern France. It is the world's largest artificial harbour after the port of Ras Laffan in Qatar. It is a military base, a fishing port, a yacht harbour, a cross-channel ferry terminal and a port of call for commercial shipping. We stayed there another day and when the wind finally died down completely, fog set in. In some ways, the fog was worse. The English Channel is 112 miles across from the Scilly Isles to Ushant and it narrows to just 12 miles across. 500 ships a day pass through it on the Atlantic/North Sea route and the U.K./Europe route making it the busiest shipping lane in the world. To help avoid collisions, traffic separation schemes have been defined and sailing from Cherbourg to Hamble involves crossing those shipping lanes at right angles to complete the 88 nautical mile voyage. Remaining alert is critical at the best of times because many of the ships don't see smaller yachts, sometimes passing dangerously close and forcing the yacht to take avoiding action.

With a maximum speed of 6 knots, I reckoned it would take us 14 hours to reach our destination. I plotted a course to take us to the Bridge buoy at the approach of the Needles Channel from where we could continue on to Port Hamble. When that was done, I started the engine, Ian hoisted the radar reflector and cast off the mooring lines and in our oilskins, we motored out of the harbour into the dense, damp, cold fog. Sitting in the cockpit clutching the tiller, with zero visibility and with ships passing all around us, it was unnerving, even scary at times. We heard the thrashing of propellers and the thumping of engines as large ships and cross-channel ferries made their way, sometimes perilously close to us. One ship sounded as if it was heading straight for us and we feared the worst. We saw nothing. Ian rushed into the cabin, grabbed the foghorn, scrambled back to the cockpit, pointed the horn in the direction of the alarmingly close ship and squeezed the trigger. It emitted a pathetic little wet fart like noise, which could never have been heard on the bridge of whatever monstrous ship was about to cut us in two. Ian squeezed the trigger repeatedly but nothing more than a dribbling burp emanated from the nozzle. We were on standby for a collision. We could see nothing and I wasn't sure which way to turn the tiller. We waited, listening, straining our eyes in the hope that we would see something. The thrashing of the propellers continued. Time stood still. We gave a huge sigh of relief when the churning sound started to recede into the distance and we knew that we'd survived. We released the tension by laughing at the ineffectual noises that came from the foghorn. Although we never once saw another ship, we knew they were occasionally far too close for comfort. In fact, we saw nothing at all until the Bridge buoy loomed out of the fog just ahead of us.

It was with a tremendous feeling of relief that we arrived safely at the exact spot that I'd set a course for, which impressed Ian so much that he vowed to always leap at any future opportunity to sail with such a skilful navigator! I didn't let on that I was as surprised as he was when that buoy appeared on our port bow! Tired from the constant strain of peering into the dense fog for hours on end, we were glad when it was all over and we'd arrived in one piece at Port Hamble. *"Captain my Captain! Our fearful trip is done. The ship has weathered every rack, the prize we sought is won." Walt Whitman.*

Rock bottom

When the thunderbolt came, it was a devastating shock. Jill told me she'd met someone else and wanted a divorce. She and I had been together twenty-four hours a day on the yachts but back in England, working apart, with both our jobs involving unsociable hours, we saw much less of each other and she had fallen in love with a staff member at the hotel. I was shattered beyond belief, even though I'd suspected that she was cheating on me. Alarm bells began to ring when I noticed that her attitude towards me had changed and she started coming home smelling of aftershave lotion; whenever I'd made any references to it she'd denied that anything was going on. Jill had always been a kind, honest, compassionate and thoughtful person and it was partly those attributes that had attracted me to her. It seems, however, that such qualities no longer applied where I was concerned and it was a bombshell to learn that she was capable of lies and deceit. To rub salt in the wound, she accused me of having an affair with one of the secretaries.

It's true that I'd had ample opportunity but was shocked and hurt to hear her unfounded accusation nevertheless. I suppose it made her feel better about what she had done. Cheats often accuse the innocent victims in an attempt to make themselves feel better about their betrayal. It is an attempt to bolster their self-worth that will have been devalued by their duplicity. To say I was utterly devastated is vastly understating it. My whole world had fallen apart and an assortment of different emotions swirled around in my head. Disbelief, anger, sorrow, shock, despondency and other painful feelings which didn't even have a name caused turmoil in my brain. I'd lost not only the wife that I loved but also what I had thought was my best friend. It felt as though I'd been hit in the stomach with a sledgehammer and a knife had been plunged into my heart and sliced it to ribbons. The pain and anguish were made much more intense because my persecutor was the one person in the world that I thought would never harm me. Mineko Iwasaki,

Japan's most famous geisha said, *"Stab the body and it heals, but injure the heart and the wound lasts a lifetime."*

My parents had been locked in an unhappy marriage but there was never any question of divorce. Such a thing was rare in working-class society, as family and the wider circle of friends and acquaintances would have been shocked and scandalised and the resulting upheaval too expensive. In 1969, a divorce reform act was passed which came into force in 1971. It made divorce easier; if neither of them contested it, couples could divorce after 2 years of separation without having to go to court. Divorce rates consequently increased and people were no longer trapped in marriages which were miserable and debilitating and were able to start again. In the wide world of human relationships feelings can change, and it was cruel to expect people to endure a life of unhappiness devoid of love and affection as was the case with my parents. However, the new laws could not take away the heart wrenching, stomach-turning, devastating trauma of those who were going through the process and even if it had been possible, I do not believe my parents would have been prepared to break their marriage vows. My sister Val is still married to her husband of more than 50 years and it would not occur to either of them to break the vows they had made. The vows I had made were sacred to me too, which may seem a little old fashioned these days. I'm not suggesting that my family was a paragon of virtue, far from it; however, it is an intriguing observation that Jill's parents were divorced, as was her brother, her uncle and her cousin who all lived together on a converted motor torpedo boat and finally Jill herself, who some years later left and divorced her second husband, the person with whom she'd betrayed me. I fully accept, nevertheless, that my own behaviour or the situation at the time may have been a contributing factor to Jill's act of betrayal although I was unaware of there being any unhappiness. After her groundless accusation, I thought about all the opportunities I'd had to be unfaithful myself and each time it had never once occurred to me to break my marriage vows. Ah well, such is life, when one door closes, another opens!

I'd hoped that we would be able to come to an amicable arrangement but once again I had to deal with members of my most despised profession, lawyers, and once they were involved all hope of an amicable settlement was sabotaged. Hate is a horrible word that I have excluded from my vocabulary for the past forty years but I could be tempted to make an exception when it comes to lawyers. It is sometimes said that the bible tells us to "Hate the sin but not the sinner," in fact, this quote comes from the autobiography of Mohandas Gandhi and I have to say that its application where lawyers are concerned presents me with a challenge. My dealings with them over the years in the U.K and in France have led me to despise everything about the profession. I loathe their callous ruthlessness, the despicable way that they lie and attack and destroy the lives of innocent victims for the sake of money and false glory, knowing full well that they are preventing or even perverting what little justice there could be by making a mockery of the law. These offensive predators are intent on robbing people of everything they can, whilst they can and are responsible for me having lost all respect for the Injustice System, (it doesn't merit the term Justice in my view.) I've never had justice and know many other unfortunate people who have had similar experiences. The French author, Gabriel Chevallier, best known for his novel Clochemerle, said of lawyers, _"The law, as manipulated by clever and highly respected rascals, still remains the best avenue for a career of honourable and leisurely plunder."_ I think that is being overly charitable. I'm sure that there may be one or two who don't fit the mould that I've created for them but if so, I've yet to have the good fortune to meet one. When the conniving rogues that Jill and I had paid had finished their devious manoeuvrings, I finished up stuck with the repayment of the mortgage on the house and the loan on the car. I also had custody of Twinkle the cat. In his book The Godfather, Mario Puzo says, _"A lawyer with his briefcase can steal more than a hundred men with guns."_

CHAPTER 2
FREEDOM

Moving on

Once I'd come to terms with the divorce I felt an immense feeling of freedom. I was able to do anything I wanted, whenever, however, wherever and with whom I wanted. I was a free spirit once more. There were two choices available to me; to continue being sorrowful or angry, in which case the only person who would have suffered would have been myself, or look upon it as an exciting new beginning and get on with my life. The decision was easy. Somebody once said, *"Holding onto anger is like drinking poison and expecting the other person to die."* Our emotions are indeed by far the most powerful creator of dis-ease in the body. Every emotion has a biochemical and subsequent physical reaction in the body, so my life rule is to attempt to dispel negativity and focus on positivity, forgiveness and love, not always with success! When the harrowing trauma was over, I eventually emerged a stronger and wiser person and these days, Jill and I are once more on friendly terms.

The house was put up for sale and I took advantage of my liberty. I joined a Buddhist group and went to regular weekly meetings to expand my knowledge and awareness and learned to meditate. Throughout my life I have studied different philosophies and religions in my search for an understanding of the universe, its purpose and my part in it. I have always had an interest in consciousness and all things esoteric - in particular the origin and meaning of dreams, a subject that I went on to study in great detail. My freedom enabled me to concentrate on improving my cooking skills and to go to pubs, jazz clubs and dances but I lacked the confidence to ask girls to dance so I enrolled for evening classes at a local dance school. Jill and I had taken dancing lessons when we were together and I'd enjoyed learning the correct steps for ballroom and Latin-American dances. The variety of activities gave me the opportunity to meet lots of interesting people and I began dating. I even began to enjoy my work. There was a major disruption at the Yacht Agency, however, in the form of the new boat sales manager, the most unlikeable person I have ever encountered in all my years on this planet. He was an overweight, married man who was one of the two salesmen at the Port Hamble office; the other being the brokerage manager. The sole aim of this person, Tom, seemed to be to upset as many people as possible during the day. He would sometimes come into the office with a sickly, malicious grin on his face and say something like "I've really managed to drop …….. in the shit," bragging as if he'd accomplished something deserving praise. Unfortunately, even animals were not spared from his spiteful behaviour. I was pleased when one day he got his comeuppance. His wife discovered a devious plan he'd had to seduce one of our very pretty secretaries. He'd invited her to a private function that he had tickets for but was stupid enough to leave the invitations where his wife could see them.

As time went on, an office manager was employed and he very soon became aware of how disruptive this unpleasant character was. Every other person in the building disliked him and wasted no time in making their feelings known to the new manager. He came to the conclusion that he had no other choice than to send a letter to the two partners in the London office with a copy to the nasty individual who had been causing so much trouble. Everyone in the office who had complained saw the letter and we were all delighted to learn that Tom was demoted to assistant to the friendly gentleman who was in charge of the brokerage section and I was promoted to New Boat Sales Manager. One phrase in the letter was especially harsh; it read, "If you don't like it, get out". Why he stayed after that is hard to understand. Another person was employed to maintain the boats that we kept afloat and after that, the office atmosphere improved. We still had to suffer the presence of Tom but with the new manager, the days became full of fun and harmony. I had my own office next to Tom and I often saw him glowering at me through the glass partition, especially when two or three of the secretaries would come in and chat and sometimes sit on my desk as we laughed and joked and flirted with each other. I wonder what had happened in Tom's past or what was going on at the time that made him so disagreeable and unliked by others.

Looking up

I was in a fortunate position, being able to intersperse my office duties with sailing. The demonstration sails on boats, occasional deliveries from Cherbourg or La Rochelle to Port Hamble and assisting purchasers to sail their yachts from Port Hamble to their home ports in the U.K. were always something I looked forward to. There were times when I was too busy to leave the office for extended periods so we employed a local road haulage company or professional yacht delivery crews to bring boats from France as well. Sometimes after a sale had taken place, I would be invited to accompany the new owners on expenses paid holidays to teach them to sail but the best trips of all were when I accompanied them to sail their yachts back from La Rochelle. They were pleasurable voyages because we called in at different harbours along the way, visiting delightful places like Les Sables d'Olonne, Belle Ile, L'ile d'Yeu, Benodet, Camaret-Sur-Mer and the Channel Islands. It was even better when Ian and I did a delivery together and ensured that we profited from the occasion as much as possible! I also took our boats on rallies so that various yachting magazines could write articles about them. Sometimes I flew in our company plane to the factory in La Rochelle where the yachts were made. There I learned about the construction techniques from the beginning to the end of the production line and was introduced to prototypes. I came to know the town and environs well and got to know one of the female factory office staff intimately, which was an added bonus!

La Rochelle is situated in Southwestern France in the treacherous Bay of Biscay. It was established in the 10th century although the area had been inhabited previously by the Romans who produced salt and wine there. It became an important harbour in the 12th century and the Knights Templar had a presence there. It was their largest base on the Atlantic Ocean and was where they kept their biggest fleet of ships. From 1154 until 1224 it was ruled by King Henry II until it was captured by Louis VIII in the siege of La Rochelle. During the 100 years' war, it came under English control again and was ruled by Edward III. Some years later a united force of French and Spanish expelled them. The French lay siege to the town and the king of Castille dispatched warships that were manned by some of the first seamen known to have employed handguns on a ship. Although Edward III sent an English convoy, in the subsequent naval battle, the English were defeated and La Rochelle then became the largest French harbour on the Atlantic coast. It remained so until the 15th century.

The French Protestants, called Huguenots, were based there in the 16th century during the French Wars of Religion when throughout France an estimated 3,000,000 people perished. In 1568, the city declared itself an independent Reformed Republic, which caused conflict with the Catholic central government that responded with a military assault in 1572. It ended with the signing of the Peace of La Rochelle in 1573. When the Huguenots rebelled again in 1622 and once more in 1625, Louis XIII and his chief minister Cardinal Richelieu resolved to end the unrest. The English, in support of La Rochelle, dispatched an expedition under George Villiers, the Duke of Buckingham and thus began an Anglo/French war between the two kingdoms. Buckingham's forces attacked the Ile de Ré in an attempt to control the approaches to La Rochelle and encourage rebellion in the city but were defeated and withdrew. Cardinal Richelieu besieged the city for 14 months until it surrendered. What took place during the Seige of La Rochelle forms part of the plot in the Alexandre Dumas novel, "The Three Musketeers."

During WWII, La Rochelle was the last French city to be liberated. The allied siege began on 12th September 1944 and continued until the Germans, who had a submarine naval base there, surrendered on 7th May 1945. The French troops entered on the following day. The submarine base was used as the setting for parts of the 1981 classic German war film, Das Boot and also for the U boat scenes in Stephen Spielberg's 1981 film, Raiders of the Lost Ark when Indiana Jones held on to the side of a Nazi submarine to hitch a ride to a hidden island base. The deep-water harbour is protected from the huge Atlantic swells by a natural barrier formed by the three offshore islands, Ile de Ré, Ile d'Oléron and Ile d'Aix. It has become a major attraction for yachts and when I was there in the early 1970s, a marina was under construction. The city of La Rochelle is an attractive place with numerous historical monuments and my trips there were considerably enhanced by frequent visits to the excellent seafood restaurants.

The numerous delivery trips I made from La Rochelle to Port Hamble in various sized yachts - from 27ft sloops to 40ft ketches - were sometimes pleasant but were often hair-raising in the violent winds and huge seas. The yachts were produced by the hugely successful Michel Dufour SA. By the time I became involved, their 15,000 square metre factory was manufacturing 300 yachts a year. They were modern, polyester, fin and skeg vessels that I had never sailed until I joined the agency. (a skeg is like a miniature fin keel to which the rudder is attached.) All of my previous experiences had been aboard long keel vessels. The traditional long keels are generally considered more stable but have more drag so typically need more sail area than the more manoeuvrable and faster fin keels. There are advantages and disadvantages for each but the modern fin and skeg arrangements are now predominantly the most popular. The yachts came straight from the factory floor, there were no navigation instruments fitted, nothing, in fact, just the basic boat. I had to take everything I needed from England so out would come my personal delivery kit. With a crew member to assist me, I would take the overnight ferry to Le Havre, where I'd hire a car and drive to La Rochelle, which could be done in a day unless Ian was with me, then it became more of a fun filled holiday! With Ian, we once didn't even get to leave Le Havre until the afternoon because we spent too much time in a restaurant having lunch. In our defence, we were delayed because there was no hire car available when we first arrived, so had to wait until the end of the morning for one to become available. When we did leave, we were so late that we didn't get very far before we booked into a hotel for the night and another meal.

What a life!

It always felt good to be in La Rochelle knowing that I would soon be enjoying the delicious seafood on offer and looking forward to another sea voyage. The yachts were delivered from the factory to the marina and I'd arrange to have the masts stepped so that I could set the rigging and prepare for sea. I attached the compass somewhere convenient so that it was easily visible; usually, I screwed it onto the lower washboard, (washboards are a series of removable boards that slot into grooves on each side of the companionway to prevent water entering the saloon from the cockpit). When everything was ready to go after a day or two, I'd cast off. It wasn't always plain sailing. The navigation skills required to negotiate the passages through the Raz de Sein and the Channel du Four can be demanding for even the most experienced sailor. The Raz de Sein, (Raz means 'race', referring to the fast flowing, hazardous current and eddies that form through the narrow passage), saved hours of extra sailing by eliminating the need to sail an extra 30 miles out to sea to avoid an extended reef, known as the Chaussée de Sein, which runs in a westerly direction from the Ile de Sein. The Ile de Sein is a small, treeless, S-shaped island only two kilometres long, barely above sea level and prone to flooding so the inhabitants live around the port area. On 18th June 1940, after General de Gaulle called upon the French to join the resistance, the entire male population of the island, totalling 130 men between the ages of 14–60, set sail for Britain in their fishing boats to join the Free French Forces. In recognition of exceptional courage, the island is now WWII's most decorated French commune, having received the *Ordre de Liberation,* the second highest

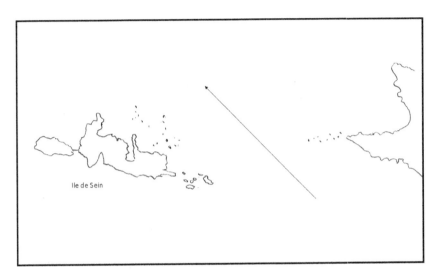

2.The Raz de Sein

honour after the *Légion d'Honneur,* as well as the *Croix de Guerre* and the *Médaille de la Résistance,* The residents were also exempted from income tax; a privilege existing to this day.

The passage through the Raz de Sein can only be attempted at certain states of the tide and in good weather conditions because of the violent seas, strong currents and numerous rocks and many ships have foundered in its perilous waters. After passing through the Raz, I then had to navigate one of the most dangerous seas in Europe, the Iroise Sea, which extends from the Chaussée de Sein to Ushant and the Moléne archipelago. It is part of the Celtic Sea, which extends from southern Ireland to the Bay of Biscay, itself a subdivision of the Atlantic Ocean. The Iroise Sea has an abundance of marine life. It was designated as France's first Marine Park and is one of UNESCO's biosphere reserves. It has more than 120 varieties of fish, accounting for one quarter of the marine mammals off the French coast. The winter storms there - and I write from experience - can be disastrous, with enormous waves and vicious winds. To help negotiate the multitude of dangers, the whole area from the Ile de Sein to Ushant has more lighthouses, beacons and buoys than any other maritime area of France. Another troublesome thing to watch for are fishing nets that can be difficult to see at night. On one delivery trip on a 30ft yacht along with the customer that I'd sold it to, I was off watch and sleeping, having left him to steer the course I'd set. It was a pitch dark night and we were sailing comfortably in a stiff breeze under mainsail and genoa.

"Tony, you'd better come up here, I don't know what's happening," he cried. I leapt out of bed expecting the worst and rushed to the cockpit bleary-eyed. I saw that the sails were still full of wind and we appeared to be sailing. I stood for a moment wondering why he'd called me before I realised that we weren't actually moving through the water as we should have been and then it clicked, we were snagged on a fishing net that had become entangled on the skeg. It took some time before we managed to free it using the boat hook, which was only just long enough to reach below the skeg. How fortunate that the owner had bought one before we left La Rochelle!

The next potential danger was the Channel du Four, a winding channel between Ushant and the other outlying islands and the coast. The passage has innumerable rocks both above and below sea level and the currents can be violent, as much as ten knots with huge swells. It is where the northwesternmost part of France juts out into the Atlantic Ocean and links the Iroise Sea to the English Channel. Vast volumes of water surge among the abundant channels between the islands and rocks and constant alertness is necessary to avoid the many dangers, hidden and otherwise and like the Raz de Sein, the passage can only be taken at certain states of the tide. Thankfully, there are a large number of lighthouses, lightships, buoys, beacons, turrets, and other natural and man-made land markers to aid navigation. Before 1825, there were very few markers and the passage would only be taken in daylight but nowadays it's safer, although still disconcerting because of the eddies and overfalls crashing around the underwater rocks. If that isn't enough to instil extreme caution, it is worth noting the words of an old Breton proverb that says, *"Qui voit Molène voit sa peine / Qui voit Ouessant, voit son sang / Qui voit Sein voit son fin."* - He who sees Molène sees his pain / He who sees Ushant sees his blood / He who sees Sein sees his end. (Molène is an island that lies 15 kilometres west of Finistère and 12 kilometres east of Ushant. It is the largest of the twenty or so islands forming the Molène archipelago and is inhabited on the eastern side by just 150 people.)

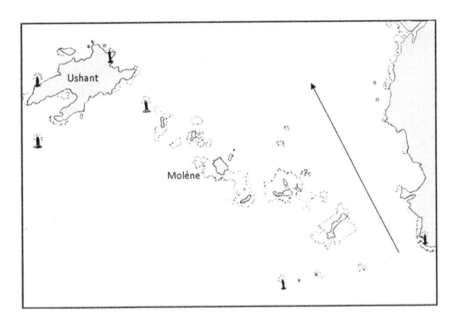

3. The Chenal du Four

My worst experience in the Channel du Four was at the end of March 1972. I had collected a 40ft ketch from La Rochelle and had a time limit to get back to the U.K. because the British government had introduced VAT on yachts entering the country after 1st April. In normal circumstances, I would have waited before entering the channel but the need to arrive before the deadline was the predominant factor because the yacht had been sold on the condition that VAT would not be applicable. It was a scary passage. There was a dark, menacing sky and a brisk wind blew against the strong tide, creating a vicious sea. In the exposed cockpit, the water being blown into my face felt like icy cold, sharp needles, which hampered my visibility. The yacht's bow rose high on the waves before it plunged downwards to disappear under the waves and then rose up like a submarine surfacing, sending volumes of water gushing along the decks. The crew member I had with me looked terrified at times and I pretended that what was happening was perfectly normal. The short passage seemed to last forever and I was pleased and relieved when we made our way into the English Channel. I wouldn't want another trip like that one! Once through the Channel du Four, the journeys in the English channel to Hamble were usually fairly easy by comparison although Ian and I once had a white-knuckle sail with a strong northwesterly wind howling on our stern. Whilst one of us was on the tiller, the other snuggled up in a sleeping bag as we raced along through the night but we soon came to when it was time to change watch. After crawling out of the sleeping bag, we were hit by a blast of cold air and a faceful of saltwater spray when we reached the cockpit. We creamed home at a breathtaking pace, arriving tired and caked in salt.

The boat shows at Earls Court, Southampton and Plymouth were essential activities for the agency. They were tiring but good opportunities to meet people and in the evenings when we were free to enjoy ourselves we played as hard as we worked, if not harder, especially at Earls Court where I met up with past and prospective purchasers. We had our own bar for entertaining, where the booze flowed freely. A past customer who'd paid for me to spend a week's holiday with him to teach him to sail came along one day and suggested that we go to a restaurant and then on to a club in the evening. He said he would pay for everything if I could arrange for three of the girls manning our stands to accompany the two of us and his friend. What a night we had. We met for aperitifs in the five star Churchill Hotel before going on to a restaurant that was out of this world, with the most beautifully prepared meal that included flowers on the plate. Then on to a club at the Hilton hotel. We danced, laughed and had a wonderful time and I became very attracted to the beautiful, long-haired girl that was my date for the night and who was constantly calling for glasses of pink champagne – I was glad I wasn't paying the bill! In the early hours of the morning when it was time to leave and the bill was brought to our host, his face drained of colour as he stared at it in horror. The expression on his face is something that I've never forgotten; I thought he was going to collapse. It must have been an astronomical amount even for him. But the memory of that night still remains with me.

During the Earls Court Boat Show of 1973 on 5th January, a message came over the public address system telling us to evacuate the building. We suspected that a bomb threat had been received from the IRA and we were right. The evacuation was orderly but we had no time to search for our coats so we huddled outside in the biting cold trying to keep warm; then we heard the explosion. There were no fatalities but a number of boats were damaged. It was the second of two bombs that exploded that day, the other being at Madame Tussauds. They were the first IRA bombs of that year. The rest of the year saw an additional 18 bombs planted, injuring 147 people and killing four guiltless bystanders, massacred by the IRA who didn't care if innocent people and young children were blasted to smithereens in the process. Their reign of terror continued unabated until the signing of the Belfast agreement in 1999. After that, dissident groups that opposed the agreement still continued their terrorist activities.

CHAPTER 3
EASTENDERS

Selling Sailing

Seated in my office, I received a phone call one day from a gentleman who said he was interested in having a demonstration on one of our 30ft sailboats, the Arpège. He eventually played a significant role in my life and we remained friends for many years.

"I'll be bringin' me wife wiv me," he said in his cockney accent, "she's very nervous cos she ain't sailed before so will yer try to keep the boat upright as much as possible?"

"Yes, of course, I'll do my best," I assured him and we arranged a date for the sail to take place.

They arrived on a Saturday morning and I was the only person in the office, which was on the first floor of the building, with our chandlery being situated on the ground floor. A force 8 gale was forecast and the wind was already strong with a light drizzle falling. They came into my office disappointed. He was a tall, well-built fellow with curly ginger hair, a rather large nose, a ruddy complexion and grey/blue eyes behind tortoiseshell glasses. His wife was an attractive woman with long raven hair, dark eyes, in smart casual wear and made up with eyeshadow and liner, lipstick and all that goes with it. Not quite what I was expecting of someone who was about to go sailing.

"Oh, whadda piddy the wevers so bad," he said after we'd shaken hands and introduced ourselves. "Now we won't be able to go out."

"Why not?" I asked.

"Well, we can't go out in this awful weather, it'll be too rough won't it?" he asked.

"It might be a bit rough but we'll be OK. I'm more than happy to take you out if you think your wife will be alright with it." I told him. They looked at each other, wondering what to do, then they looked out of the window at the black sky, the drizzle and the moored yachts moving in the wind, neither of them speaking. He turned to her and said, "What do you think love?" She shuffled around nervously, looked out of the window again and then looked at her husband and then looked at me.

"Are you sure it will be alright?" she asked, hoping for reassurance.

"Yes, we'll be alright but we may heel over a bit. I can't guarantee to keep the boat upright but it will be safe" I said with confidence. They'd travelled down from London and I didn't want to let them down. The husband put his arm around her shoulders.

"It'll be fine love if Mr. Edwards says so. He knows what he's doing" he assured her. She looked at him, then at me.

"All right," she said. We left the office and walked to the pontoon. The riggings on the yachts moored in the port were clanging against the masts in the wind, making a dreadful din but the drizzle had almost stopped. I climbed aboard first and held out my hand to assist the woman, Anne, as she climbed up after me. Her husband, Keith, followed. They looked ill at ease.

"Have you sailed much before?" I enquired.

"Not really," Keith replied.

"That's no problem, I'll do everything and if I need you to help I'll explain what I want you to do," I went to the foredeck, pulled a jib out of the sail locker, hanked it on to the forestay and attached the sheets. I returned to the cockpit where Keith and Anne stood looking uneasy and started the engine, then I let go the mainsheet, allowing the boom to swing free in the wind. I climbed onto the coachroof, removed the ties from the mainsail and hoisted it enough to allow me to put a reef in, then lowered it again and replaced the ties. I returned to the cockpit once again, cast off the mooring ropes and motored slowly out to the middle of the river. I turned the bow into the wind and throttled back till the engine was just ticking over.

"Here," I said to Keith, "You take the tiller and keep us headed into the wind like we are now whilst I hoist the sails." I went on deck, removed the ties once more and hoisted the mainsail. Next, I went to the foredeck and hoisted the jib. The sails flapped wildly in the wind and the boom swung from one side to the other as I made my way back to the cockpit.

"Right, bear away a bit now so that I can set the sails and we'll tack our way out to Southampton Water," I said. He gave me a puzzled look.

"Pull the tiller towards you," I explained. He obeyed and as we swung around I hauled in the mainsail sheet and the port jib sheet, switched off the engine and we were off. I'd set the sails so that we wouldn't be at too uncomfortable an angle. We heeled over slightly one side then the other as we tacked our way down the river. Once we were out into Southampton Water I was able to put the boat through her paces. The wind was much stronger than it had been when they'd first arrived at my office.

"Are you both OK?" I enquired.

"Yer, I fink so" Keith replied. They were both wedged up on the windward side of the cockpit.

"Shall I get her sailing a bit harder then?" I said. They looked at each other.

"Yeah, go on then," Keith said. I hardened up on the sheets and headed out further into the channel. The boat sailed beautifully, she was a joy to handle and we took off. My two passengers started to relax. We sailed around a bit in a freshening wind. I was enjoying myself and began to show them just what the boat was capable of - and then it started to rain. Not long afterwards, the wind strengthened, approaching the gale-force that had been forecast and the rain came down harder. They sat, getting soaking wet in the cockpit, watching me as I stood fighting with the tiller. The rain poured down and I was wet through but showed no sign of returning.

"Would you like to go back?" I asked them.

"No, carry on" Keith replied. They squinted at me through the rain that pelted down on their faces. They hadn't expected to find themselves in such circumstances when they'd left London that morning and they giggled at the situation they were in. Then there was a sudden, violent gust of wind that threw the boat over almost to the gunwales.

"FUCK!" Keith shouted and Anne screamed as they both grabbed hold of anything within reach to steady themselves. They looked at me wild-eyed. I smiled and when they realised that I wasn't in the least bit concerned they started to laugh, possibly to disguise the fear they'd felt. After that, we had a wonderful time sailing around and they began to enjoy it as much as I did. When they'd had enough we went back and moored up to the pontoon. I stowed the sails and we went ashore, dripping as we climbed the steps to my warm office. We were thoroughly soaked and windswept. I went downstairs to the chandlery, grabbed some towels, a bottle of our own brand whisky and some glasses, then went back up to join them. They were thrilled with the experience they'd had and they didn't stop chattering about it whilst we stripped off as much as we decently could in each other's company, dried ourselves and hung our wet clothes on the radiators. The whisky was poured and we sat at my desk, tingling from the exposure to the wind, rain and salt spray, whilst doing our best to empty the bottle. I was amazed and surprised at how well Anne had reacted to everything. I began to like them both very much. When we felt we'd had enough whisky, Keith invited me to a restaurant for lunch. We got through two bottles of wine and finished with cognac and that became a regular routine whenever Keith and I got together after that day.

"Thank you so much, we've had a fabulous day and I'll be in touch with you," he said in his broad cockney accent. When the time came for them to head off back to London, we shook hands, they drove off and I went home pleased with the day.

A week later Keith called me. After the initial pleasantries, he said

"I'm not really interested myself but a friend told me that there is a larger model boat that's 35ft long that he's interested in."

"Yes, that's right, I can arrange a sail anytime," I told him. He asked a few further questions and I did my best to sell him the idea of the larger vessel, which was my own personal favourite from the range that was built at the boatyard in La Rochelle. After a few days of reflection, he called me again and we went for a much gentler demonstration sail on the 35ft yacht. That day was entirely different, there was a light wind and the sun was shining so we took a bottle of wine and sandwiches from the chandlery to enjoy in the cockpit. After the sail, we had another lunch together and he left saying that he'd be in touch when he'd had time to think things over. When the call came, I very soon realised that he was serious about going ahead with the purchase. He asked the price and what extras I would recommend.

"We have the one that we sailed on that I can let you have with a good discount and it has wheel steering instead of a tiller so you will be getting a bargain," I told him. We discussed more details and he agreed to go ahead with the purchase and thus began a lasting friendship. I could not have imagined then that we would become partners in a sailing project in the Mediterranean less than two years later

Georgie-two-boats

The agency was experiencing financial difficulties and decided to downgrade. The chandlery was closed and its staff paid off together with our secretaries and the office manager, leaving just the accountant, one secretary, the boat cleaner, the obnoxious Tom and myself. We vacated the Port Hamble offices for a smaller one a little further away at the outer edge of the village. The accountant, the secretary, the boat cleaner and I refused to work with Tom; he was just too unbearable and so he was sent to the London office. From that moment on the remaining four of us worked together successfully in our new office. It was a lot smaller than we were used to but we'd had it refurbished entirely, having chosen the style and materials ourselves. There was a small reception area on the right-hand side of the entrance, with the secretary's office behind it. On the opposite side of the reception area was the accountant's office, my office behind his and a small kitchen area at the back. The offices were panelled with rosewood. We were comfortable and fortunate that next door, there was a very good, popular restaurant called "The Seadog", where it was convenient for me to take clients to lunch. In addition to dealing with customer enquiries and taking them on demonstrations, a lot of my time was spent visiting Port Hamble boatyard to supervise the fitting out of the boats that we'd sold with the extra equipment that they needed and dealing with the suppliers and the delivery crews that brought our boats from La Rochelle. I did fewer deliveries myself because I was needed more in the office but I was happy and as well as weekdays, often worked at weekends whenever it was required.

It was during that time that George contacted me. He was a successful, local businessman who owned an Arpége that he'd had for a number of years and wanted to upgrade to a newer model. He'd shortlisted to two yachts, one was an Ecume de Mer, on offer

29

from a different agency and the other, marketed by us, the brand new Dufour 31. It was a first-class yacht that I liked very much, which made it easier for me to sell. After a number of meetings and conversations, George decided he preferred the Dufour 31, which pleased me but he was reluctant to commit because of the financial circumstances of our agency.

"What happens if I pay for the yacht and the agency goes bust before it's delivered?" he asked.

"I really don't expect anything like that to happen in the near future if at all," I assured him and it was true as I understood it at the time. He looked at me not knowing whether to believe me.

"We're talking about a lot of money that I could lose if I go ahead and I haven't sold my Arpége yet."

"Let me look into the matter further for you and I'll call you when I have more news." He agreed and left. Over the course of the next week, I made phone calls, had discussions with the accountant, with whom I was on friendly terms, (we went to clubs together) and quizzed the two partners in the London office. After all, my own job was on the line too. Satisfied that the yacht could be delivered before any drastic decisions were taken by the two partners, I called George and promised him that I personally would follow every aspect of the deal from beginning to the end to make sure that he would get delivery of the yacht. I was not prepared to lie and pretend that the company finances were secure.

The deal was concluded, the contract was signed, the funds transferred to us and his Arpége was put up for sale. True to my word, I made constant phone calls to the London office and to the Dufour office in La Rochelle. I discovered that our London office hadn't paid the La Rochelle office for the yacht so I swung into action and ensured that it was ordered, paid for and delivered to Hamble for George. He took delivery of the Dufour 31 before his Arpége was sold so had the expense of keeping two yachts for a while, which was not an ideal state of affairs. George and I became close and subsequently life-long friends. Like me, he was an ardent jazz enthusiast, a lover of good wines and enjoyed eating out in restaurants. We often lunched together and had many laughter-filled days and nights. I dined with him and his wife from time to time and reciprocated by arranging my first dinner party since Jill had left me. To make up the numbers, I invited my sister-in-law, Sue, who I liked very much and visited often. Sue was and is a kind, thoughtful, caring person who devoted a large part of her adult life to working for Oxfam. She was divorced from Jill's brother and had no desire for any material possessions, her energies being devoted to helping others. Her overwhelming interest was her charity work. We got along very well and I was looking forward to an enjoyable evening. It was indeed memorable but for all the wrong reasons.

I made a special effort to make sure the evening went well and prepared simple French cuisine. The main course was *moules marinières* – mussels cooked with shallots, white wine, butter, parsley and cream. It is worth remembering that any mussels that are open before being cooked should close after being tapped firmly and after cooking, any that remain closed should be discarded, otherwise, they can cause serious tummy upsets. I had candles lit on the table and smooth jazz playing when George and his wife, Pauline arrived. I explained that Sue was my sister-in-law, that she was a humanitarian who cared deeply for others who were less fortunate than ourselves and that she had a good sense of humour. I wanted them to know what to expect when she arrived and introductions were made. I'd explained to Sue beforehand that George was a client, had bought a boat from me, had a totally different lifestyle to her own and wouldn't necessarily agree with all of her ideas and values but he was a valued friend with a terrific sense of humour. I'd thought of everything in advance so what could go wrong?

The evening went well, I was pleased with my culinary efforts, everybody enjoyed the meal, the conversation had been convivial, facilitated no doubt by the free-flowing wine and we relaxed with cognac afterwards and that's when it happened. Sue was passionate about her work and had a tendency to become over immersed in the injustices of the wars, famines and sufferings in third world countries. She went on about all the problems that existed and George responded. He understood about problems, he had one of his own.

"I have a problem at the moment. I have two yachts ...." He never finished what he wanted to say. Sue was incandescent with rage!

"You have a problem because you have two yachts?" she bellowed and she went on and on berating him and her eyes bore into him. He never had the opportunity to explain. He had a problem because he still hadn't sold his Arpége and had already bought the Dufour 31 but compared to the problems of the unfortunate souls that Sue and Oxfam were involved with, it was of no relevance. I thought her ranting would never end. At one stage, Pauline left the table and disappeared. George sat red-faced and became more and more uneasy as he squirmed in his chair, looking like a very naughty boy being scolded for his misdemeanours. Each time he tried to say something, Sue blasted him again with more verbal abuse. Upstairs, I heard the toilet flush several times. I had remained silent throughout, not knowing how best to calm the situation. Pauline had been absent for a long time so I went to look for her. She was nowhere in the house. I opened the entrance door and looked outside. It was bitterly cold and she was bent over in my front garden vomiting, making strange noises as she strained to empty her stomach of the meal. She hadn't been able to make it back up the stairs to the toilet in time so she'd taken the nearest escape route.

"Are you alright?" I enquired. A ridiculous thing to have said on reflection.

"Eeeeurgh!" she replied and again, "Eeeeugh!" and she vomited over my plants some more. I went back inside. Sue was still haranguing George, who still sat staring, dumbfounded.

"Let's listen to some more jazz," I said, hoping to quieten things down. I put on a lively Kenny Ball record.

"Let's dance," George said to Sue, standing up and holding his hand out to her.

"I don't think so!" she replied and then things settled down a bit. I realised I'd made a gigantic error in bringing them together. Pauline staggered into the room and grasped the table to stop herself from falling. She was ashen-faced, her hair was dishevelled, her clothing loosened and her speech incoherent when she tried to speak and stop herself from vomiting at the same time.

"I want to go home," she murmured to George as she bent over the back of her chair. Oh no, I thought to myself, she's going to vomit on the carpet. I rushed around to steer her back outside before she spewed out whatever tiny portions of the meal remained inside her.

"Ooooh, take me home," she pleaded. George leapt to his feet. At last, he had an excuse to escape his tormentor.

"I'd better get Pauline home, sorry to break up the party so soon," he said. I walked with them to the door.

"Well, that went well," I whispered to him and he giggled. Pauline groaned and leant on him. He made his way to his car with Pauline teetering alongside him. He helped her get inside, got inside himself and drove away. I went back inside. Sue was on her feet, preparing to leave.

"That didn't go as planned," I said and she smiled. I walked her to the door, we said our goodnights and I cleared away. Before going to bed, I went into the toilet and there was evidence of Pauline's stomach upset. I suspected the mussels may have been responsible and I know that she didn't eat mussels again for a long time afterwards. When I got into bed, I went into fits of laughter and to this day, whenever George and I meet we talk about that night and laugh.

Night terror

One day I had to visit an office that was a short walk away. I went through the entrance door where two secretaries were seated, one facing me and the other with her back to me. I chatted with the one who was facing me and we flirted with each other in a playful manner as we concluded our business. The other one, hearing our banter spun around to face me. My jaw hit the floor! She wore a very short skirt, revealing an amazing pair of legs. She had long, shiny, jet black hair, wide, sparkling, intense green eyes and bright red lipstick. The combination was utterly striking. She laughed as she looked up at me staring open-mouthed. I didn't hesitate for a moment.

"Wow, if you're not doing anything this evening would you like to spend it with me?" I said.

"Are you serious?" she asked, smiling up at me with a twinkle in her green eyes.

"I certainly am," I assured her. She stared at me for a while, weighing me up.

"All right then," she replied.

"Where will I meet you, I can call by your house if you like?"

"No, let's meet here," she suggested.

"Great, seven o clock OK for you?"

"Yes, all right," she agreed, riveting her laughing, green eyes on mine and giving me a cheeky, seductive smile that made my knees go weak.

I said goodbye and returned to my office feeling on top of the world. She was absolutely stunning.

Seven o clock came and on the dot, I arrived in my nice new Toyota Celica to see her already standing there with a mature woman. She came over and I went out and opened the car door for her to show her what a perfect gentleman I was so that she would never want to leave me.

"Who was the woman that you were with? "I asked.

"My mum, she came with me because I wasn't sure you'd be here." Silly girl! She was gorgeous and I wouldn't have missed that date for anything. Her name was Virginia.

She had a terrific sense of humour and we laughed a lot together. On our third date, she came home with me and stayed the night. I cooked us both a meal and we finished off a bottle of wine, then we relaxed for a while before we shared a bath and went to bed and made love. Then we both slept.

A piercing, blood-curdling scream shocked me into wakefulness. I shot up into a sitting position. Something flew past me in the dark and there was another earsplitting scream of abject terror that penetrated every fibre of my body and must have woken the rest of the neighbourhood. My heart pounded. I switched on the light. Virginia was hysterical, gibbering from fear. I saw nothing.

"What's the matter, what happened?" I asked. The blood had drained from her face. She didn't answer. She was sitting up, shaking. "Tell me what happened?" I asked again.

"There......." She was panting and on the verge of tears

"There what? She took several deep breaths and flung her arms around me. "Tell me what happened, "I implored her. She released her hold on me, sat back and took a couple more deep breaths.

"There was something on the bed," She was distressed. I took hold of her, caressed her and asked again

"What was on the bed?" She took another deep breath.

"It was alive, it moved." I looked around.

"There's nothing here," I reassured her.

"I put my hand out. I felt it and it moved."

"It's all right," I murmured, releasing my hold on her.

"It leapt in the air when I screamed."

"And that's why you screamed again, when it leapt in the air?"

"Oh, Tony, it was horrible." Traumatised, she flung her arms around me again and held me tightly.

And then I laughed.

I'd forgotten to tell her that I had a cat called Twinkle who liked to sleep with me. I held her voluptuous, naked body against mine and did what I could to calm her down and explain what had happened. Her scream had petrified Twinkle who'd flown off the bed and disappeared to who knows where. We remained sitting and cuddling for a while and then we lay down to try to sleep. Virginia had difficulty dropping off because she took some time to recover from the horror she'd been through. I had difficulty because I couldn't stop laughing. We didn't see Twinkle any more until we went downstairs in the morning.

I liked Virginia very much and we continued dating for a while longer until she started telling me how much she enjoyed being with me and when the word love was mentioned I felt that it was starting to get too serious, too soon. And so it was with sadness that I had to gently explain my feelings to Virginia. I liked her very much but I didn't love her. After having been cheated on and dragged through a distressing and costly divorce by Jill, I was in no hurry to get involved in a serious relationship again, if ever, and I thought far too much of Virginia to ever want to hurt her. We continued seeing each other for a while longer before I reluctantly, sadly, let her go for her sake, not my own. At that time I wasn't in the right frame of mind to give her what she wanted. She was so lovely she deserved to find a loving partner and I sincerely hope that she has done so.

She showed no mercy

I had a few brief flings with other girls, some lasting longer than others and one situation became awkward. I met a girl at a dance and learned that, like me, she was a lover of jazz and blues. We talked about our favourite artists and the concerts we'd been to and I told her about my good collection of jazz records. We got talking about big band jazz, which I love and inevitably the names of Count Basie and Duke Ellington came up.

"I have an album with both bands dueting," I told her.

"That sounds interesting," she said

"It's great, it's called Battle Royal, you'd enjoy it," I said.

"I'll look out for it and look forward to listening to it sometime."

"Why not come back to my place now and I'll play it for you," I suggested hopefully as I also had a burning desire to get to know her more intimately. She looked at me for a while with a half-smile on her luscious, full lips and a naughty twinkle in her eye before allowing herself a full smile and agreeing to accept my hard to resist offer.

"OK," she said. It started to look promising. We left the dance and headed home. When we arrived, I poured us each a drink and we sat for a while chatting. I went to my record collection to search for the album. She was watching me as I flicked through each one. I couldn't find it. I looked again and again. It wasn't there. I'd brought her home specifically to listen to that one record and it wasn't there and she was looking at me expectantly. Then I realised what had happened. Jill had been into the house and helped herself to a selection of the records without consulting me.

"I'm sorry but it doesn't seem to be here," I said. She gave me a look that left no doubt in my mind that she thought I'd lied to her just to get her into bed. "Somebody must have borrowed it but never mind let me play you this one," I said quickly as I placed a Maynard Ferguson record on the turntable. As it happened, the evening went well but it could have turned out to be quite different and I was getting frustrated with Jill coming in and helping herself to anything she wanted without having the decency to discuss it with me first or to check if it would be convenient. Mostly I was absent when she did so but I could very easily have been caught in a compromising situation. After our years together I was surprised that she behaved as she did, it seemed so out of character to the Jill I thought I knew. She even took my wedding ring that I'd left on the bedside table.

Next, I met a multiple-orgasmic nymphomaniac called Ruth, at least that's what I assume she was and if she wasn't then she certainly gave a very convincing impression of being one. If she wasn't then I'm not sure I'd want to meet the real thing. Well, what an experience it was and I learned a few things! Alfred Kinsey, the sexologist said, *"The only unnatural sex act is that which you cannot perform."* Ruth was of the same opinion. After the first time that we'd made love, which was the first time we'd met, I asked her if she'd orgasmed, "Three times," she replied. I didn't bother to ask anymore after that.

At times it was inconvenient to say the least, like the time we were told to leave the premises because she wouldn't take her hands off me. I was hoping for an enjoyable evening in a pub and was on my first beer when she started rubbing me all over and shoving her hand where it shouldn't have been. I tried to resist but realised that I was not going to succeed and it wasn't very long before I no longer wanted her to stop. *"License my roving hands, and let them go. Behind, before, above, between, below;"* From John Donne's, To His Mistress Going to Bed (1595)

"Get out of here you two, we don't want any of that bloody disgusting stuff in here, get out!" the pub landlord demanded. I'd become so enthralled that I hadn't even noticed the only other four customers sitting at the bar. I was embarrassed beyond belief. It was a pub I hadn't been to before so they wouldn't have missed me when I never went back! We left and went straight home for another sleepless night. Then there was the occasion when I'd reserved a table for us at one of my favourite restaurants. I called at her house and when she appeared at the door she looked devastating. She had shoulder-length blonde hair and beautiful, seductive, pale blue eyes, perfectly made up with expertly applied eyeshadow and liner and red lipstick on her inviting lips. She certainly knew how to make herself attractive and I wasn't expecting the surprise that she'd planned next. I had been looking forward to a good night out with her and what I knew would be a delicious meal. We went to the car; I started the engine then turned and gave her an admiring glance. She flung her coat open to reveal scant, sexy, black lace underwear and suspenders and that was all she wore beneath her coat. The look she gave me sent electrifying tingles throughout my body. I released the handbrake, engaged gear and as fast as it was safe to do so, headed straight home for another sleepless night and so it went on and on for some weeks until we both began to tire of each other. No matter what plans I made for the two of us there was only ever going to be one exhausting outcome but I did get some respite from her incessant demands on my body whilst I was at work. I decided that a nymphomaniac was fine for a while but I was in no hurry for a repeat performance and even at the last moment before we parted I had to satisfy her sexual appetite. *"Sex without love is a meaningless experience, but as far as meaningless experiences go it's pretty damn good."* Woody Allen.

CHAPTER 4
CHANGE IS IN THE AIR

The power of thought

I called Jill and asked her to take charge of Twinkle whilst I took time out to visit our friends Bob and Tina in Majorca. Bob and I had studied for our Board of Trade Yacht Master Certificate at the same time at the Southampton School of Navigation in Warsash. We both passed our exams and received our certificates at the same time. Bob took command of a yacht with his wife Tina as his crew and they spent a year based in the United States and the Caribbean. They later took command of a yacht in the Mediterranean and were based in the same harbour as Jill and me at Port Gallice in Juan Les Pins. The following year they changed over to another yacht that was based in Palma, Majorca and when that job finished they stayed in Majorca. They bought a house there in a remote area, with no electricity or water, had a child and opened a yacht agency close to the harbour in Palma. That is where I went for two weeks. I already knew Palma because Jill and I had been based there aboard a cutter in 1967 and had spent the month of August sailing around the island, visiting the beautiful creeks and harbours. Bob and Tina's house was small and basic. It was situated in a difficult to access and unbelievably pretty area on the vertiginous slope of a deep valley overlooking a beautiful cove, with the blue sea receding into the distance. It was idyllic. Bob worked hard to keep the agency running but with plenty of competition from well-established agencies, it was becoming increasingly difficult for him to continue.

Whilst I was staying with him he discovered a water source at the bottom of the valley. He installed a container to catch the water and he bought a pump powerful enough to convey the water up to the house. He purchased lengths of metal tubing and he and I connected it all up. It was a difficult undertaking as the mountainside was so steep and covered in undergrowth, but with perseverance and much sweating and cursing, the task was completed before I returned to the U.K. He was over the moon when the system was connected up to his generator and water gushed from the tap when he turned it on. Until that moment he'd had to order lorry loads of water to be delivered and emptied into a holding tank. His euphoria came to an abrupt halt when we discovered that the exhaust from the generator had started burning the parched shrubbery outside the shed. Bob quickly shut it down; we doused the smouldering brush and over the next couple of days cut it down to prevent a reoccurrence.

My thoughts played havoc with me at times as I recalled certain moments with Ruth and I weakened to the extent that before I left Majorca, I sent her my door key and asked her to be there when I got home. When I arrived back in the U.K. Ruth was duly waiting for me at home and we readily fell back into a relationship once again. We stayed together for a few weeks until we decided that the relationship was never going to be any more than a manic sex romp and that we needed to get on with our lives, so for the final time we parted on good terms and I had a chance to recover from the exhaustion.

By mutual agreement, Jill didn't return Twinkle when I got back. I'd become very attached to Twinkle and it had been a nice feeling to have her meet me each time I arrived home from work and to have her curled up on my lap, purring with contentment as I stroked her soft furry head - but I don't suppose Twinkle was too upset.

A fine romance

At the evening dance classes, we swapped partners constantly and I'd partnered a beautiful Indian girl a few times. After one particular dance was finished and we stopped to change partners, she held onto my hand, making it known that she wanted me to stay with her. I turned to look at her; she smiled and pushed her slim, warm body against me. We gazed into each other's eyes. She was exceedingly attractive with a curvaceous, slim, supple body, long black hair and such penetrating, dark, seductive eyes that I almost melted when she gazed at me. Her look needed no verbal communication, the message was so clear that I became aroused. We danced together a few more times and each time she held onto my hand to keep me with her. I asked her if she would like to spend some time with me when the classes were finished.

"I might," she said, with a bewitching smile.

"I'd prefer it if you would just say yes," I said. She looked at me, turned to face me and took hold of my other hand.

"All right then, yes," she said. And so began a wonderful relationship that I have never forgotten. She was a widow, just a few years older than me; an intelligent, professional woman with a successful business. She was called Asha, which means hope and she only worked for a few half days a week so we spent a lot of time together and became very attached to each other. The first night we spent together was awesome and she made it plain that she was willing to please me in any way that I desired.

"If there is anything you would like me to do or any books you would like me to read, you will let me know, won't you?" she said.
She paid for us to go on trips, visiting different parts of the country, staying in opulent hotels and eating in extravagant restaurants. I offered to pay my share but she insisted that I shouldn't. That was just as well since I was paying off the mortgage on the house and the loan on the car out of my salary alone, whereas initially Jill and I had both contributed. Asha and I were happy together but the open hostility we often encountered from other members of Asha's race astonished me. They didn't hide their disapproval of our relationship and I felt uncomfortable at times. However, we were never aware of any objection at all from other members of society. Her calmness impressed me; no matter what adverse circumstances arose she just smiled and accepted them. The Buddha said that we must learn to accept disappointments with a smile. Asha was a shining example of how to react to disappointment and I have since learned to do the same myself. (Mostly!)

The house sold and after the conniving lawyers had finished their underhand activities, Jill took half of everything even though I'd been paying off the loans alone. With the money I received, I put down a deposit on what was advertised as a two-bedroom, luxury apartment in Netley Abbey, an old-fashioned village southeast of the city of Southampton on the eastern shore of Southampton Water. The small apartment block was just a few feet from a shingle beach overlooking Hythe and Fawley on the opposite side of the water and my apartment, on the top floor of the two-story building had a view over Southampton Water. The village of Netley, commonly known as Netley Abbey, is flanked by the Abbey proper on one side of the village and on the other side, The Royal Victoria Country Park. There were just a few quaint shops on the opposite side of the road.

The Abbey, a medieval monastery, was founded in 1239 to house Cistercian monks. In 1536, during the dissolution of the monasteries by King Henry VIII, it was converted into a mansion for a wealthy Tudor politician and remained as a country house until the beginning of the 18th century, when it was abandoned. It slowly fell into ruin after being robbed of its stonework, which was used for building materials. It was gifted to the nation at the beginning of the 20th century and is now a tourist attraction cared for by English Heritage.

4. The Dufour 35

The Royal Victoria Country Park was acquired by the Hampshire County Council in 1966 and was opened to the public in 1970. Before that, it was the location for the Royal Victoria Hospital, built-in 1863 on the recommendation of Queen Victoria, who visited it on many occasions. At the time, on completion, it was the world's longest building. However, when they took over, the Council demolished the buildings, leaving only the chapel. The park now comprises 200 acres of mature woodland and grassy open spaces, as well as a small shingle beach, all ideally situated on the shores of Southampton Water. I enjoyed my time at Netley Abbey. It had everything I needed and I enjoyed being able to stroll along the beach just a few paces from my door.

An offer I couldn't refuse

The unavoidable outcome of the yacht agency's financial problems came to pass. Our Hamble office was closed down at the beginning of 1975 and I was unemployed. The London office remained open for a while longer until that also eventually closed, leaving only the office in Antibes on the Côte d'Azur open. I had remained friends with some of the people that I'd either sold boats to, taken on demonstrations or that I'd helped to sail in other ways so had plenty of opportunities to wine and dine with them and continue sailing from time to time, which was a good thing as I disliked being idle and I loved sailing. I wondered what my future held, having settled into a comfortable, enjoyable life in the U.K. I had more free time to spend with Asha and we become closer by the day. She didn't want me to work, preferring to keep me with her as much as possible and she was happy to pay for anything that I needed. It worked very well for a while until I began to feel uncomfortable at being a kept person. I told her how I felt and she assured me that it was exactly what she wanted and she hoped that we would go to India sometime, where she had nutmeg farms and other businesses and properties. She was happy and we continued to enjoy each other's company.

Keith and Anne came to Port Hamble as often as they could to sail their boat but mostly Keith came with friends or alone and he would invite me to lunch or dinner whenever it was convenient. The first demonstration I'd taken him and Anne on had impressed him very much and he often told his friends how I'd taken them out in a force eight gale and torrential rain without the slightest hesitation. He was impressed with my knowledge and experience of boats.

Over lunch one day he became enthusiastic about the idea of taking his Dufour 35 sloop to the Mediterranean.

"D'ya fink we'd be able to charter 'er out?" he asked me.

"I don't see why not" I answered

"I'd only be interested if you were with me," he said in his cockney accent, "Would you be interested?"

"I think so; it depends on the arrangement we'd have between us because I need to earn money."

"I wouldn't want it any other way. I wanted to suggest it to you but didn't know how you'd feel."

"Well, it sounds interesting," I said.

"Think it over then and when you've come to a decision we'll get together and discuss it in more detail," he said. We finished lunch and as always with Keith, we went on to Cognacs afterwards, with both of us becoming more impassioned at the prospect of sailing together in the South of France.

I didn't mention anything to Asha because I knew she would be unhappy to learn that I may be going away. We had a superb relationship but unsatisfactory from my point of view because she paid for everything, which made me feel uneasy. The sea was my profession and I yearned for the thrills of sailing once more. It was nine days later that Keith called.

"Ave ya decided if ya wanna accept me offer?" he asked.

"Yes, I've given It a lot of thought and I think it would be a good idea," I told him.

"Right, why don't you come up to London and we'll discuss it over lunch."

"Sounds good to me," I said. We arranged a time and date and I drove there to meet him, explaining to Asha beforehand that I may well be leaving her for the summer season but that I would come back to visit her as often as I could. Keith and I had actually discussed the possibility of me staying there with the boat permanently but I saw no point in telling Asha that until I knew for certain that it would be the case. She took it badly. There were tears in her eyes and I was upset for her since we had become so fond of each other. She had often talked about our future together but I was uncertain that I was ready for another permanent relationship so hadn't committed to anything.

44

"What would you want as a salary?" Keith asked as we scoffed our way through a mouthwatering lunch and an equally good bottle of wine. I told him and he agreed without question.

"What do you think we would be able to ask as a charter fee?" he asked.

"We should be able to get at least £100 a day," I told him.

"That sounds fair enough to me," he responded.

"It's customary for the skippers to also get a cut of the charter fee to give them an incentive," I said.

"Of course, that won't be a problem," he assured me, "How much would you want?"

"I would think £20 a day would be reasonable" I suggested.

"I'll give you £25 and on top of that I'll arrange for you to acquire shares in the boat so we'll become equal partners in the venture on a 50/50 basis," he said and so the deal was agreed and we shook hands on it.

"Will you make all the arrangements to have the boat taken down to the South of France by road haulage and sort out a berth and everything else that needs doing - is that OK?"

"No problem, I'll keep you informed on progress," I said and thus began a friendship that would endure and lead on to further undertakings.

We'll meet again

I fixed a date for the boat to be loaded and delivered with the road haulage company that the agency had used, two men that I'd come to know well. Meanwhile, I fitted it out with everything that I thought I would need and charged it to Keith. The next task was painful; I had to tell Asha that I would be leaving her. I chose what I thought would be the most appropriate moment, following dinner in our favourite Indian restaurant as I was about to say goodnight after taking her home. I knew that it would be a challenging moment for us both and it was. We sat in the car outside her home when I dropped the bombshell.

"But you don't need to go, I have enough money for you to not have to work," she said holding on to me and looking at me with her beautiful, dark, tear-filled eyes.

"I do, I can't spend my life living off you and I need to be doing something." I held her hands and wished it could have been different. I knew she would do anything I asked and that made it even more difficult for me.

"We can find something for you to do here; I can set you up in a business doing something that you like," she said, "Just tell me what you want."

"I don't want to do anything except sailing. I'll go away for this season and then I'll come back and we can rethink but I've given my word and everything has been finalised. I promise I'll call you as often as I can and I'll come back here whenever possible. I'll have plenty of free time to see you in the winter months and in any case, you can always come out and visit me in the South of France," I said. We held each other tightly for a long time, neither of us wanting to let the other go and I could feel her lovely body trembling as she sobbed. I stroked her long, black hair as I waited for her tears to stop, then we said goodnight. I sat and watched her until she'd entered her house then drove home feeling drained. When we had both come to terms with the new arrangement we continued as usual and made each day as memorable as we could. Asha bought me many gifts and I felt uncomfortable accepting them. I asked her not to but it gave her pleasure and she was happy as long as I was with her. Our last ecstasy filled night together was unforgettable. The next day, I locked up my apartment and left. *"The story of life is quicker than the wink of an eye, the story of love is hello and goodbye...until we meet again." Jimmy Hendrix.*

CHAPTER 5
THE OPPOSITE CITY

Return to the Med

The four-day overland trip with the road transporters went well, although there was one strange incident when we'd parked for the night in the middle of a car park in a small, quiet village. We were woken at two-o clock in the morning by the noise of a car circling us at high speed. We went outside to see what on earth was going on. The car was being driven by an elderly lady. The driver's window was wound down and the car screeched around us with the tyres squealing and the engine roaring. She had her head out, screaming unintelligible nonsense and shouting about how she carried out oil changes on her vehicle using human blood. To say the least this was disconcerting and we were relieved when she finally left. The rest of our trip was uneventful until we finally arrived at Port Vauban in Antibes on a bright sunny day.

The marina had been under construction when I was last there a few years earlier in 1971. It is now the largest yachting harbour in Europe, with facilities to accommodate more than 2,000 yachts, including yachts of more than 100 metres in length. The original old natural harbour was once part of the Greek city of Antipolis, which was established around 400 BC by the Phocaeans, ancient Greek seafarers who had also founded the city of Massalia (Marseille) in 600 BC. Antipolis, (the opposite city), was so-called because it was situated opposite Corsica and was a convenient stopover point between Corsica and Massalia. It suffered repeated attacks from Ligurian tribes in the second century BC but after the Greeks appealed to Rome for assistance, the tribes were defeated. Rome strengthened its control over the Mediterranean coast and occupied Antipolis in 43 BC. The town remained under Roman occupation for the next 500 years. They built fortifications, public baths and aqueducts and developed Antipolis into the largest town in the region. The remains of their constructions are still visible today. When the Western Roman Empire began to crumble in 476 AD, Antibes was captured by Barbarian tribes and there followed a prolonged period of instability and destruction. In the 10th century, Seigneur Rodoart, a wealthy nobleman who had been awarded Antibes by the King of France, defeated the occupying tribes, built fortifications and offered protection to the city. It prospered for the next 200 years until wars and epidemics again caused chaos sending the inhabitants inside the fortified city walls for protection. Gradually peace started to return by the end of the 14th century and when at the end of the 15th century, the Comte de Provence, who then owned the region, died and bequeathed the land to King Louis XI of France, relative stability was established.

For centuries, nearby Cap d'Antibes, consisting of wild scrubland and pine forests, was considered unsafe and the land worthless. Although there was already a hotel called the Hotel du Cap-Eden-Roc on the western end of the Cap d'Antibes, which had opened its doors in 1889, it needed a hard-working family of Italian immigrants to recognize the potential of the rest of Cap d'Antibes and its interior as the beautiful place it really is. They arrived in 1892, a family from Calabria on the toe of Italy, impoverished and looking for work. They had decided to travel to join relatives living in Antibes, where work was supposed to be plentiful and life was good. The Paolinos were industrious and had as their financial head a savvy matriarch who managed their investments and pretty much everything else. Little by little she bought up parcels of the worthless land until they owned large areas of it. Even though she was paying high-interest rates, in the region of 15 to 20%, she knew that the price of the land was bound to increase. The ground was cleared and nurtured and was to become the base of her son Francesco's enterprise propagating and growing roses. His daughter Louisette married Francis Meilland, the son of a rose growing family near Lyon and himself a brilliant hybridist. This brought two major rose growing families together who are still leaders in the field, with the name of Meilland being the most well-known as it comes from the male line. They still have premises in Antibes, as well as large experimental laboratories in Le Cannet-des-Maures in the Var.

Europeans, notably English and Russians, discovered the natural beauty of the area. They built luxurious villas and the harbour once again became active with a thriving fishing industry. By the time of WWI, most of the fortifications had been demolished, new residential areas were built and Antibes was connected to Nice by a railway. It has continued to grow and develop ever since. Pablo Picasso arrived in 1946 and stayed for six months. He painted, drew and crafted ceramics and tapestries, some of which are now displayed in the Picasso museum which is situated on the ramparts. The port is named after a French military engineer, Sébastien le Prestre de Vauban who was in service to King Louis XIV. He was considered the preeminent engineer of his time and it was he who designed and built the fortifications next to the port.

I was glad to be back there. It felt like home as I basked in the sunshine and savoured the familiar smells of France and once more enjoyed being surrounded by the sounds and the atmosphere of a vibrant yacht harbour. We'd driven all through the previous night so that we would arrive in the early morning. It was early April and everywhere there was a great deal of activity. Crews were preparing the yachts for the coming season and I was impatient to arrange to get the sloop launched, rigged and moored so that I could settle in and visit the agencies in the hope of them finding me plenty of charters. I went to the Capitainerie and arranged a berth for the season, then visited the boatyard and persuaded the boatyard manager to launch the yacht and step the mast that same day. By the evening I'd aligned the mast, secured the stays and shrouds and was nicely settled in.

The yacht had a comfortable interior. There was a double bed in the fore section. Aft of that, on the starboard side, was a shower cubicle and on the port side a toilet and washbasin. Wooden doors separated that cabin from the saloon, which had a settee/single bunk on the starboard side, astern of which was a good-sized chart table with seating area and radio equipment. On the port side was a dinette area with a table that could be lowered to make a double bunk. Behind the dinette area, there was an extra-wide shelf which could double as a single bunk. The table had collapsible side sections so that it could be enlarged and be used by people sitting on the opposite settee. Astern of the dinette was an L shaped galley with a good-sized gimballed cooker and oven. Deckside, she had an attractive sheer line, low coachroof and a reverse transom. Deckside, she had an attractive sheer line, low coachroof and a reverse transom. There was a large cockpit with wheel steering, plenty of high-quality instrumentation on a console above the cabin entrance hatch, a folding cockpit canopy for protection and a comprehensive suit of sails stowed in the sail locker. A 30hp Volvo diesel engine provided mechanical propulsion. She was a quality yacht, sturdy, easy to handle and fast. I was ready to sail and slept well that night, pleased to hear the gentle lapping of the water on the hull and the halyards tapping against the mast.

I soon started to make friends with other Captains and met some of those that I knew from my previous years sailing in the Mediterranean. I reintroduced myself to the charter agencies that I knew and made contact with the agency that I'd worked for in Hamble. A small motor yacht was moored next to me and some days a remarkably pretty, 30-year-old girl called Marjie would go aboard to clean it for the Russian owner. We exchanged pleasantries and I learnt that she lived aboard her own sailboat on the opposite quay to me and that coincidentally she and her husband had bought the vessel, a 28 ft Great Dane sloop through the yacht agency for whom I'd worked. She was a happy girl, always smiling and had the most amazing eyes that seemed to change colour according to what she wore or the time of day so that it was difficult to know exactly what colour they actually were. They were extraordinary and I found them mesmerising. I tried my best to get to know her better but she didn't seem interested so we continued with our small talk whenever she was on the boat next to me and I continued looking at her when she was stretched out in the sun on the deck of her own boat. Our conversations became less frequent when I moved to another mooring next to a Grand Banks motor vessel a little further away. It was owned by two couples, Harry and Sue and Ted and Pam. They had spent time in Africa before setting up a car hire business in the U.K. and what fun they were, we laughed and joked constantly.

Brief encounter

In May, Keith flew down for a weeks holiday and we sailed as much as we could whenever the weather was favourable. When he went home I went sailing by myself and as I got to know Marjie, the girl with the amazing eyes, better, I invited her to come for a sail to the Iles des Lérins, west of Cap d'Antibes and a few miles offshore from Cannes. I'd also invited four other girls that I knew who were involved one way or another with the agency that had made me redundant. The weather was perfect that day. There was not a cloud in the dazzling blue sky, the sea was calm and sparkling under the fierce sun and there was a light breeze. When we'd cleared the harbour entrance, I hoisted the Genoa and mainsail, switched off the engine and we had a terrific sail. We dropped anchor between the two islands where we swam and enjoyed a good lunch comprising various products that we had all contributed. It had been a long time since I'd left the lovely Asha behind in the U.K. and I was missing female company. I called her regularly on the phone and each time it was disturbing to hear her pleading with me to return. I'd hoped that by inviting so many lovely girls to spend the afternoon with me it would lead to a date with one of them. I wasn't thinking of being unfaithful to Asha, even though I had never given her any reason to believe that our relationship would ever be permanent. I was still smarting too much from the effect of Jill's adulterous affair, the loss of some of my personal items that she'd helped herself to and the costly divorce. I just wanted to have a female companion from time to time. I prefer female company and will share my personal theory as to a possible explanation.

In the 1960s, neuropsychologist, neurobiologist and Nobel Prize winner, Roger Wolcott Sperry, identified hemispheric characteristics following his split-brain research. The brain is split into two hemispheres, left and right, each one being roughly the size of a clenched fist. The left hemisphere is sequential, analytical, critical, logical, linear, factual, mathematical and habitual. The right hemisphere is imaginative, intuitive, sensitive, amorphous, emotional, creative and artistic. Both hemispheres work independently with the left hemisphere being the dominant one in 95% of the population. However, information travels from one hemisphere to the other via a thick bundle of nerve fibres called the Corpus Callosum. Whilst a female brain is slightly smaller than the male brain, the Corpus Callosum in females is larger than in males. The larger Corpus Callosum contributes to a more integrated brain function and an enhanced capacity to access right hemisphere characteristics. I suggest that is why I find females are generally more intuitive, more in touch with their emotions, more imaginative, more open to new ideas such as natural healing methods, spiritual and esoteric matters, vegetarianism etc. The left hemisphere controls the right side of the body and the right hemisphere controls the left side of the body. I am left-handed and to an extent ambidextrous so according to research carried out in 1985 by neuroscientist Sandra Wittelson, my own Corpus Callosum and that of other left-handed and ambidextrous people would be 11% larger than a right-handed male, therefore, we may have the potential to perceive things differently because there would be less distinction between the two hemispheres. Perhaps that is why I am more at ease in female company because our shared larger Corpus Collosum made it easier for me to discuss with them subjects that interest me. Of all my male friends and acquaintances, there are very few, with whom I'd feel comfortable talking about my spiritual and other interests. As an aside, it has been suggested by Anthony Peake in his book "The Daemon," that our consciousness resides in the left hemisphere and our spiritual self, (Daemon) in the right hemisphere. *"In each of us there is another whom we do not know."* - Carl Jung."

Maybe the world would be safer, more caring, more advanced and more spiritual if more right-brained women were in positions of power. The left brain, male-dominated world that we live in limits progress by excluding women and deprives itself of ideas from around 50% of the population, a lot of which could be of a right-brain nature. The Catholic Church is a good example. However, according to the early Christian (Gnostic) Gospels discovered in the Nag Hammadi Codices, The Gospel of Mary attests that Mary Magdalen, a visionary, was a close associate of Jesus and was the first woman apostle. She was the apostle to the apostles. The sacred scriptures of the three major religions that originated in the middle east, Judaism, Christianity and Islam, are similar and all uphold the equality of man and woman. The Old Testament states "Man and woman are created equally in God's image and have dominion over the earth." Gen. 1:26-27. Jesus talks of men and women as equals. Matt. 12:49-50, Mark 3:34-35, Luke 8:21. The Koran also teaches that God, (Allah,) created men and women as equals and the obligations of each and God's treatment of each shall be the same. K 33:30-36, K 16:99, K 92:4. Granted that the church gave us much in the way of science in times past but only when it didn't call into question its own authority, strict dogma and rigid beliefs. If it did it was deemed heresy and the so-called heretics were burned at the stake, tortured by the "inquisitors" into confessing the errors of their ways or incarcerated for life. This had a powerful effect and held back scientific progress for centuries. When people began to question the authority of the church and were no longer in fear of retribution, women were allowed to contribute and science was able to advance.

Of course, there are other cultures that exclude women and some of them are consequentially less advanced than cultures where the potential of women's broader perceptions are encouraged .*"On the other hand, mere critical thinking, without creative and intuitive insights, without the search for new patterns, is sterile and doomed. To solve complex problems in changing circumstances requires the activity of both cerebral hemispheres: the path to the future lies in the corpus callosum." –Carl Sagan.*

5. Marjie and me

The girl that I got closest to during the day was Marjie, who had a perfect, shapely body, a captivating, laughing face and a lively brain. In the days that followed, we got to know more about each other. She was married but separated and had a French boyfriend in Saudi Arabia and I had the lovely Asha waiting for me so neither of us was looking for a romantic relationship. It was a perfect situation, we each had our own boat moored on separate quays so we could be friends and enjoy each other's company without getting too involved and without feeling guilty. I visited her sometimes and sometimes she visited me. We'd share a drink and chat and say our goodbyes. It was a perfect relationship.

CHAPTER 6
GREAT EXPECTATIONS

Half-shafted

I was offered a two-week charter taking a young couple on a cruise to some local areas. The Dufour 35, classed as a cruiser/racer, was my favourite yacht from the Dufour range and we had some splendid sailing and visited exquisite creeks and harbours. The charterers were enchanted with the places we visited and the stimulating passages between each stopover. They helped me to hoist and to lower the sails and the charter was as good as I'd hoped it would be. I had the time of my life and my joy was intensified by the knowledge that I was getting paid for it. The couple were disheartened when the time came to return to Antibes and they wished they'd chartered the yacht for a longer period. The last sail was invigorating. There was a good, late afternoon breeze and we were on a broad reach. The sturdy yacht rode the waves well. The sun beat down from a clear blue sky and the scenery was spectacular with the blue Estérel mountains in the distance. When we reached Port Vauban and moored up and the time came for them to leave, they gave me an extra payment in appreciation of all that I'd done for them. I felt good and was optimistic that the season would be a success.

In anticipation of more charters and more money, I bought a second hand MG Midget from a Skipper who dealt in old cars and anything else that would augment his already more than adequate income. He skippered a large motor yacht for a famous comedian/actor. He was renowned among the other yacht crews and I knew him well and liked him in spite of his dubious reputation. I knew that I was taking a chance in dealing with him but he had what I wanted. Although I persuaded myself that I was getting a reasonable deal, I really knew that I was probably being robbed - albeit in a charming way. He was, I suppose, a loveable rogue; a typical Eastender with a very broad cockney accent, known to everyone as "Well-Spoken Fred." His father had been "a motor breaker" as he called it so Fred knew everything there was to know about cars and always had a large selection of them for sale or repair that he kept on the quay at the stern of his yacht. He had been in France for many years but still hadn't got round to occupying himself with the French language. He was often in trouble with the port authorities who would have preferred it if the charming old quay backed by a charming stone wall wasn't cluttered with cars in varying states of decrepitude. Once I was moored close by and was sitting in the saloon when suddenly a figure came bursting through the doorway and started crawling towards me on hands and knees at top speed. I was dumbfounded and at a loss for words at the unusual and unexpected intrusion. It was Well-Spoken Fred.

"'Ave they gone?" he begged me breathlessly from a lying position as he collapsed on the floor.

"Has who gone?" I enquired.

"The Customs, they're after me agin," he gasped. I looked out and saw people milling around his cars. One of them pointed along the quay.

"Somebody's heading this way; you'd better stay where you are," I told him. At that moment he did a stupid thing, he raised himself enough to peer through the window to see for himself. As soon as the top of his head was spotted he was summoned to the quay to face the wrath of the authorities. They knew exactly where he was anyway; they'd seen him racing for a hideaway and scarpering up the gangplank of a yacht further down the quay. He'd been doubled over in the hope of making himself inconspicuous and had hoped that even if he had been seen it would be assumed that he was hiding on that yacht. Ah, but Fred was crafty, he then scrambled over the other yachts until he'd reached mine. He slunk along the side deck until he reached the saloon doors and then stumbled in. I heard the commotion and the exchange of words as he was ordered for the umpteenth time to remove the unsightly cars. Fred didn't understand a word that was said to him but knew exactly what they were ordering him to do. He had insufficient French to reply but did his best as he fumbled for the right words.

"je – je – je -move the fuckin' lot," he said.

Anyway, I was delighted with the MG Midget, a small, green, two-seater sports car. It gave me the freedom to explore the area and I felt good racing along the mountain roads in a fast, open-topped car.

One day, on my way to shop at Maison Robert, where I had become friendly with one of the girls who always got to serve me before any of her colleagues and slipped a few extra items into my bag, I met the ravishing, petite Marjie, with the perfect, bronzed body and the mesmerising eyes.

"When are you going to take me out to dinner then?" she asked cheekily after I'd told her of my successful charter, the money I'd made and the car I'd purchased. I hesitated for an entire half of one second before I smiled at her cheekiness and said,

"How about tonight?" and she agreed.

"Do you have a favourite restaurant?" I asked her.

"Yes, I know one, I ate there recently and it was quite good," she replied. So that evening we went to dine together and had an enjoyable evening but I wasn't impressed with the restaurant. A few days later, I was on my way to make one of my regular phone calls to Asha and met Marjie again so I proposed that we go to a much better restaurant.

"I've been told about a very good restaurant at St Martin de Vésubie up in the mountains, what about tomorrow night, it's the 14th of July, Bastille Day, so there should be plenty of festivities going on to make it a good evening," I said. - July 14th is a national holiday throughout France. It was instituted in law in 1880 to commemorate two events, 1; the storming of the fortress prison, the Bastille, in 1789, which resulted in the end of the monarchy and 2, the *Fete de la Fédération*, to celebrate the unity of the French nation. St Martin de Vésubie is known as Nice Switzerland because of its cooler summer climate. It is located at an altitude of almost 1000 metres in the Maritime Alps, north of the Vésubie valley and lies at the convergence of two alpine torrents, the Madone de Fenestre to the east and the Boréon to the west. It is a key gateway to the Mercantour National Park

"OK, what time?" she asked.

"Why not come around to my boat for a drink first, say half-past five because it will take an hour and a half to drive there," I said.

"Alright I'll see you then," she affirmed before she went on her way. I continued on my shopping trip and to chat to Asha on the agency telephone. She asked me once again if I could go to the U.K. to be with her and I explained once again that I couldn't afford to be away and miss the opportunity of a charter but I would be home in September.

That evening, I sat waiting in the cockpit basking in the sunshine and saw Marjie approaching wearing a cotton evening dress. She looked spectacular and I was looking forward to getting to know her better. An hour later, after a gin and tonic, we walked to the MG that was parked close by, settled in and set off for the drive to the Alps. We had a pleasant drive along the coast with the hood down. There was a warm evening breeze, a clear sky and a sparkling sea. The engine of the MG purred and there was hardly any traffic on the roads. When we reached the vicinity of Nice Airport, I turned north to join the Route du Mercantour and after 700 metres we came to a red traffic light so I stopped in the inside lane. Another car drew up alongside me in the outside lane. The young male driver stared at me and I knew he was as determined to pull away before me as I was determined to leave him behind. We continued exchanging glances. The light changed to amber. We each started pushing down on the accelerator pedal, revving up ready for a racing getaway. The lights went green. We both slammed down the accelerator pedals to the floor and released the clutch pedals. The engines screamed at maximum revolutions. The car alongside me shot forward and the tyres screeched as it disappeared into the distance. So did the other cars that were behind me. The MG remained stationary with a screaming engine. Bewildered, I took my foot off the accelerator, jiggled with the gear lever and pressed and released the clutch and accelerator but nothing I did would make the car move. Embarrassed, I had to ask Marjie to help me push the car out of the line of oncoming traffic and park it somewhere nearby. Even though she was wearing a long dress and sandals, she didn't hesitate. We climbed out and pushed until we found a suitable place to leave the car. I had hoped to impress Marjie and although the evening wasn't how I'd hoped and planned, she's certainly never forgotten it! The car wasn't going to get us anywhere. I knew there was a small bar two kilometres away to the north so we set off to walk there, feeling conspicuous in our evening attire. We were hot and sweaty when we arrived. I asked the proprietor if I could use his telephone to call a taxi. He found that amusing.

"You must be joking," he said, "It's 14th July, nobody is going to come for you. You've got no chance at all, it's almost eight-o-clock and everybody will be sitting down to eat and looking forward to the festivities." He was right, after a couple of phone calls, I hadn't found anybody prepared to help us. I called the Capitainerie at Port Vauban to ask them to get Harry or Ted to call me back. Almost half an hour later the phone in the bar rang and the proprietor passed it to me. It was Ted. I explained our situation and asked if one of them could come and pick us up and he agreed. We went outside and sat on a wall so that he would see us and not drive past the bar. We waited...and waited...and waited. One hour and a half later nobody had arrived. We found out later that they thought I was joking. That's the price that's paid when constantly playing practical jokes on each other. I suggested to an understanding and forgiving Marjie that we walk the five kilometres to Nice airport to find a taxi. It took us another hour to get there and thank heavens, we found an available taxi.

"I'm so sorry about all of this," I said to Marjie, who unbelievably and fortunately for me, found it amusing and laughed.

"I'm starving and we won't find anywhere to eat now, I'm not sure what we can do," I said.

"I might be able to find something for us to eat aboard my boat," she replied.

We arrived in Port Vauban Antibes at 23h30, ravenous, tired, sweaty and so pleased that we'd made it home. Marjie invited me aboard her sloop and we sat for a while exhausted, then she looked in the lockers for some food.

"All I've got is a tin of Heinz spaghetti from my emergency stores and two Mars bars," she said.

"I don't care what it is, I'm so hungry I'll eat anything," I replied.

"I've got some whiskey if you want one," she said.

"What a wonderful idea. I'm really sorry about tonight's fiasco," I said once again.

"It doesn't matter," she said and laughed. I wondered how she really felt after having accepted my offer of a wonderful meal in a highly recommended restaurant and we had to make do with a small tin of spaghetti between us and a Mars bar each that she fried to try to make them more interesting. It was well after midnight by the time we ate. The next day, I arranged with friends to tow the car back to Antibes where I discovered that the half shafts had broken.

CHAPTER 7
A LESSON IN TRUST

At least it started well

My next charter was to take a young French couple, their au pair and two friends sailing for ten days. They were jovial, friendly and easy to get along with, which was just as well since we were all going to be sleeping in the restricted space of a 35ft boat. They arrived fairly late in the morning of the first day and by the time they'd boarded and unpacked their luggage and provisions, they were anxious to set sail. It was a glorious, hot, sunny day. The afternoon sea breeze, which is a regular feature on the Côte d'Azur, was blowing fairly strongly from the south-west and the forecast for the following day was for the cloud to build up and the wind to swing round to the east. The decision was taken to head off to Villefranche bay for the night, a mere ten nautical miles away to the east, where it would be totally protected from the wind. I started the engine to motor out of the berth and as soon as it was practical, hoisted the mainsail and genoa so that we could sail out of the harbour. When we were clear of the entrance, we had a stimulating sail to the bay where we anchored offshore from the town for the night.

Villefranche bay, with a maximum depth of 17 metres is one of the deepest natural harbours in the Mediterranean. The entrance to the bay has a depth of 95 metres and extending out to sea, it increases to more than 500 metres, forming what is known as the Canyon of Villefranche. The town is surrounded by hills rising to a height of 577 metres. The Greeks and later the Romans used the natural harbour, which they called Olivula Portus, as a stop-over en route to settlements around the Western Mediterranean. It came under repeated attack by Barbarian pirates and when in the 9th century, Saracen pirates built a stronghold there, the inhabitants fled to the safety of the surrounding hills where they founded a new village, Montolivo. In 1225, pirates were still a problem, and the Count of Provence, Charles II of Anjou, realising the strategic importance of the site, encouraged the inhabitants to return by offering them exemption from taxes. This lasted until the 18th century, hence the name Villefranche (free port). At the same time, the new port of Nice was built and Villefranche's maritime trade decreased, but it still remained an important naval base. From the 19th century onwards, it became more and more a winter residence for the wealthy. There are a number of restaurants along the waterfront and the old harbour, which dates back to the 17th century is now a yacht marina. The Chapelle St Pierre in the old harbour dates back to the 16th century, but was restored in 1957 and decorated by Jean Cocteau with murals depicting the life of the Saint and of local fishermen. We had a very peaceful night there and slept well after enjoying a good but hastily prepared meal

The next morning it was overcast. I looked up at the grey sky and out to sea, I could see white caps so knew that the wind had increased during the night. I ate a good breakfast in the cockpit whilst I waited for the charterers to rise, then prepared for sea. They were excited when they came on deck and chattered non-stop as they ate breakfast in the cockpit and discussed their plans.

"We'd like to go to St Tropez today if that's OK" one of them said.

"That'll be OK, there's a good wind blowing and it's in the right direction so we should have a really good sail," I told them. As soon as breakfast was finished, I pulled the number two genoa from the sail locker, fastened the hanks to the forestay, connected the sheets and the halyard, put a reef in the mainsail and hoisted it so that we were ready to go. I asked one of them to haul in the anchor. When it was clear, I called to him to hoist the genoa and another of them winched in the sheet. I hardened up on the mainsail sheet and we took off at a rate of knots. When we cleared the sheltered bay we felt the full force of the wind and the waves. The wind was abaft the beam so we were on a broad reach on course for St Tropez and we rode the waves well at a good speed. I expected to complete the 40 nautical miles in about five hours and hoped to reach our destination before the expected storm struck. It was a thrilling sail. We were thundering along on a southwesterly course and had passed the Iles de Lerins. Despite the gloomy weather, the charterers were delighted, animated and eager to reach St Tropez. I was exhilarated, feeling the steering wheel trembling in my hands as we effortlessly sliced our way through the water, which made a satisfying gurgle as it raced past the hull. The wind was on my back and I took a deep breath savouring the delicious smell of the sea and in my locker below, several thousand francs in cash that I'd been paid for having the time of my life. Things couldn't get better. They didn't, they got immeasurably worse.

One foot from death

"This is fantastic," one of the charterers said as the rest of them gathered around me in the cockpit. "I'd love to take the wheel; may I steer for a while?"

"Maybe later, it could be a bit tricky because we have to keep the wind on our port quarter," I said.

"I know all about that, I'm an experienced sailor", he assured me. I'd heard these sorts of comments before from people who thought they were experts but who still had plenty to learn. The wind had increased in strength since we'd left Villefranche and the clouds were menacing. As much as I was enjoying myself, I was eager to reach our destination.

"I'd prefer to continue steering myself for a while as the weather is deteriorating and I think we should get to St Tropez as soon as possible," I told him.

"You can trust me, I know what I'm doing," he insisted. I looked at him and wondered if I could really trust him. I was unsure but he was paying a considerable amount of money and I wanted to keep them happy.

"All right, you can take the wheel for a while but make sure you hold the course and keep the wind where it is," I said as I reluctantly moved to one side to let him steer. I stood forward of the wheel by the cabin entrance, looking ahead.

The next thing I knew, I was lying in the cockpit, semi-conscious with three of the charterers huddled over me. One of the girls was applying compresses to my head. They were chattering insanely, panicking. I could see their worried faces. Whatever had happened had terrified them. As I slowly regained full consciousness, I became aware of the sails flapping wildly with the boat pitching up and down and the so-called expert sailor spinning the wheel in all directions. I gingerly pushed the charterers away and stood up to assess the situation. I felt warm liquid running from my head into my eyes and down my left cheek. It was blood. Dazed, I took the wheel and steadied the boat.

"We have to get back to Cannes as soon as possible," I was told, "You need to get to the hospital." I looked around to ascertain where we were and then told them to harden up on the mainsail and genoa sheets as I spun the wheel to head for the entrance to the old harbour of Cannes. With the wind now on our beam, the sea conditions were uncomfortable. We heeled over and smashed our way through the waves. I stood steering with the girl tending the wound on my head until we'd almost reached the harbour. I told them to drop and stow the sails and I started the engine. Due to the urgency, I moored alongside the ferry terminal. When the mooring ropes had been made fast and I'd switched the engine off, I collapsed onto one of the cockpit seats and from then on was unable to move. One of the girls, who fortunately was a nurse, related to me what had happened whilst she cleaned up the blood from my head and face and continued to apply the compress.

The expert sailor had gybed the vessel. A gybe is a sailing manoeuvre where the vessel, running with the wind on the stern and the mainsail out on one side, is turned slightly so that the mainsail boom travels through 180° and ends up on the other side. When done intentionally, it is a controlled manoeuvre. The mainsail sheet is hauled in tightly as the stern swings around and then is freed off again when the wind is on the opposite side. When done unintentionally, which is what had happened, the uncontrolled mainsail boom flies across to the other side wildly as the stern passes through the wind. The boom struck me and sent me flying with such ferocity that I somersaulted and smashed my head on the cockpit winch. It knocked me unconscious and ripped a portion of skin from my head. Then I was flicked overboard. My back slammed onto the stanchions as I disappeared from sight but by a miracle, the au pair girl managed to grab hold of one of my ankles. She held on with both hands until the others helped to pull my unconscious body back on board.

Once we were moored up one of the charterers ran to the port office and asked them to call an ambulance. Shortly afterwards I heard the siren of the approaching ambulance and soon the paramedics were strapping me up to a stretcher and I was taken to Brousaille hospital in Cannes. *Ernest Hemingway said, "The best way to find out if you can trust someone is to trust them."* Well, I'll be very careful about trusting someone again when they tell me they're an expert at something, especially if my life could depend on it.

Stitched up and broken

The journey to the hospital is vague in my memory but once I'd been rushed to the emergency room, I remember only too well what happened. As I lay on the trolley surrounded by hospital staff, I heard them discussing what they should do.

"Do you have insurance?" was the first question I was asked, not "What happened or where does it hurt or how are you feeling?"

"Yes, I should be insured," I replied. Then they asked me for details so I told them the situation and that they would have to contact Keith and also gave them the contact details of the agency that I used to work for and who had passed on the charter to me. One of them went to verify the facts and two others started to clean me and shave my head. They gave me an injection and began sewing the flap of skin back on my scalp. Putting the ten stitches in my head took longer than expected and the effects of the local anaesthetic began to wear off. I winced each time the needle pierced me and the stitches were pulled tight.

"We have to give another injection," one of them said.

"We don't have confirmation about insurance," another said. So they carried on stitching me up regardless and when the anaesthetic had worn off completely, I could have done with a glass of whisky and a stick to bite on. They x-rayed me and generally attended to me reasonably well after that. They placed me on a bed in a ward and gave me the results - three broken ribs and a couple of damaged vertebrae.

The next day I was visited by the unbelievably lovely Heather, who worked in the agency and whom I knew well from when I worked there myself. She was compassionate and took care of everything. She found a replacement Skipper to continue the charter, collected the cash that was lying in my locker, and made sure that Keith and Marjie were aware of the situation. For the first few days, I was unable to move without a great deal of pain. I couldn't even sit up. Food was brought and placed by my bedside and that's where it stayed. French nurses do not get involved in personal domestic duties, patients were expected to be cared for by family members and I had nobody. One of the cleaning ladies took pity on me and poured my hot soup into the plastic bottle with a spout that I could place between my lips. She lifted my head and put the spout to my mouth. I recoiled and gasped as the scalding contents poured onto my face and neck. She'd forgotten to screw the cap on the bottle. The reflex action as I reacted sent waves of pain through my protesting broken ribs.

After that, Marjie came to see me each day to tend to my needs, travelling the 12 kilometres from Antibes on the moped that she'd been bought by her French boyfriend. I had no complaints about the food. Each day I was brought a three-course meal with wine at midday and again in the evening. (Sadly, things have changed now. I was taken to hospital five years ago with more broken ribs after an accident and the food was atrocious – that's progress!) Unusually for me, I didn't have a big appetite since I wasn't moving much so it was mostly Marjie who profited from the food. It would have been thoroughly miserable had she not devoted so much of her time to me.

One day she made the mistake of coming with Harry from the boat next to mine. The intention was well-meant and I appreciated the fact that he'd taken the time to visit but it was excruciatingly painful for me. Harry, Ted, their two wives, Marjie and I never stopped laughing when we were together and they were almost incapable of being serious. From the moment he came in he was wisecracking and each time I laughed I almost fainted from the pain but in spite of my pleas not to make me laugh, he couldn't help himself. He walked to the window and gazed out as he tried to stay calm and not make me laugh.

"Oh, that's handy having the cemetery so close," he said. I saw his shoulders rising and falling as he giggled silently at his own remark. Then Marjie laughed and that made him laugh louder, which made me laugh and the pain was excruciating. It was such a relief when they left.

As the days passed, Marjie helped me walk, first by allowing me to lean on her and later by accompanying me whilst I walked unaided. There was very little privacy in the hospital and as Marjie and I were walking the length of the ward, a determined and fierce-looking nurse came at me with a syringe in her hand. Not a very agreeable sight at the best of times.

"Time for your injection," she said and pulled down my pyjama bottoms before plunging the needle into my buttocks. Then she disappeared to probably skewer the next unfortunate soul. I stood there in full view of the other patients waiting for Marjie to pull up my pyjama bottoms for me. I was mortally embarrassed but grateful to be alive.

CHAPTER 8
IRRESISTIBLE YOU

Close up and personal

Keith contacted me and told me that he had chartered the boat to a friend for a week's cruise and wanted to know if he should employ another Skipper. As a result of the accident, I'd already lost 10 days commission and didn't want to lose another seven days. I told him I'd be OK. However, I knew that I wouldn't be able to manage on my own so asked Marjie if she would like to crew for me. She agreed and just 12 days after the accident, I was back on board the yacht, which had been returned to Antibes by the replacement Skipper. Marjie joined me and we waited for Keith's friend to arrive. I'd called Asha and explained why I hadn't been in touch. I told her about the accident and the charter and that I wouldn't be able to call her again for another week. Once again she asked me to go back to the U.K. to be with her and I agreed to visit her as soon as possible.

The charter went well. We had an enjoyable week's cruising and after having visited the naturist island of Ile Levant, the four of us spent much of the remainder of the cruise *à poil,* - the French expression for in the raw. Being in close confinement for the week, Marjie and I got to know each other better and remained close afterwards. We met more people when we returned to Antibes and spent more time together, socialising, dining in restaurants, and inviting each other to our respective yachts for drinks and meals and Marjie helped me when I had work to do aboard the yacht. I kept it in perfect condition; after all, it was in effect my boat as

Keith had promised me a 50% share in it. To polish the hull, I squeezed the inflatable dinghy between my boat and the one next to me so that it was wedged in position. When I wanted to move along, I went to the bow of the dinghy, spread my arms to push the two yachts apart and used a backwards walking motion with my feet to move the dinghy forward. When the stern of the dinghy was beneath my feet, I let go the two yachts. They floated back together, wedging the dinghy firmly in place so that I could continue working on the hull. It was a good system, so much so that Harry asked me to explain it to him so that he could clean the hull of his boat. I did and he tried out the method himself. The first stage went well enough but when he walked the dinghy forward he moved his feet too quickly. The buoyant dinghy shot forward, he panicked, let go with his arms, fell flat on his back in the dinghy as it shot out into the middle of the harbour with Harry flapping around trying to get upright. Then he discovered he had no paddles so had no way to get back. Marjie and I laughed so much that by the time we stopped long enough for me to throw a rope to him, he'd drifted almost to the opposite jetty, all the time waving his arms and yelling for us to help him. We hauled him back in and had a good hearty laugh.

Marjie and I sometimes took the Dufour 35 for a sail and we had some wonderful times together. When all the other boats came back into the harbour at the end of the day, we'd cast off, hoist the sails and in the light, warm evening breeze, sail away to a deserted, sheltered creek and drop anchor for the night. They were moments of pure joy. All alone, we spent a long time swimming naked in the calm, blue, warm sea that we had all to ourselves. We enjoyed evening meals in the candlelit cockpit, savouring the warm, still summer air, beneath the clear skies, filled with millions of twinkling stars and listening to the sound of the cicadas on the shore. If we were close to a town or port, the lights shining along the shoreline were enticing enough for us to get into the dinghy, start the outboard motor and go ashore for coffee and cognac after the evening meal. During those blissful nights we slept peacefully, the only sound was the gentle rippling of the water. In the mornings, we swam before breakfast, then swam again afterwards and relaxed until yachts left their harbours and began to arrive for the day. That was when we weighed anchor and returned to Port Vauban.

One evening we decided to anchor at the Iles de Lerins between the two main islands, Ile Ste Marguerite and Ile St Honorat. We'd spent nights there before and had told Harry and Ted how calm and peaceful it was so they asked if they could join us in their boat. They were friends and fun to be with so we agreed. At the end of the day, we both set off and dropped anchor a short distance from the tiny harbour of Ile St Honorat. We dined on Ted and Harry's boat and afterwards returned to our own boat for a nice quiet night's sleep. It wasn't to be. We should have known that when Harry and Ted were around serenity was nonexistent. In the middle of the night, we heard an engine start up. It thumped away for a while and then stopped. We forgot about it and went back to sleep. Then it happened again. Sometime later the same thing happened. When it happened a fourth time and we heard shouting, we went on deck to find out what was happening. It was our friends. When they'd dropped the anchor, it had hooked on an underwater cable that ran between the two islands. What little wind there was, was enough to send them sliding along the cable towards the other island. They started the engine to reposition themselves to where they'd dropped the anchor only to slide back again and so it went on until they decided to try to free the anchor. They hauled it up until they could see the cable hanging from it. Pat put a boathook under the cable and tried to lift it off. Ted was on the flying bridge. Marjie and I were doubled up with laughter watching them.

"Pull, pull," he was shouting to Pat but the cable was too heavy for her to lift it clear of the anchor. Harry came on to the foredeck to help her. Whilst Pat kept hold of the boathook and cable, Harry dropped the anchor, which plunged to the seabed. It had cleared the cable that then became too heavy for Pat to hold. The boathook, still hooked to the cable, shot through her hands at great speed and embedded itself in the sea-bed like a spear. At last, peace reigned and Marjie and I were eventually able to get some sleep after we'd stopped laughing. Fortunately, the water is very shallow between the islands and they were able to retrieve the boathook the following morning.

Bye-bye love

I spoke with Asha constantly, she was a wonderful, generous, caring person and I was very fond of her. Her feelings for me were more than mere fondness so I felt enormous guilt because I was developing strong feelings for Marjie and Asha didn't deserve to be deceived.

"When will you come home?" she asked for the umpteenth time.

"Well, we have no more charters booked and it's looking unlikely that we'll be offered anything for a while, so maybe I could fly back for a few days," I said. I was confused and needed to sort myself out because I didn't know what I wanted any more. The last thing I wanted was to cause anybody any harm in any way. I cared deeply for the lovely, kind, thoughtful Asha and also for the equally loving, kind and thoughtful Marjie with the amazing laughing eyes.

"Let's think about it overnight. I can come anytime and I'll call you tomorrow," I told her. The next day, when I called her, she told me she'd booked a return flight for me for a long weekend. I was surprised but was looking forward to seeing her again and to have the opportunity to get my life in order. As a youth, I'd had the good fortune to have lived through the cultural and sexual revolution of the fabulous swinging 60s and had had more than my share of all that it had to offer but had never before been unfaithful to a girl that I'd been in a relationship with. There was, however, one exception, which happened at the beginning of my relationship with my ex-wife Jill and although there was no excuse, the circumstances at the time were complicated. I did not like feeling guilty and I knew that when I met Asha I would know what I had to do. What I was doing was not right and it had to be resolved. When the time came, a friend took Marjie and me to Nice airport, then left the two of us to say our goodbyes. We stayed for a long time with each other, finding it difficult to part, so long in fact, that I missed my flight and had to take the next available one. I managed to get a message to Asha who had been waiting for me at the other end. When I did arrive she was not at all upset; on the contrary, she was forgiving and happy to see me. She looked radiant, which made me feel even more guilty. We hugged and kissed for a long time before going to the lavish hotel that she'd booked for us for the night and after an extravagant meal we went to our room - we had a lot of time to make up for. In bed, the adorable Asha pulled me on top of her and I was unable to satisfy her because I was so consumed with guilt and thoughts of the bewitching girl I'd left behind in Antibes. Asha realised that something had changed.

The next two days were a mixture of emotions for both of us as we came to terms with the change in our relationship. Back home in my apartment, I was missing Marjie already. I was pleased to be with Asha again but my feelings for Marjie were stronger. I realised that it was a mistake to have returned to the U.K. and that the kindest thing to do would be to tell Asha what had happened and how I felt. When she called by at the end of the afternoon to drive us to an Indian restaurant she was bubbling with excitement and looked so enchanting in her brightly coloured sari I couldn't bear to spoil the occasion for her. We had an enjoyable, intimate evening together despite the disapproving stares of the Indian waiters and proprietors. On the way home, she pulled up outside a Mercedes showroom and parked so that we could see the cars on display. There were two gleaming Mercedes-Benz 450 SL sports cars on show, one red and the other white. They were beautiful, two-seater cars with detachable roofs.

"What colour would you like?" she asked. I looked at her in amazement and saw that she was deadly serious. "I want to buy you one," she said.

"I can't let you do that," I told her.

"I want to," she replied, "We can call by tomorrow and order one."

"No, let's wait," I said. I felt a terrible sadness knowing that I was responsible for creating such a horrible situation for us both and that the adorable woman beside me was prepared to go to such lengths to keep me with her. "Let's go home now and we'll talk tomorrow," I said.

We spent the next day together and had a good time but by the evening we were both subdued and that's when I told her what she had suspected. I had met somebody else. With Asha, I would have had a comfortable life but it would have been restricting. She wanted me to be with her constantly and preferred either that I didn't work or that I worked as little as possible since she had sufficient money to keep us. With the adventurous, unconventional, intelligent, sensational and perpetually laughing Marjie, I had no idea what the future would be like, only that it would undoubtedly be full of constant change and much laughter, which appealed to me. We laughed so much when we were together it was sometimes uncontrollable and even painful as we struggled to contain our mirth. Laughter is an international language available to us all and it has proven health benefits. It increases the blood flow, releases endorphins, which can diminish pain, reduces the production of the stress hormones, adrenalin and cortisol and strengthens the immune system by producing antibodies. A study in 2000, found that people with heart disease were 40% less likely to laugh than people of the same age without heart disease. *"Always laugh when you can. It is cheap medicine."* – Lord Byron.

My heart ached as I held Asha close and she sobbed and sobbed. I have never forgotten and will never forget the sorrow in her tear-filled eyes when she looked at me as we said goodbye. The pain I caused her that day still haunts me and if I haven't already paid the price then I surely will one day. I believe in the spiritual principle of cause and effect (karma), which is a key concept of Buddhism, as well as Hinduism and Sikhism. Reincarnation is the belief system of all three and although most Christians do not believe in reincarnation, they still believe in the principle of cause and effect, *"Be not deceived; God is not mocked: for whatsoever a man soweth, that shall he also reap." Epistle to the Galatians, 6:7* and there are numerous other references to the same concept in the Bible, *Proverbs 22:8. "Whosoever sows injustice, will reap calamity,"* is another. However, there is evidence suggesting that reincarnation played a role in early Christianity and according to a 2009 survey in America, 25% of Christians now express a belief in it. Since there is no proof either for or against reincarnation, just as there is no proof of a God, I keep an open mind. Religion is a faith and the definition of faith is "a belief in something without proof of its existence." The law of the Universe is that every action has an equal and opposite reaction and nobody escapes. People may suspect that they've managed to get away with an unkindly act but in time they will feel the effects. However, I'd trusted my inner guidance and made my choice. Life is an endless cycle of making choices, some we win, and some we don't and we have to live with the consequences. Asha had offered me love and I'd rejected it. *"Farewell, thou art too dear for my possessing." Shakespeare, Sonnet 87.*

CHAPTER 9
DREAM GIRL

Marjie was waiting for me when I arrived at Nice airport. She looked spectacular and I was pleased to be back. Her husband, Dave, had taken her boat to sail it back to the U.K. and they had agreed on divorce proceedings so Marjie moved in with me. She felt that she had been responsible for the breakdown of her marriage by having an affair with a Frenchman in Rhyad so decided that she would take nothing whatsoever from her husband. He had the boat and everything else he wanted so she finished up with nothing at all, not that her husband was in any way malicious, in fact, I found him to be charming and understanding. Giving up everything she had was Marjie's way of atoning for her infidelity but she did receive half of the proceeds when their house was sold. Her compassionate, loving, extraordinarily generous behaviour towards her husband was in stark contrast to the way Jill had treated me. Jill will have found a way to justify her act of betrayal and will have a different perception to my own but either way, it is as it is and had it not been so I may never have met Marjie, the girl of my dreams. Marjie is a unique and very special person who would never knowingly say or do anything to hurt another being, animal or human and I love her deeply, much more than I could ever describe. We have been together for 46 years and although we are both now in our mid-seventies, we still behave like a couple of lovesick teenagers. I swear she gets prettier each year and I tell her so throughout each day. Although Jill's infidelity was extremely distressing to me at the time, I am pleased that things turned out as they did.

As a child, Marjie had no interest in the usual girlie things like dolls, apart from a big blue teddy bear called Bobby that her mum bought at Rosie's second-hand stall in Nuneaton market, which is also where a lot of her clothes were bought. Her lack of interest in traditionally accepted pursuits of girls in the 1950s transformed into having no desire to have children. However, she did love making her own clothes, an interest that was inherited from her mum. From her dad, she inherited an interest in photography. She got him to make up a stand to house a modified old bellows camera, which she used as an enlarger and developed and printed films in the bathroom, a large upstairs room at the back of the house. (The toilet was outside at the end of the backyard.) She joined Nuneaton photographic society and went weekly from school with her friend Meghan and entered all the competitions, mostly for black and white photos, which were mounted on special boards using an iron-on backing paper to avoid creases.

After leaving grammar school, she took up clothes design as a career, becoming an assistant designer for Denham Knitwear at their factory in Atherstone, which enabled her to travel one or two days a week to Leicester Art College to study dress design. Later, she became chief designer at Hinckley Knitting Company, not far from her hometown, Nuneaton. She stayed there until she married Dave in 1965. Unlike my own unhappy childhood, where the only literature in the house was an old copy of a Mrs. Beeton's Cookery Book, Marjie had, among other books, two sets of Children's Encyclopaedia and following instructions, distilled water using household items, constructed weather forecasting tools and made all manner of other things.

Like many other children before and since, she was inspired by Arthur Ransome's 'Swallows and Amazons' series of books and had long wanted to learn how to sail. Imagine her delight when just recently we were invited to sail on Arthur Ransome's old boat, the 'Nancy Blackett', now run by The Nancy Blackett Trust. The beautiful red sailed cutter ("Goblin" in Ransome's book "We Didn't Mean to Go to Sea") is moored at Wolverstone Marina on the River Orwell in Suffolk and we had a lovely day out with two of their skippers, John Smith and Simon Jackson. John is the sailing secretary for the Trust and organised our visit, for which we are both really grateful.

Marjie's desire to sail was frustrated by many factors – distance from the sea being one of them. Finally, she went on a Youth Hostel sailing holiday on a ketch called Kelpie, in Salcombe, Devon, where she met her husband. He was studying physics at Brighton Polytechnic and when they started corresponding, he travelled to Nuneaton at weekends to see her as often as he could. They bought a foldaway canoe and with that, at weekends, went camping on the River Wye in Wales, taking her mum and dad's old ridge tent. The River Wye is very popular among canoeists and kayakers. From its source at Plynlimon, in the Welsh mountains, it flows for 216 kilometres to join the Severn estuary with the last 26 kilometres, from Redbrook to Chepstow, forming the English/Welsh border. Sometimes they arrived late on Friday night, pitching the tent in the dark and getting what sleep they could before daylight when they assembled the canoe, packed all their camping equipment and food into it and set off for the day. At the end of the afternoon, they would choose a spot to set up camp for the night. On one occasion, they'd stopped, dragged the canoe onto an open, flat piece of land and started to unpack. Dave was pulling the tent out of the canoe when Marjie noticed an idyllic spot on the opposite side of the river. It looked appealing because it was backed by trees and resembled an island as the river bent around it.

"Actually, we should have stopped over there. It looks much better. It would be amazing to spend the night there. Like being on an island," she said.

"Well, I haven't unpacked everything yet. There's no reason why we shouldn't. We'll take across what's left in the canoe now and come back for the rest." They set off for the opposite bank with the half-filled canoe, unloaded it, then returned for the rest of the gear which they hastily threw into the canoe as the light was fading. They clambered in and started paddling once more, looking forward to settling down for the night. In an instant, they were thrown into the depth of the icy cold river. The shock took their breath away. The canoe had capsized. Gasping for breath as they resurfaced, it took them a few moments to take stock of the situation. Their possessions were being carried away by the current. They splashed around in the fading light to right the canoe and rescue what they could. Soaked to the skin and shivering from the icy cold water, they made their way to the chosen spot on the river bank where they once again dragged the canoe ashore and unpacked. Chilled to the bone and shivering in their wet clothes that were clinging to their bodies, they went scavaging for firewood among the trees. With the fire lit, they spread their wet belongings around the flames in a vain attempt to dry everything out. They hastily erected the tent and changed into dry clothes. Dave set up the paraffin cooker and Marjie opened a packet of Vesta curry, tipped the contents into the aluminium saucepan and measured in the water. They sat around the fire, devoured the meal and regretted not having taken more care with weight distribution when they'd repacked the canoe. Later, when night fell and they were tucked up in their sleeping bags, Marjie, shivering uncontrollably with her teeth chattering, thought what a stroke of luck it had been that the sleeping bags and clothes were in the first load. Shortly after that trip, for whatever reason, Marjie contracted yellow jaundice.

Marjie's great grandfather had owned a trawler, the St. Cecelia, based in Lowestoft. It was a hard life and not one of his seven sons followed in his footsteps but somehow, an interest in boats was in her blood. She impatiently looked forward to the two weeks every year when her family went to stay with her grandparents for the summer holidays in Felixstowe, a mostly unspoilt Edwardian seaside town on the North Sea coast and now Britain's largest container port, although in those days the port was just a small affair. Nevertheless, Felixstowe itself is still the same, apart from the towering black derricks on the skyline to the south of the town. Marjie used to go lobster fishing with a local fisherman called Billy Newson who doubled as a river pilot. He was based at a place called Felixstowe Ferry, set at the mouth of the River Deben, two miles northeast of Felixstowe. The hamlet even now has a timeless atmosphere, with its collection of residences, shacks and houseboats, a pub, church, boatyard and sailing club, as well as a shack selling an amazing variety of locally caught fresh fish and shellfish.

Billy's eighteen-foot clinker-built motorboat would be loaded with a pile of hoops which had nets underneath and a cord across the top into which a piece of fish was inserted. They'd motor round in a large circle, dropping the hoops and then go round again picking them up. The catches weren't bountiful but any they did catch would be sold – usually after being boiled in a large pan on a gas ring in Billy's hut. The hut looked out over the estuary and Billy always kept a weather eye out to sea, on the lookout for any craft flying the international code flag G, which has three yellow and blue vertical stripes, indicating that they needed a pilot. The mouth of the River Deben is treacherous with a fast-flowing current and constantly shifting shingle banks which stretch out from the entrance. On the other side of the river, connected by a foot and bicycle ferry is Bawdsey Manor. Built in the 1880s, it was sold to the Air Ministry in 1936 and became a secret WW11 establishment where Sir Robert Watson-Watt developed radar. Billy came from a family which had lived there for generations, and his name comes up many times in a wonderful new book, called 'Felixstowe Ferry, Yesterday, Today and Tomorrow', which we bought in the Ferry Boat Inn when we recently visited Felixstowe.

Sea wife

After Marjie and Dave married, they moved into a 22ft caravan pitched on the top of the cliffs at Peacehaven on a site called Rushy Hill Caravan Site, where other newlyweds lived with their children as well as retired folk and a few eccentrics, including a man who walked along the clifftop playing his bagpipes and a trapeze artist who'd set up a trapeze in his garden. The site was very exposed and the caravan used to get buffeted in gales making it impossible to leave a glass or mug on the table for fear of it landing on the floor. It was a small comfort that the van was anchored down with strong cables.

Students were given grants in those days, which were used principally for accommodation but by buying and renovating a caravan cheaply, Marjie and Dave had money left over for more exciting things – like buying boats. Dave spotted an abandoned Merlin Rocket parked at a local sailing club. (These are 14 ft. racing class dinghies that were created in 1951 for racing in the North Sea and inland waterways.) They traced the owner, went to see him and asked if he wanted to sell it. He agreed, delighted no doubt to be rid of it. They painted it, sorted out the rigging and used it for a while before they decided to replace it with a GP14, a "General Purpose" dinghy designed in 1949 as a racing/cruising dinghy, which went on to became a world-class racing dinghy. Although in better condition than the Merlin Rocket it still needed renovating. The GP 14 provided them with the opportunity to travel longer distances but again, having no engine, it often took them a painfully long time to return home. Their next undertaking was to buy a Debutante 21 ft. sloop, which they kept moored at Newhaven. Debutantes were seaworthy bilge-keelers, built of cold moulded marine plywood with high topsides and cambered flush decks. They had two bunks, a quarter berth and a cooker and sink area, which made them good for coastal cruising and one has also been sailed across the Atlantic. The Debutante allowed Marjie and Dave to go further afield. They regularly sailed across to France and the Channel Islands, where the tides can be tricky, especially around Alderney. The cross-channel passages took a couple of days because the Debutante was a slow vessel and not good at pointing into the wind and it wasn't unusual to have to set off for work immediately after they got back. They had some amazing adventures – "the smaller the boat, the greater the adventure." I've had many amazing adventures myself in much larger vessels and know only too well the mishaps, the fears and the joys that can be had from sailing.

Their income was augmented by the wages Marjie earned as a technician in the Pharmacognosy department at the Polytechnic where Dave was studying. The department dealt with the study of natural medicines obtained from plants, and she enjoyed her work as it was a subject that interested her. It was the start of a lifetime interest which later on led her to acquire diplomas in Iridology, Radionics, Aromatherapy and Reflexology. She and I have never stopped being interested in nutrition and health and are convinced that healthy eating is a major contributor to a healthy life. Whilst employed as a technician, Marjie attended a one day a week course for the City and Guilds Technicians Certificate, covering biology and chemistry as well as making things, a natural pursuit for Marjie. She was in her element playing with optical apparatus, woodwork and glass blowing and had such an aptitude that she became the favourite pupil. These days, I never know what she's making next. I hear machinery starting up and bangs coming from all over the place and wonder to myself, "What on earth is she up to now?" She is the sort of person who doesn't believe in buying anything if she can make it. What a unique and amazing person she is. Sometimes she will disappear and become so involved in a project and I won't have a clue where she is and it can have unfortunate outcomes. I once turned out the light and locked the door of our large semi-buried wine cellar that is entered from the garage that is annexed to our house. I hadn't realised that she was in there involved in another of her little ventures. I'm so used to her disappearing that it didn't occur to me to check the wine cellar first. It happened at a time that our good friend, Georgie-two-boats was staying with us and he and I were so involved in joking and laughing that we couldn't hear Marjie's shouts to be let out. She was locked in there for a couple of hours before I happened to walk by and hear her hammering on the door croaking my name. She was not happy with me when I let her out!

After Dave finished his Master's degree and realised that he couldn't continue as a student forever, as enticing as the prospect seemed, he joined the Royal Navy as a "Schoolie", (someone already qualified in a subject, who is allowed to join as a Lieutenant and serve as a lecturer.) Before he was let loose on the students he had to undergo a short naval training, which took place at Portsmouth. He had to learn about the varied duties of a Naval Officer, including parade ground marching and what it meant to be 'Officer of the day'.

Marjie and Dave were not the sort of people to conform to a conventional lifestyle. The very thought of a nice little bungalow was anathema to them so they bought a 12 ton Hillyard, a Bermudan sloop with a central cockpit, an aft cabin, a saloon with standing headroom and a small forward cabin. They sailed from Birdham Pool to Portsmouth in the Hillyard, called "Lady Bear" and obtained an offshore mooring at Camper and Nicholson's yard at Gosport, which lies to the west of Portsmouth. Dave attended his naval training at the base in Portsmouth and Marjie got a job as Senior Technician at Portsmouth Polytechnic. She lived on her own except for weekends and to get ashore, had to row the short distance to the quay in the dinghy each morning to catch the ferry across the harbour to Portsmouth. At night, she'd climb into bed in the cosy aft cabin and in the warm glow and gentle low hiss of the Tilley lamp that hung from the deckhead, read sailing books, anticipating the time when she could emulate the seafarers that she read about. With a mug of hot cocoa at her side and the gentle lapping of water on the hull, things didn't get much better.

At the end of Dave's training, because of his sailing experience, he was posted to Dartmouth where the Navy had five 43ft sail training yachts which had been built especially for the college in the 1950s by Morgan Giles of Teignmouth. There was always a need for officers to skipper them in their spare time and Dave took charge of the 'Martlet', so they set sail in Lady Bear for the River Dart early one cold January morning.

The River Dart has two sources; the West Dart originates at Lower White Tor and the East Dart at Kit Rock, Whinney's Down. Each source flows down to Dartmeet, where they converge and then on to Totnes where the river becomes tidal, after which, there are no more bridges and all crossings are by ferry. At the estuary, which is a large submerged valley open to the sea, Kingswear lies on the east bank and Dartmouth, where the Royal Britannia Naval College is based, is on the west bank. The area is a natural, deep water harbour that is popular with yachtsmen but it can be surprisingly rough when gales blow. They tried a variety of moorings. The first one was upriver and one morning when a strong gale was blowing, the dinghy, including the engine, became swamped by the waves breaking over it so they had to be taken ashore by the boatmen at the naval shipyard. They stayed in a flat at the college which was kept for visitors until they found a more suitable mooring. Afterwards, they bought a second, inflatable dinghy,and took the yacht to a less exposed spot very close to the College in Old Mill Creek. Beaching legs were bought and bolted to either side of the boat to hold it upright when the tide went out and on the first night when the water level dropped, one of the legs sank into the mud and the boat slowly keeled over on its side, creaking as it did so. It was at an alarming angle and any possibility of staying the night on board had to be abandoned. Tired from lack of sleep, they clambered out and dropped down into the soft, slimy mud. They made their way to the shore, squelching as the mud sucked at their feet. In the pitch dark, they scrambled through the trees up a bank and walked up to the college and Dave's 'cabin'. All officers were allocated their own small rooms, called cabins, which were meant to be used when they were on night duty. The steward was already used to seeing ladies evening dresses in the wardrobe but was even more surprised the following morning to find the lady as well. They couldn't risk the same thing happening again and once more had to find another mooring immediately.

The next mooring they tried was on the Kingswear side of the river, which meant that the two dinghies worked overtime taking them backwards and forwards across the river. Dave left for work early one morning in their original wooden dinghy, leaving Marjie on board. A short while afterwards the wind increased until it was a howling gale. The remaining dinghy, the inflatable, had taken off and still attached by its painter, was flying, kite-like, in the air, the sail covers were coming loose and items on deck were being blown around. Not knowing what to do first, she ran along the decks trying to restore order. Soon afterwards, she was relieved to see the long-suffering guys from the boatyard approaching in a launch. They helped her and took her ashore. Dave had sent them when he realised what was happening. That night was spent in the guest apartment that once again saved the day.

The final attempt at finding a mooring on the river ended in failure. It turned out to be too close to the chain ferry known as The Higher Ferry, which was unusual in that whilst it used chains on the river bed for directional purposes, it was propelled by paddle wheels. It served as a bridge joining up the A379 from one bank to the other. The mooring was on the opposite bank to the Naval College, near Kingswear. The mishaps which occurred in that location culminated in having to be rescued once again by the Royal Navy! Dave was on a sail training trip, and Marjie was on board with Dave's brother Gerald who was visiting on holiday. Before leaving, Dave had borrowed a sailing dinghy for Gerald to use and had put down a mooring for it near the Lady Bear. One windy night before Gerald arrived, the dinghy dragged its mooring, which then got caught on one of the underwater ferry chains. Marjie doesn't recall how that problem was resolved, but it did result in the dinghy losing its jib so when a few days later Gerald and Marjie decided to explore upriver, they only had the mainsail and as there wasn't much wind it took them a long time to reach the wide bend in the river at Dittisham. When they turned around to sail back to Dartmouth the wind had dropped almost completely. Progress was so slow they resorted to employing the only paddle they could find, taking turns at paddling, which was tedious. Night had closed in and all was black when they reached the Lady Bear exhausted. Gerald's holiday was more of the outward bound than the relaxing rest he'd been hoping for.

Late the following evening there was a violent thunderstorm echoing around the hills when Gerald made the disturbing discovery that he'd run out of cigarettes. To Marjie's horror, he decided to set off in the tender to go in search of his fix on the opposite shore. By the time he returned it was after 10 o'clock and the weather had deteriorated. Later some cadets arrived in a naval launch and told them that conditions were going to get even worse and they would have to move to the pontoon where the cadet training minesweeper HMS Walkerton was moored. Much to the relief of Marjie and Gerald, the cadets offered to take charge and move them.

When Dave returned, he persuaded the college to let them move alongside the dockyard quay. At high water, they motored over and moored up. To make sure that the boat would always lean into the quay, Dave borrowed some heavy lead weights from the divers and placed them along the side decks closest to the wall. It was the height of luxury. No more worrying about the weather and having to go ashore in the dinghy. It was fine until one day the divers came and took the weights away without telling them. Dave was off sailing at the time so Marjie was on her own yet again. She had by this time got a job in the college library as an assistant. Apart from shelving books and chasing late returns, she had the enjoyable task of deciding which books to buy on sailing, as she knew more about sailing than the librarian did. When she got back to the boat after work she was shocked to discover that she couldn't get on board because the boat was leaning out from the quay, with only the bar taut mooring ropes stopping it from crashing onto the mud. There was an apartment occupied by a naval petty officer and his family close to the quay, so she knocked on the door and was invited in for tea whilst she waited for the tide to come in – hoping that the ropes would continue to take the strain. So many mooring disasters, storms and sleepless nights could have convinced a lesser person to have given up boating forever but they pale into insignificance compared to what happened next.

CHAPTER 10
NEVER SAY NEVER

The voyage that never was

They'd made plans to sail to Brittany for their summer holiday; the yacht had been prepared ready to set off and the last thing they had to do was top up with petrol so they went to the fuel jetty and filled the tank. When that was done, they cast off and motored into the middle of the river to pick up a mooring buoy and wait for a favourable tide the next day as the weather forecast was for a storm that evening. The sky was overcast and there was a light breeze blowing as Dave steered the boat towards the buoy. Marjie was on the foredeck coiling up the mooring lines.

A bone-rattling explosion shattered the peace and tranquillity of the neighbourhood. Stunned, Marjie spun around and looked in the direction of the cockpit. Dave was no longer there! Flames were shooting in the air. She ran along the side deck in a panic, frantically searching the water for Dave. She saw him swimming towards the fuel jetty and was overcome with relief. When it was evident that he was safe, she decided that the best course of action was to abandon the burning vessel so she leapt in the water herself. The fuel hose on the jetty had been exceptionally powerful making it difficult to regulate so some of the petrol had spilt into the cockpit and found its way to the fridge pilot light. When Dave had been blown out of the cockpit, he'd been catapulted into the river hitting his arm on the boom on the way up. Marjie swam ashore where a growing crowd of people had gathered after seeing and hearing the explosion. They helped her onto the fuel jetty where she sat dazed.

Some of the crowd had gathered around Dave who was lying on the jetty. He was charred and shaking, covered in burns and was in a severe state of shock. Marjie's left wrist was swelling rapidly. It was broken but she hadn't realised it at the time. She sat alone on the quay unnoticed until a kind man who she vaguely recognised as a local yacht designer, took pity on her. He understood that although she wasn't as badly hurt as Dave, she did need a bit of comforting even so. Marjie will always be grateful to him.

Whilst that drama was happening on the fuel jetty, another one was unfolding elsewhere. The Lady Bear, still on fire, was drifting in the middle of the river and there was a race going on to get to her. Salvage laws state that the first person to get a rope attached can claim if it can be proven that the vessel would have perished otherwise. As she was on fire at the time they would have had a good case and could have claimed salvage. The amount would have depended on the value of the vessel and the danger that the salvors had been exposed to. Fortunately, one of Dave's fellow officers had been on the college quay on his own boat at the time it happened so he jumped into a naval launch, raced out to the stricken vessel and got a rope attached before anyone else. There was a large jerry can in the cockpit which had been filled with petrol as a reserve. It had no label on it and looked as if it contained water. This same naval officer was not happy when he found out that he had escaped a conflagration by deciding not to use it. He stayed on board and waited for the fire brigade who drove onto the Lower Ferry, which transported them to the scene of the fire as was customary in such circumstances. The ambulance took forever to arrive and by the time they finally got to the hospital the storm had arrived in full force. It was so bad that the anaesthetist was unable to get into work so they were kept waiting on trolleys in a corridor for several hours, wet through and mostly being ignored. At one point, Marjie looked down at her left hand and noticed that her engagement ring wasn't there. It was the final straw; she started crying and feeling sorry for herself. Noticing Marjie's distress, a nurse who happened to be passing by, went over to her.

"You're not to upset your husband," she scolded. Dave was lying on his trolley not saying very much and still looking in a bad way.

In the early hours of the following morning, when the anaesthetist finally arrived they were attended to separately. Without being told what was happening they were put into separate men's and women's wards. Marjie was upset and worried about Dave as no one had thought to tell her how he was. When she heard someone moaning in pain in the adjoining ward she assumed it was him. A nurse gave her some painkillers and sleeping pills and she finally went to sleep. The next day she was relieved to find out that Dave's burns were only superficial but he had a broken right arm and damage to his right leg. Friends at the college responded to the accident with various acts of kindness. A few of the wives washed and ironed some of Marjie's clothes that they'd recovered from the debris and white foam on the remains of the Lady Bear. Although Marjie was grateful for their kindness, she was embarrassed to discover that the clothes they'd found had been the old 'workers' that had been shoved to the bottom of one of the cupboards. What must they have thought! Another kind act came from one of the college lecturers who was going on holiday so loaned them his house, which solved and removed the urgency to find alternative accommodation. As far as the guys at the naval boatyard were concerned – they were probably holding a party to celebrate that their rescue services would no longer be required!

The Lady Bear was moored at the dockyard awaiting the arrival of the insurance assessor; when Marjie and Dave went there the next day to take their belongings off, they were shocked at the amount of damage. The cockpit and stern of the vessel were badly damaged and planks at the bow, where Marjie had been standing, had sprung apart. Below decks, everything was covered with water and foam. They were later told by their insurance company that Lady Bear was damaged beyond repair. However, we have recently discovered that she does still exist, owned by a family who has widely travelled around the Mediterranean and self-taught their children. So someone at some time must have bought the wreck and repaired it.

For the next several weeks, they each had one good arm, her right and his left so between them were able to drive and help each other to eat. It would be understandable after an accident like that and the endless other mishaps and disasters that had occurred that Marjie and Dave would never want to set foot on a boat again. Not so. When they received the insurance money for the Lady Bear, they bought a new Hurley 22, the most popular model that was built by Hurley Marine Company Ltd. George Hurley was a carpenter and shipwright who set up his own business in 1946 working from a shed in his backyard. He moved to new premises when the business expanded and in 1958, began to build the well-known Silhouette sailboats. In 1964, with the injection of extra capital by other directors joining the firm, a new factory was built in Plympton. There they constructed fibreglass boats designed by Ian Anderson, the kindly gentleman who went to Marjie's assistance after the explosion of the Lady Bear. The officer in charge of the college boats was so impressed with the design of Dave and Marjie's Hurley 22, he ordered a few of the bilge keel version for the cadets to sail. Dave was delighted because when there were any Hurley 22 races organised, he and Marjie always won, which was gratifying even if they did have an unfair advantage because a bilge keel is never a match for a straight keel.

6. Antifouling the Hurley 22

They rented a house in a narrow road called Above Town in Dartmouth with lovely views over the river and out to sea. It had its downside, however. Whenever they wanted to go anywhere, they had to either head steeply upwards or steeply downwards so when a married quarter became available, they decided to take it. It lacked character but it was such a treat for them to be able to park easily and to not have the steep hill to deal with every time they went out. After a couple of years at Dartmouth, Dave was posted to Portsmouth so they sailed there in the Hurley 22. Marjie got a job as a technician at Portsmouth Technical College in the Home Economics department, where students were taught how to clean, wash and iron correctly – not things which were of much interest to her. Whilst there she took the opportunity to add to her qualifications by completing City and Guilds Advanced Dress, having already done the basic course earlier on one of her day release days when at Hinckley Knitting.

The beginning of the end

After three years in the Navy, Dave decided a change was needed and chose to get a teaching qualification so that he could teach in further education colleges and Polytechnics. Marjie applied for the same teaching course to add to her qualifications. The course was for anyone with a qualification in their own subject and Marjie's design and dressmaking certificates were sufficient for her to be accepted. In the summer of 1971, they sold the Hurley 22 and moved to Huddersfield where they bought a house in the nearby village of Kirkburton. A year later they both had their teaching certificates. Marjie started working as a dressmaking and crafts teacher at a secondary school in Barnsley and Dave got a job at Huddersfield Polytechnic teaching Physics.

They missed sailing but filled their leisure time by buying a couple of horses. Marjie had spent a lot of time riding when she was younger and it was she who was eager to rekindle memories. They became friendly with a farmer, Stanley, at the end of the road and sometimes helped him with his milk rounds and menial farm work as well as occasionally accompanying him to the pub on Friday evenings, the one night he allowed himself some time off. Stanley took them to a local horse fair and helped them choose Taffy, a beautiful, dappled grey Welsh Mountain pony; perhaps he was the best choice of those on show but he did have an unfortunate habit of landing on all four feet when jumping, which became noticeable when a rider was showing off his paces in an adjoining ring. He also had some other bad habits as Marjie discovered later – like taking off at top speed with the bit between his teeth and galloping through the undergrowth at an insane speed. She found that the only way to stop him was to try and reach an open space and steer him in ever-decreasing circles until he could go no further. Nevertheless, she was delighted with him, the first horse she had ever owned and together, they went exploring near and far in the countryside close to home. Dave, who had never ridden before, decided that he was missing out so they looked around for another, larger horse for him and bought a big, solid bay and called him Sancho. Dave took to riding with ease and Taffy and Marjie were no longer alone on their expeditions. Unfortunately, Taffy always wanted to be in the lead and once there, the sound of thundering hooves behind him triggered the bolting reflex in his brain so she had to always make sure she was in the rear. If they were riding along a track and it looked like Taffy was set on overtaking, she would shout to Dave to steer to one side and block her path.

Although they were both working, the end of the month always saw them struggling and when Dave saw an advertisement for a teaching job in Saudi Arabia, with high pay and free accommodation he went for an interview. Some weeks later his letter of acceptance arrived. Marjie was dubious because it meant a big upheaval and above all, would mean parting from her beloved Taffy. Not only that, Dave would have to work there for three months before she could join him. Nevertheless, that's what they finally decided to do. They sold both horses to a girl who was setting up a livery stable and arranged for her and her assistant to share the house with Marjie. Dave warned people not to mention Taffy to Marjie as she would find it difficult to hold back her tears at the mention of his name. The distressing image of him locked in a stable on his own, barely able to see over the door is etched in her mind even now. He was used to being free in a field with his companion Sancho and they had become so attached to one another that it was very difficult to go off riding with one and leave the other behind. The one left behind galloped up and down the fence whinnying. Taffy's new owner sold him to a girl who did a lot of hunting and Marjie hopes she managed to get used to his eccentricities and that he was happy again. Owning and loving animals seems to be wrought with guilt and sadness. Having to live a human life makes it difficult sometimes to combine that with what would be best for the animal.

The French connection

Finally, the three months had passed, Dave returned and Marjie met him at Manchester airport. It was almost like picking up a stranger, even though they'd corresponded frequently, they'd both had so many different experiences since they'd last been together. When the time arrived for them to leave for Saudi Arabia, they took a flight from Heathrow to Riyadh and on arrival they were taken through teeming traffic and blaring horns along a road lined with date palms to a hotel in the centre of town. It had quite basic accommodation and an unwelcome wake-up call the following morning when the Muezzin called the Adhan through loudspeakers at the mosque close by. After breakfast, they were picked up by a tanned guy driving a jeep and taken across desert roads to the Airbase run by BAC who was responsible for training Air Force cadets and the maintenance of the aircraft. The unaccustomed sights and smells in the blistering heat made Marjie really feel that she had arrived and the adventure had begun.

The next day she was introduced to her new horse, a beautiful Arabian stallion called Dashran, which means playboy. He lived up to his name when she first got on his back and Dave said,

"Take your hat off".

She was unprepared for what happened next. Dashran had obviously suffered from mistreatment in the past, because he immediately swivelled around 360 degrees on his hind legs, expecting to be hit. She was shocked and annoyed at Dave for playing that trick on her. At least she knew never to take her hat off again, or indeed make any sort of movement in the air above Dashran's head. She was introduced to other people at the stables, including the grooms and met Dave's horse Ajeeb, meaning wonderful, who had a predilection for dates and managed to eat the flesh and leave the stones in his manger. Their house was in a small gated complex with a pool, approached along rough unmade tracks and from the roof they could look out over the airport.

Life followed a pattern of getting up very early as Dave's work commenced before it got too hot and finished at lunchtime. After lunch, they rested and then drove in their old American car to the stables for the afternoon. Shopping was done in small supermarkets on the way home. Marjie started work as a secretary for the BAC housing department. They didn't have much choice in staff and would take people like her with no experience who couldn't type. She left after a while as she fancied starting up a dressmaking business from home. She bought an industrial sewing machine, which she housed in the spare bedroom. There were a few questions from the CEO who wasn't too keen on employee's wives setting up businesses from their free accommodation but a precedent had already been set by another wife who was running a successful hairdressing business. Unfortunately, Marjie's business wasn't as successful. Making individually designed clothes takes a lot of time and if she'd charged the true cost no one would have been interested - so when she was offered a job in another office working for a French firm doing geological surveys (mainly searching for water), she was pleased to take it. Her job was to correct their English reports and their spoken English.

Hankering after another boat, Marjie and Dave pored over advertisements in yachting magazines until they found one which suited them, a Great Dane 28ft sloop, which happened to be for sale in the London office of the agency that I had worked for. They had no choice but to buy it unseen and decided to take the risk, as they had corresponded with the owner, who was a vicar. How could anything go wrong if the vendor was a trustworthy man of God?

The boat was moored at Ile des Embiez, a small island near Toulon. They flew to France for a holiday and landed in Marseille, where they hired a taxi to take them to the small, picturesque fishing port of Le Brusc, which was the starting point for the ferry that sailed regularly between Ile des Embiez and the mainland. The island is less than one square kilometre with a coastline of six kilometres, moorings for 750 boats and a population of just ten permanent inhabitants. It was purchased in 1958 by Paul Ricard, the founder of Ricard, the anise-flavoured aperitif that is very popular in the southern region of France. He is buried on the highest point, 57 metres above sea level and each year on the 9th July, his birthday is celebrated on the island. Everything went more or less smoothly until they boarded the boat late in the evening and discovered that all the crockery, cutlery, pots and pans had been taken off. The wooden racks where everything had been housed were empty so the first task the following day was to take a bus to Toulon and visit the chandleries on the waterfront to replace the missing items. Their stay in Embiez was marred by the weather. Mostly it rained and when it didn't rain, the Mistral blew. They listened each day to the weather forecasts hoping for an improvement. It always sounded much better further east, nearer the Italian border so as soon as they came off the slip after having antifouled the keel, they set off for Antibes in search of sunshine. The further east they travelled, the more the weather improved and they were pleased with their decision. They were allotted a mooring and stayed in Antibes for the rest of the holiday, going out occasionally for day sails.

When they returned to Riyadh, Marjie continued working for the French company and unfortunately for her and Dave but fortunately for me, it was the beginning of the break-up of their marriage. When she met Dave he was a sensitive, thoughtful, gentle person but as time went on he became more dynamic, more domineering. She felt in a way that he was ashamed of her, and he often interrupted and corrected her whenever she had an opinion or spoke when they were with friends. Her boss, a charismatic, handsome, manipulative Frenchman focused on Marjie's vulnerability. She was very naïve and flattered that anyone should think her worthy of attention and an affair began. The next time she and Dave flew back to the boat for a pre-arranged holiday with friends from England, she stayed on the boat when the holiday was over, and Dave flew back to Riyadh alone.

CHAPTER 11
A NEW COMMAND

Heading South

Marjie and I'd had a brilliant summer together in Antibes but I hadn't been offered any more charters and Keith didn't have another opportunity to use the boat himself, so when the season finished he called an end to our joint venture. It hadn't worked out as we'd hoped and I agreed to contact the same boat haulage company that had brought the boat to Antibes and arranged for them to take her and us back to the U.K. I arranged to sell the MG Midget back to Well-Spoken Fred who, it must be remembered, was from a long line of East End "motor breakers." What was I thinking? But I had no choice. I wanted to sell it quickly and nobody else would have been interested knowing of its provenance. He offered me considerably less than I'd paid for it in the first place. In fact, about the same price that I'd paid him to replace the broken half shafts - so effectively he was getting it for nothing.

"Is that the best you can do?" I asked. I wasn't too surprised to learn that it actually was the best he could do.

When the time came, we stocked up on duty-free booze and hid the bottles inside the hollow mast after it had been taken down and lashed securely along the deck. The vessel was loaded on a trailer and we set off. As usual with the U.K. customs officers in those days, it was a tiresome, irritating process when we arrived. The female officer searched everywhere in a determined effort to find contraband, even in the anchor chain locker in the bows. Not a single part of the boat escaped her scrutiny – except the inside of the mast. At the end of the extensive and fruitless hunt, she conceded that we had no duty free goods that were being smuggled in. Disappointed, she left us with the all-clear. Her parting words as she descended the ladder were,

"I expect you've hidden it all inside the mast." We feigned shock that she could possibly think that we would do such a thing!

We moved into my apartment in Netley Abbey and Keith continued to pay me until the end of the year - by which time we'd applied for and been offered the command of a 59ft motor yacht which we were to take to Greece. It was based at La Napoule in the South of France, where the owner of the yacht also had an apartment close to the port. We'd decided that we didn't want to have any other crew so had sought a position on a yacht that we would be able to manage on our own. 59ft seemed an ideal size and we couldn't wait to return to the blue waters and blazing sun of the Mediterranean. When the time came, we packed our bags, locked up the apartment and travelled to the market town of Nuneaton to spend some time with Marjie's parents before we left for France.

Nuneaton's market was established in 1226 and is still going strong to this day. Other important industries were coal mining, which began in the 13th century and the textile industry that was established in the 18th century. Both grew extensively after the Coventry canal opened in 1789. Nuneaton suffered heavy bombing during WWII due to its munitions factories. The heaviest raid, on May 17th, 1941, killed 130 people, destroyed 380 houses and damaged a further 10,000. The Nuneaton area had been Marjie's father's stomping ground since his birth in the nearby village of Oldbury in 1910. He left school at 15, and his diaries for that year outline his many activities - joining the scouts, the Civil Defence, the Red Cross, the Operatic Society, taking piano lessons as well as evening classes in drawing and mathematics. His activities on Sundays involved going to different churches in the area with his friends. He met her mother whilst on holiday in Felixstowe and after their marriage, she left her hometown and joined him in Nuneaton. Although most people at the time thought that it was a waste of time educating girls – after all, they'd only get married anyway - Marjie's parents, in spite of limited funds, made sure that she and her elder sister, Jill, made the most of the wonderful free educational opportunities that were available at the time.

We said our goodbyes to Marjie's parents at 09h00 Monday 8th March 1976, when a chauffeur-driven car pulled up outside their house to take us to Loughborough. There we collected the company car, an executive, 3.0 L Ford Granada estate, filled with equipment for the yacht. We started on the journey to La Napoule with the large sum of money that had been handed to us and the car packed to maximum, including a refrigerator for the apartment. We set off along the M1, stopping off in London for lunch and then going on to Gravesend to visit my parents. I was heartbroken to see my dad sitting in his usual chair, close to the television, looking frail and connected to an oxygen bottle. We stayed with them a short while, said our goodbyes and continued on our way to the coastal town and major ferry port of Dover.

It was a bitterly cold evening when we arrived and as we had a three-hour wait for the ferry and were on an all-expenses-paid trip, we parked in the town to have a meal in a warm restaurant.

"Where you wan' sit?" The waiter asked in a foreign accent that sounded very much like Manuel from Fawlty Towers.

"The warmest place," Marjie said

"Par me," he said

"The warmest place," Marjie reiterated

"No unerstan, where you wan' sit?" he asked again

"We'd like to sit in the warmest place."

"You wan' sit here?" showing us a table near the door.

"No – we – want - to – sit – in – the – warmest - place," she insisted, speaking slowly and precisely

"Where you wan' go? " It was ridiculous and plain that we were never going to get through to him.

"Come on," I said to Marjie having seen an available table in the corner and off we went with the waiter trotting along behind us.

"You wan' sit 'ere?" he asked.

"Yes." His limited vocabulary didn't extend as far as "warmest place." After recovering from the shock of the eye-watering prices, we ordered the meal, pleased that we weren't paying for it ourselves. It was more than forgettable, it was awful but the unexpected entertainment compensated for the lack of culinary expertise. I wonder if John Cleese ever visited the same restaurant and based his fictional character, Manuel, on the antics of the waiter that we had that day. We laughed as he scuttled around each table, straining to understand and communicate with the customers, some of whom became a little irate with him. And then, every so often, another individual dressed in overalls and carrying a paint pot walked past our table in one direction and then back again. I don't know if he actually did any painting. What a strange evening we had but at least we were reasonably warm. Not so in Calais.

The gateway to the Estérels

We arrived at 22h30 and booked into the Windsor hotel. The proprietor gushed about how wonderful his hotel was and how proud he was of the new fittings that had been installed and they were impressive – what a pity they didn't function. The room was icy cold, as was the bed and there was no hot water. We couldn't wait to check out the next morning and get underway in the warm car. We drove to Dunkirk to take the motorway and were surprised to see that the pavements were covered in ice - but that was nothing compared to what was about to happen. It started to snow and then snowed some more until it became a veritable blizzard and the motorway traffic was reduced to one lane. We crawled our way through the blinding snow at no more than ten miles per hour, passing an untold number of accidents. South of Paris the weather improved and we were able to make up some of the lost time, arriving in Orange at 19h30. The hotel we found there was a vast improvement on the last one. We had a hot bath and then went down to the restaurant for a meal of trout, followed by quail, followed by apple tart. Oh, it was so was good to be back in France!

After breakfast, we drove to La Napoule, situated at the western end of the bay of Cannes where the vivid red rocks of the Estérel Mountains begin. As we entered the port it felt as if we'd been transported into summer. White yachts at their moorings were jostling each other in a light breeze, the people wore light clothing, the busy shops had their doors open wide, with goods displayed outside on the pavement and the cloudless sky was an intense blue. We found the Picchiotti and unloaded enough equipment from the car to allow Marjie to squeeze into the back so that we could go to Nice airport to pick up Dennis, the Managing Director of the company that was registered as the owner of the vessel. It was customary for luxury yachts to be registered in the name of a company, very often in an obscure tax haven. Panama was the most popular at the time. In the 1970s, the U.K. Labour Government was in power and the Chancellor of the Exchequer, Dennis Healey, crucified the rich with unbelievably high taxes. Rather than pay ruinous Corporation tax, it made more sense for them to invest some of their profits in a company yacht – supposedly for business entertainment. Yacht owners exploited every possible loophole to avoid paying taxes. Almost everything that was purchased for their yachts was tax-free. Even their cars would sometimes be registered as the yacht's tender to avoid paying any tax on it. Leona Helmsley, an American billionaire, nicknamed the "Queen of Mean" who had a notorious reputation for being tyrannical, once said, *"We don't pay taxes. Only the little people pay taxes."* Although a highly derogatory statement, it is accurate in the sense that it is generally the average working family who are the ones that contribute their fair share of taxes. One of the yacht owners that Marjie and I worked for once told us, "If I ever have to pay any tax, I'll sack my accountant." They justify their actions by distinguishing between the fine line of tax avoidance, that they consider they're entitled to exploit and tax evasion, which is a criminal offence. Having said that, I can't complain about any yacht owner that I've worked for, in fact, some of them have been very good to me and in any case, you could say that I profited from the results of their behaviour.

We went to the apartment with Dennis and unloaded the fridge, then went back to the boat to unload the remainder of the equipment. Our hearts sank - what a mess! The yacht was filthy and piled high with all manner of bits and pieces that had been stowed inside and to add to our disappointment, it had started to turn cold outside and we'd been expecting warmth. Dennis considered the expense of running the yacht too large a drain on the company finances and would have preferred it to be sold, so to make a point, he had a tendency to overspend. We checked into the Sofitel hotel, which had a rooftop terrace with a swimming pool and is situated on the seafront in Cannes, next to the attractive old port. We stayed the night and had a delicious meal in one of the many enticing restaurants on the Quay St Pierre. The following day we took Dennis to the airport. He returned to the U.K., we moved onto the yacht and set about preparing the boat for the passage to Greece.

Righting Wrongs

Over the course of the next few days, we began to discover all the faults. Vital navigation charts were missing, the cushion covers we had brought from Loughborough were too big so the company that made them had to be contacted to make the alterations, the echo sounder didn't work, the intercom system didn't work, some of the electrical sockets didn't work, and the oven couldn't be used at the same time as the rings. I was busily engaged in trying to fix them when it started to rain and the electricity supply cut out. I stopped what I was doing so that I could rewire a faulty connection and waterproof the plug that went into the socket on the quay. All this was taking place on a boat that was crammed full of bits and pieces that had been removed from their normal positions and stowed inside for the winter, together with all the things that we'd brought down from the U.K. Why the lamps, doorknobs and ashtrays that are normally fixed in position had been unscrewed and stacked up I don't know. A lot of the boat equipment had also been stored in the owner's apartment so we were constantly going backwards and forwards to search for things. When the sun shone for two days, we concentrated on the outside, screwing on life ring holders, wooden dodgers around the aft deck and fastening in position wooden lockers that had all inexplicably been removed. Then the rain started again and it was accompanied by thunderstorms so we went to Antibes to collect the liferafts that had been sent there to be serviced.

The new generator starting battery that we'd brought down from Loughborough had the wrong terminals and the new air-conditioning pump we'd brought was the wrong size. Throughout all of this, I was cursing and wondering what had possessed me to return to skippering private yachts. I was having difficulty getting everything to work, so decided to call in professional firms. It was gratifying to know that it wasn't just me – they didn't have much success either. However, after a week of nonstop aggravation and hard work, things started to get repaired. The sun shone once more and we gave a tremendous sigh of relief. Then one of the electric toilets stopped working.

"Right, that's it!" I said, "I've had enough, we're off to Gréolières-les-Neiges for an afternoon skiing."I knew the resort well, having skied there many times before. Created in 1963, in the hills above

Grasse, it's the resort nearest to the coast, just less than 70 kilometres away so we could get there in a one and a half-hour drive. From the summit of the Cheiron ridge, there is a magnificent 360° vista of the snow-capped Maritime Alps, the Côte d'Azur, the Italian Riviera, and on a clear day, Corsica. We were looking forward to some well-earned recreation. We set off and shortly afterwards it started to cloud over. By the time we reached Gourdon, a medieval village perched high on a rocky spur, 13 kilometres from Grasse, the cloud was low and dense and it started to rain again. Disappointed, we turned around and decided to spend some time in Grasse but it was impossible to find a parking spot, so we went to Antibes to visit friends. When we got there, we discovered that they'd moved so we returned to the boat and sat inside with a bottle of wine, listening to the heavy rain drumming down on the deck, feeling miserable. The following day was still unsettled but we decided to try Gréolières-les-Neiges once more and then it started to rain again and it turned out to be another unsuccessful day of arriving at places too early, too late, unable to park and an awful meal in a restaurant.

Monday 22nd March we were up early. I'd arranged for the boat to be slipped and anti-fouled at Port Pierre-Canto at 10h30. We filled the water tanks, stowed everything for sea and motored out in the rain, wondering when the sun would shine for us. It was not the South of France weather we'd expected. Clear of the harbour entrance, I pushed the throttles forward to cruising speed and we discovered that the port engine would only reach 1500 rpm whereas the starboard one was running at 2800 rpm and also the steering was stiff. What else can go wrong we wondered? Although we arrived at 10h30, we had to wait until 16h00 before we were eventually lifted out of the water and chocked up ashore.

We accomplished a considerable amount whilst at the boatyard. Repairs were carried out on numerous faults and I noticed that the stern gland looked as if it hadn't been touched for a long time, so I repacked it. (The stern gland is designed to grease the propeller shaft and keep it watertight at the point where it passes through the hull. The packing consists of a length of wadding, sometimes impregnated with a lubricant that is wrapped around the shaft three or four times and then compressed by tightening the gland nut.) I had no idea then of the trouble it would cause us once we started cruising. When all the jobs had been completed the yacht was launched again three days later and we made our way back to La Napoule with the steering and the port engine working normally. Dennis contacted us to say that we wouldn't be going to Greece and that we were to prepare to make our way to Naples instead.

The next day we finally made it to Gréolières-les-Neiges and had an enjoyable day skiing and a delicious lunch in a restaurant. It was Marjie's first attempt at skiing on real snow. When we knew we'd be joining the Picchiotti, she'd taken lessons on the artificial ski slope in Southampton because she knew that I was a keen skier and that we'd be visiting the resorts in the Maritime Alps and Italy as often as possible.

At Gréolières-les-Neiges, she mastered the nursery slopes in no time and it wasn't long before she found them too easy so I took her on a more difficult piste. We were a little too hasty. She found the piste too steep and too narrow so spent a lot of time picking herself up after falls. She also got a little too confident on the téléski and fell off halfway up a steep slope. She tried to grab hold of the empty téléskis as they passed her whilst simultaneously trying to stay upright and point her skis uphill, not an easy thing to do when the hill is covered in slippery snow and the skis want to shoot off in reverse. Each time she grabbed a passing téléski, she was jerked uphill before she had time to point her skis in the right direction so promptly fell off again. When she tried to get upright after the fall, the following téléski that she didn't get time to grab, smashed her on the head and knocked her down again. I, meanwhile, having been on the téléski in front of her and not knowing she'd fallen off, was standing at the top of the piste wondering where she could be.

After a long wait, I realised that something was amiss so pointed my skis downhill and skied down off-piste, in deep powder snow to look for her. I followed the line of the téléskis as closely as it was safe to do so until I spied a lump rising and falling on the same spot in the distance. I zoomed towards it. When I got there, Marjie was sitting in the snow exhausted, rubbing her head and on the verge of tears. I swished to a stop beside her, crouched down, kissed, cuddled and comforted her and helped her to her feet. She was surprised. She'd expected me to tell her off, which apparently is what her ex-husband Dave would have done. I helped her on to a téléski and waited until she'd successfully been whisked away uphill then skied down to the bottom of the piste to get a téléski back up to meet her at the top. We both set off together for the descent.

Despite the numerous falls, she made it to the bottom safely. After all the setbacks, one more ski on the nursery slope restored her confidence. Back on the yacht, she had a hot bath, I massaged her and after dinner, she went to bed with a headache. Bright and early next day the sun was shining and it was hot so we went off for another day's skiing. That night we both slept well.

We started work again on Monday morning and for the next six days toiled non-stop to get the boat into some sort of working order. We cleaned the yacht from top to bottom, fitted the aft deck awning and freed jammed doors. In addition, I discovered that the limber holes in the frames under the floorboards were either non-existent or blocked and water had accumulated behind individual frames. Once I'd cleared them, the water was able to flow freely again along the whole length of the boat so that I could pump it out - and then the bilge pump stopped working. Why did I return to skippering yachts? I tried to buy a replacement bilge pump but the ones for sale were 12 volts and I needed one of 24 volts. A lot of time was wasted driving around and eventually, I had no choice but to dismantle the pump and do what I could to get it running again, but it wasn't perfect by any means.

Marjie cleaned the entire interior and together we painted the outside superstructure a glistening white. Next, we mounted the outboard motor onto the tender, a fibreglass Dell Quay Dory, which we took for a trial spin. At least that worked! The Dorys were tough, buoyant, stable boats with a cathedral hull and our one was fitted with wheel steering. They were built by Dell Quay Ltd at Chichester in West Sussex from the mid-60s onwards and were virtual replicas of the popular American Boston Whaler. After that, there was very little left to do before we set off. I telephoned the Picchiotti boatyard in Viareggio for the umpteenth time to ensure that new engine starting batteries would be waiting for us when we arrived, we took on bonded stores, changed some of our French francs into lire and I ordered the refuelling lorry for the next morning so that we could cast off bright and early.

Alexandria

Genoa

France

Imperia
Sanremo
Monaco
Antibes
La Napoule
Saint Tropez

Iles d'Hyeres

Viareggio
Pisa

Adriatic Sea

Porto Ferraio

Calvi

Santa Stefano
Porto Ercole

Corsica

Italy

Ajaccio

Bonifacio

Anzio

Tyrrhenian Sea

Porto Cervo

Ponza
Ventotene
Ischia
Capri

Naples

Sardinia

Arbatax

Cagliari

Sicily

N. Africa

7. Italy and the Islands

CHAPTER 12
DESTINATION NAPOLI

Finding our sea legs

We were up early. The sky was a brilliant blue, there was not a cloud to be seen, no wind and it felt good to feel the heat from the sun. We stowed everything for the sea passage whilst waiting for the fuelling lorry to arrive. It didn't come. I called them.

"Ah yes," I was told, "it's broken down and we can't come until tomorrow." I was not happy and told them exactly what I thought of them. They clearly thought I was a force to be reckoned with because they acquiesced and said they'd send a different lorry, which took a long time to arrive. Whilst we were waiting, we took the car and our moped to the underground garage in the apartment block where the owner had his flat. When the lorry arrived and the fuel tanks were full, we slipped our moorings at 11h30 on 3rd April to begin our adventure, sailing to Naples on a luxury motor yacht and getting paid for it. Could life be any better?

The yacht was extremely well built to a traditional design and we felt confident. There were three cabins, the owner's stateroom aft with toilet and shower, a double bed and a bath beneath a single bed. Steps led up to the well-appointed saloon and at the other end of the saloon, more steps led down to the galley. Forward of the galley, there was another double cabin, with its toilet and shower and forward of that, an additional twin cabin with its own toilet and shower room. The crew accommodation with shower and toilet was in the forepeak with access via a hatch on the foredeck. Air-conditioning and heating were fitted throughout. The engine room housed a 15 kilowatt Kohler generator and twin 300 hp V8 turbocharged General Motors diesel engines that gave us a maximum speed of around 20 knots and a cruising speed of 15 knots. She was fully equipped with everything needed for navigation and we were looking forward to having the yacht to ourselves for the journey. We had plenty of time to get to Naples so we decided to have a leisurely cruise around the coast, calling in wherever we pleased, weather permitting.

8. The Picchiotti Mistral

The first port of call was to be Imperia as we'd never been there before and it was an ideal starting point for crossing the Gulf of Genoa. There are two ports at Imperia, Oneglia, which was established around 935 AD and Porto Maurizio, which was once a Roman settlement. The more touristic side of the city is based around Porto Maurizio and its marina whilst the port of Oneglia to the East has an old fashioned air with beautiful colourful buildings lining the quay. Between the two centres lies the river Impero after which the city was named. The two ports were combined, together with some of the surrounding villages, to create the city of Imperia in 1923, at the decree of Mussolini, the founder of Italian fascism.

The trip went well. It was choppy and the wind increased the nearer we got to Imperia but not enough to concern us. We chose to moor for the night in Oneglia. Berths were limited but we spotted one between two much smaller boats. By that time the wind had strengthened and was blowing onto our beam making the manoeuvre difficult. The yacht didn't have single lever controls, there were two separate ones for engaging the gearbox and throttle on each engine. I motored slowly into position, throttled back to tick-over speed, pushed the port gear lever forward, the starboard into astern and pushed the throttles forward to spin the boat around. I then put both engines into astern to back onto the quay. Marjie stood by on the aft deck with a boat hook and grabbed the permanent mooring line that ran underwater from its anchoring spot to the quay. She ran to the bow with it to make it fast but it was too short. It was meant for much smaller vessels. She let it fall back into the water and I motored back out to drop the anchor.

"Let go," I called to her when I was in position and put the engines into astern as the anchor dropped and the chain payed out. Except it didn't. The anchor gypsy was jammed and Marjie was pulling the chain to try to get it to run free. Consequently, when we reached the quay there wasn't enough chain out so the anchor didn't hold. We had to go out again and repeat the procedure, making sure that a sufficient length of chain lay on the bottom to hold us. When we'd finally moored safely I went off to the port Captain to register our arrival and it took ages. Reams of forms had to be typed out by the staff in quadruplicate and endless questions were fired at me. In those days, it was always a long drawn out process entering Italian harbours, even more so in places like Oneglia where not many yachts chose to go and I understood why they didn't want to be there. When we went ashore in the evening after dinner, we weren't impressed. It was untidy and quite grotty. It's much better these days.

The following morning when I went to check the engines, I noticed that the port stern gland, that I'd repacked before leaving, was leaking so I tightened it before we cast off. That should have been a warning of things to come. However, at the time I thought no more of it so started the engines, leaving them ticking over in neutral. When all was ready, I cast off the stern lines and Marjie, on the foredeck, switched on the electric winch and hauled in the anchor chain, which pulled us clear and out into the harbour and that's where we stayed because the anchor had hooked itself over other boats mooring chains. It took us twenty minutes to clear and hoist it before we could set off for Genoa, the capital of the Ligurian region and Italy's largest and busiest port. There is often a depression over the Gulf of Genoa and the city itself has a reputation as a windy city. We felt the effects of it as we rode a huge swell but I was pleased with the way the vessel coped with the rough sea. It felt good to have such a seaworthy boat but nevertheless, we were pleased when we arrived and gained some respite. The only mooring we could find was alongside a commercial jetty, which was very dirty, with coal on the quay. We couldn't wait to leave for Portofino the next day. When we did, it was overcast and there was still an uncomfortable swell but the journey went well as we headed southeast to arrive at the unbelievably attractive town set in a stunning natural harbour. In the inlet, submerged at a depth of 17 metres, there is a two and a half metre tall bronze statue of "Christ of the Abyss," depicting Him with his head and hands raised skywards, offering a benediction of peace. It was placed there in August 1954 in memory of Dario Gonzatti, the first Italian to use scuba equipment, who died in 1947. It's meant to protect fishermen and scuba divers, although it's a shame that the rest of us don't get to see it!

Despite the grey sky, it was still a delightful place to be. I spun the boat around to back onto the quay and called to Marjie to let go the anchor. She released the brake and nothing happened. The chain gypsy didn't move and once again the anchor stayed where it was. She pulled the chain with her hands and managed to get the anchor to drop. I went slowly astern whilst she continued to pull the chain free, paying out enough to allow me to reach the quay and attach the stern lines. When she switched on the electric winch to tighten the anchor chain, we realised that the anchor hadn't held so we cast off, went back out and tried again with the same result. On the third attempt, the anchor dug in and we were able to moor up securely and relax before cleaning off the disgusting oil and coal dust from our night in Genoa. To reward ourselves afterwards, we strolled ashore along the continuous line of pastel coloured houses, restaurants and cafés until we arrived at the small cobblestoned Piazzetta overlooking the harbour. It was lined with attractive and inviting seafood restaurants with no prices shown on the enticing menus displayed outside. We found what we thought would be an appealing place to eat and installed ourselves at a table near the window. A waiter brought us the menu. We looked at it, then at each other. That was the moment we made our excuses and extricated ourselves as inconspicuously as possible The next place we tried seemed cheap by comparison but it was still scandalously expensive for a mediocre meal. With the idyllic setting, I suppose we shouldn't have been too surprised. Italy in those days was a place where you could easily get parted from your money.

As was the case in France, Italian politics was strongly influenced by 'Eurocommunism'. We were there just before a general election which was held in June 1976 and was the first to be held after the voting age had been lowered to 18. The Christian Democrats only held onto power because there was a concerted effort, using tactical voting, to keep out the Communist party led by Enrico Berlinguer. It meant that all minor parties lost votes. However, the communists were still very popular and increased their vote share. From our perspective, there was a general feeling of being unwelcome, and we'd had one or two unpleasant experiences. We were welcomed with shouts of "Capitalist!" when we arrived or there were surly looks and a lack of the usual help in taking the ropes when mooring up. It was customary for shoes to be left at the end of the gangplank before going on board and it wasn't unusual to find that they'd finished up in the water when you went back ashore. But it was still a fabulous country to be in for all that and I never tire of going there. *Robert Browning said, "Open my heart and you will see, graved inside of it Italy."*

The city of yacht construction

The next day we cast off at 08h30 to go to Viareggio, on the coast of the Tyrrhenian Sea in northern Tuscany, where we were to have the new engine starting batteries installed. The sea was calm and the sun was shining in a clear blue sky. It was a shame that an otherwise idyllic trip was marred by Italian naval vessels passing close and forcing us further out to sea, all the time bellowing at us in Italian. We had no idea what they were saying but gathered from the sign language that there were submarine exercises taking place and they wanted us gone. They became aggressive and kept forcing us further and further out to sea putting us way off course so that Viareggio turned up in the wrong place. It was a relief when we saw it on the distant shoreline and even more of a relief to find a mooring available in the crowded harbour when we arrived. There were lots of yachts berthed there to have work carried out before the season started and there was a heavy smell of diesel in the air. But, as ever, it was exciting to be in a new place.

9. Packed like sardines in Viareggio

Viareggio is a well preserved Belle Epoque beach resort known for its seemingly endless sandy beaches stretching for ten kilometres and its Carnival, which sadly we'd just missed. It was started in 1873 by the local bourgeoisie as a protest about high taxation but has since developed into one of the largest and most popular international carnivals. The floats carry gigantic 40ft papier-maché caricatures of big political, cultural and showbiz names with an emphasis on cruel satire. They are amazing machines with movements that become increasingly complex each year.

It is thought that the city's name is derived from the Latin, Via Regis, meaning King's Road, which refers to a mediaeval road that linked a beach fortification to the inland city of Lucca. The first marina, the Marina of Lucca, was completed in 1823 and the fifth and final one, Marina di Madonnina, which accommodates 500 yachts, was finished in 1970.

In the early 19th century, Viareggio's craftsmen began building small fishing boats on the banks of the Burlamacca canal. Over the years the industry grew, eventually becoming an internationally renowned shipbuilding centre. Today, Viareggio is the world's main luxury yacht producing city, with the famous shipyards of Azimut Benetti, Codecasa, Rossinavi, Perini Navi and Cantiere Picchiotti, our destination. They all build their own versions of yachts appealing to the luxury market. Cantiere Picchiotti was one of Italy's most renowned shipbuilders throughout the 19th and early 20th centuries. I attempted to contact them about our batteries but to no avail. All the telephone calls we'd made before leaving La Napoule had served no purpose.

The port stern gland had been leaking throughout our journey, which meant that I had to empty the bilges far too often with a pump that wasn't working properly. In fact, there was so much water in the bilges at one stage, I was alarmed to see that the generator starting battery was underwater so I removed it, took it to a small workshop near our mooring and asked them to flush it out and check that it was still usable. That was a good move because they said that they could also supply me with the new engine starting batteries at half the cost of that quoted by Cantiere Picchiotti. I was disappointed that a new bilge pump was unavailable so I took the faulty one to the workshop, got them to overhaul it then fitted it back in position. On the way back, I ordered fuel and as soon as I was on board, repacked the stern gland to satisfy myself that it would no longer leak. High hopes! Marjie had visited numerous shops in town and stocked up with galley items and anything else she thought she would need. It was a nice feeling to be able to buy anything we wanted without having to worry about the cost. That's just one of the many advantages of being in command of a luxury motor yacht! The batteries were fitted and in the evening we went ashore with other crews for a meal and took over the restaurant. We put all of the tables together and had a riotous time.

The following day it was raining, a strong wind was blowing and the sea was rough so instead of leaving we concentrated on trying to repair all the things that still weren't working. I stripped, cleaned and re-assembled the bilge pump once more to satisfy myself that all was as it should be and it seemed to function better afterwards, which was a relief. I freed the anchor chain gypsy that had been jamming so that the anchor could be dropped without Marjie having to pull it out by hand, a dangerous thing to do. I still had difficulty repairing the intercom system and there were so many other things that weren't working. It seemed that the yacht hadn't been maintained properly for a number of years and the previous Skipper had been of little help to me. Whenever I had asked for his opinion on anything before we left La Napoule, I had soon reached the conclusion that he didn't know a great deal.

The next morning, Thursday 08 April, we woke at 07h00 and by 07h30 we were underway. The wind had decreased, the sea was calmer than the previous day but the sky was still overcast. When we were south of the port city of Livorno, on the west coast of Tuscany, the wind strength increased and we started to roll around with the waves crashing onto the decks but we were making good time. Things eased a little by the time we reached the island of Elba so I decided to continue on to Porto Santo Stefano, on the northwestern promontory of Monte Argentario, which was a further three hours away. The calm spell didn't last and as the wind increased the sea conditions worsened and we had a very uncomfortable time until we finally entered the harbour at Santo Stefano. There were no available berths and nobody around on the quay so we moored up close to the Giglio ferry. Marjie had to climb into the Dory hanging in the davits and leap from it to the quay with the mooring line clamped between her teeth because she needed both hands free.

10. Making Landfall

Fish and prawns aplenty

That evening, the wind started to howl and there were even whitecaps in the harbour. The fierce, ear-splitting wind and huge surges of water created a very disagreeable motion lasting all through the night. By the next morning, the wind strength had increased further. The boat was surging violently back and forth. The stern lines at each quarter and the two springs twanged when they were stretched bar tight by the back surge from the quay that sent us forward and then the swell swung us back again so that we almost crashed onto the quay. We hauled in some of the anchor chain to pull the vessel further away and then were unable to get ashore. The strain on the mooring lines was so great that the starboard fairlead was ripped from the deck and the stern swung around to port. Then the stainless steel spring shackle broke on the port stern rope. Some Italians on another yacht nearby just watched and offered no help. Fortunately, a couple of youths passed by so we threw them another mooring line, which they attached to the quay for us. There was mayhem in the port, the wind was screeching and there were whitecaps with spray flying in our faces. A tanker decided to leave and several yachts had to cast off and make way for him. One of the yachts had his anchor chain hooked onto the tanker's anchor chain and was motoring around trying to free it. Shortly afterwards the Giglio ferry came in and had difficulty manoeuvring in the atrocious conditions. The Captain timed it wrong and crashed onto the quay, missing us by just a few feet. As we couldn't get ashore we had to eat what we had on board. We didn't sleep much that night, worrying whether the mooring lines and the anchor would hold as the wind screamed and the surging continued unabated.

There was no change the next day and once again the violent movement prevented us from getting ashore. I noticed a berth available on the opposite quay that was protected so we cast off, hauled in the anchor and motored across as quickly as possible before another boat could beat us to it. We moored alongside a fishing boat and the contrast to the opposite, exposed quay was remarkable. We hardly felt the effects of the violent wind and the fishermen were much friendlier. They helped us moor up and gave us a huge box of freshly caught sardines and prawns and the calmer conditions allowed me to re-bed the damaged fairlead.

I woke early, at 06h00 the next morning in the hope that we could cast off and head south as it seemed calmer. I considered whether it would be prudent to set off, but by 08h00 the wind had picked up once more and the fisherman recommended that we stay in port because the wind was forecast to continue for at least another day. We profited from the extra day in port to clean, polish, repair and buy any extra bits and pieces that we thought we might need. The fisherman gave us another large box of assorted fish and I spent a considerable amount of the day, gutting and cleaning them so that Marjie could make a delicious "soupe de poisson," a recipe that originates from Marseille fishermen using the fish that were not considered good enough to sell. It has a unique flavour that is brought about by the use of the wonderful herbs of Provence. Once Marjie had made it, there was so much that most of it had to be frozen for later dates. When we'd finished our chores we explored the town.

At 08h00 the next morning, we weighed anchor, cast off the mooring lines and set course for the 130 mile trip to Anzio but we hadn't got very far when the starboard engine overheated. I shut it down and went to investigate whilst we floated around, wallowing in the swell that remained from the previous few days of strong wind. I found nothing seriously wrong, started up again and continued onwards to Anzio. The further south we got, the calmer the sea became, the sky cleared to a brilliant blue and a fierce sun beat down on us all the while until we finally entered the harbour and moored up on the main quay, only to be told that we had to leave by 06h00 the next morning. We explored the town a little that evening and set off again at 05h30 the following day for Naples, with the starboard engine running slightly hotter than the port one throughout the trip.

CHAPTER 13
NAPOLI

A dangerous place?

We arrived at the small port of Santa Lucia, which is huddled between a small rocky island and the mainland on the eastern side of the bay of Naples and from where we had a good view of Mount Vesuvius, arguably the most dangerous volcano in the world in the most densely populated volcanic region in the world. There have been several eruptions since the disastrous Pompeian one in 79 AD. The latest period of activity was between 1913 to 1944 when there was a major eruption that destroyed several villages. At the time, the United States Army Air Forces 340th Bombardment Group was based at Pompeii Airfield and 88 of their aircraft were destroyed. Because Vesuvius is an active volcano, which will erupt again, it is constantly monitored by the Osservatorio Vesuvio in Naples and plans are in place for a mass emergency evacuation when the next explosion takes place.

A smartly dressed man signalled to us from the quay, beckoning us over to where he stood. I obeyed and when we arrived, three of his accomplices took over the mooring operation. I'd become accustomed to giving out large quantities of Italian lire to helpers on the quays and wondered what the four of them would expect, pleased that it wouldn't be my own money that I'd be giving away. The very smartly dressed man was clearly in charge and what a character he was. He was tall with a deeply tanned face and a large hooked nose on which were perched black sunglasses with shades all-around almost to his ears. His jet black hair was combed straight back and looked as if it was held in place by what I assumed was a generous dollop of greasy Brylcream. His attire was flawless, from his expensive, beautifully tailored suit to his shining black, equally expensive shoes. He had the air of someone who was used to being obeyed and he was the epitome of charm when he welcomed us.

"Anything-a you need-a, you ask-a me", he said.

"Could you send an engineer to check one of my engines? It's overheating."

"No problem-a, I speak-a to my friend" and within an hour an engineer was aboard, in the engine room, cursing in Italian whilst he looked for the problem, which turned out to be a plastic bag caught in the seawater filter. He presented me with an astronomical bill, which I refused to pay.

"Leave-a this-a ta me," said the mafioso looking gentleman who'd beckoned us in. They discussed together and then mafioso came and told me to pay him less than half, which I did as it seemed more than reasonable. We now had a friend in Naples, or did we?

"Where can I get duty free fuel?" I asked him and he explained that duty-free was only available to vessels of 50 tons or more. Feeling pleased that we'd arrived in Naples, we had a good lunch, drank a little more wine than we should have and went to sleep it off. We awoke to the sound of rain but walked into town to explore Naples and look for a suitable restaurant for our evening meal. We'd been eating in restaurants a lot since we'd first arrived in France and didn't intend to stop doing so in Italy.

Yesteryear and now

During the five days before the owner was due to arrive, we had a lot to do to get the boat ready – cleaning, polishing and buying provisions. It was going to be the first time we would meet him and we wanted to make a good impression. It took us two attempts to find the supermarket and when we finally managed it we bought so much that we had to get a taxi back to the boat. All the searching, on foot, meant that we saw quite a lot of Naples, one of the world's oldest continuously inhabited urban areas.

There is a vast volcanic zone west of Naples called the Phlegraean Fields that was inhabited in Neolithic times. It consists of 24 volcanic structures and craters and around 150 pools of boiling mud and steam rising from openings in the earth's crust. The Greeks first settled in the region around 2000 BC. In the 9th century BC, the port of Parthenope was established on the island of Megaride. The island is no longer called Megaride and is now joined to the mainland but it is the very same place where we were moored. Parthenope, a siren in Greek mythology, (the name means "maiden voiced") supposedly threw herself into the sea and drowned after her singing failed to entice Odysseus. (Marjie sympathised with Odysseus when she first heard my singing but fortunately, I was able to overcome my disappointment and good sense prevailed.) Anyway, Parthenope's distraught body washed up on the shore of the island and the area was named in her honour. By the 6th century BC, the name Parthenope also applied to a plain on the mainland and the inhabitants of the nearby Greek colony of Cumae built Neapolis (New City), near the old Parthenope.

Neapolis prospered under Greek rule but the Romans conquered the city in 326 BC. Under Roman rule, the port of Naples continued to thrive. They built roads to connect the city, now called Napoli, to the rest of Italy. The port was enlarged and the city expanded with the building of Roman villas, aqueducts and public baths. Christianity arrived later and the apostles Saint Peter and Saint Paul are said to have preached there. When the Western Roman Empire went into decline, the whole of Italy was taken over by the Ostrogoths, who were one of three Germanic states, which included the Visigoths who occupied Spain and the South of France and the Vandals who occupied North Africa, Corsica and Sardinia. In 546, Naples once again became part of the Byzantine Empire, also known as the Eastern Roman Empire until 763, when it switched allegiance from Constantinople, the capital of the Byzantine Empire, to the Pope who had been of more assistance than the remote Constantinople. There followed a volatile period as relations with the Byzantine empire deteriorated and various pretenders feuded for supremacy. In 999, when Norman adventurers began to arrive, they were employed by Naples as mercenaries to assist in battling its rivals. There followed a troubled time with power alternating between France, Sicily, Germany and the Popes.

Spain took over in 1503 and Naples became part of the Spanish empire. The Spanish paved the roads, restored old buildings, built new ones and fortresses, strengthened and expanded the walls and made Naples the largest and best-fortified city in the Spanish Empire. By the 17th century, it had become a major cultural centre and the largest European Mediterranean city. It fell into decline, however, when In 1656, the Bubonic plague killed almost half of the 300,000 inhabitants. Then in 1798, a civil war erupted when French revolutionary forces entered the city and the inhabitants were divided between those seeking change and those who supported existing conditions.

Emperor Napoleon conquered Naples in 1806 and installed his brother, Joseph Bonaparte as King. Later, in 1808, his brother-in-law, Joachim Murat reigned until 1815, when Napoleon was defeated. The throne and the Kingdom then went once more to the Spanish Bourbon Dynasty, a royal house originating in France. It held thrones in Spain, Naples, Sicily and Parma. The Kingdoms of Sicily and Naples were combined, creating the so-called Kingdom of the Two Sicilies, with Naples as the capital. An uprising in Sicily in 1860, provided an opportunity for Giuseppe Garibaldi, an Italian general and nationalist, to invade and take Sicily. He proclaimed himself Dictator of Sicily and went on to take Naples, entering by train and descending in the square that now bears his name. He was instrumental in bringing about the unification of Italy, with Naples becoming part of the Kingdom of Italy in 1861, thus ending the Bourbon rule. The Kingdom of the Two Sicilies had been wealthy and when a large portion of its wealth was taken as a contribution to the new Italian treasury, the economy collapsed, which led to an unprecedented 4,000,000 people emigrating from the Naples area between 1876 and 1913. Although the population of Naples grew less than some of the other major cities, it was still the largest city in Italy.

Between 1834 and 1884, 48,000 people died from 12 outbreaks of cholera and typhoid due to poor public health conditions, followed by another major cholera epidemic in 1885, largely due to the poor sewerage infrastructure. The government decided on a radical transformation of the sewerage system and to replace narrow streets with wide, airy avenues - but widespread corruption, speculation and excessively long, complicated bureaucracy resulted in it taking several decades to complete.

During WWII, Naples was the most heavily bombed city in Italy and the first to rise up against the Nazi occupation. The uprising took place in September 1943, when the people forced the Nazis out in what was known as "The four days of Naples". When the allied forces arrived, the city was already freed so they pushed on to

Rome. The fleeing Nazis burned the University library and destroyed the city archives.

The Camorra

Although government funding has helped the Neapolitan economy, unemployment is very high and organised crime is rampant, with many deaths resulting from the warring gangs and families. Much has been said and written about the dangers of visiting Naples and many tourists shun the city for that reason. Italy is the fifth most visited country but only 13% of its visitors venture to Naples and some areas are best avoided. The Camorra crime syndicate is made up of 100 individual clans that have kinship ties but unlike the Sicilian Cosa Nostra that has a pyramidal structure, they feud with each other, so if a crime boss is arrested or assassinated new clans form, making it difficult to defeat. The Camorra first appeared during the years 1799 – 1815 when there was a power vacuum at the time of the French Revolution.

After the 1848 Sicilian revolution against Bourbon rule, the dissenters who sought a liberal government were defeated and realised they needed the support of the local populace. They paid the criminal leaders of the city's poor, the Camorra, to assist in the overthrow of the King. The police chief recruited the head of the Camorra, Salvatore de Crescendo and appointed him head of the municipal guard. Their power grew. In 1869, Ciccio Cappuccio succeeded Salvatore de Crescendo and was nicknamed, the King of Naples. The Low Camorra's power base was originally among the poor but then came the High Camorra, from the middle classes, focusing on trade, public works contracts and government and political meetings. Both the Low and the more dangerous High Camorra, dealt with each other, exchanging favours and promises. They relied on the strength that comes from the streets, using violent and underhand methods to exploit wherever they could, be it smuggling, blackmail, robbery, extortion, money laundering, counterfeit products, or illegal construction work etc.

It appears that they control pretty much everything in Naples and are referred to as "The System". They have investments in the city's hotels, restaurants and shops and run protection rackets. Tom Behan in his book, "The Camorra", writes,

"From the rich industrialist who wants a clear road into politics or administration to the small shop owner who wants to ask for a reduction of taxes; from the businessman trying to win a contract to a worker looking for a job in a factory; from a professional who wants more clients or greater recognition to somebody looking for an office job; from somebody from the provinces who has come to Naples to buy some goods to somebody who wants to emigrate to America; they all find somebody stepping into their path, and nearly all make use of them."

There is a trade-off between local politicians and public officials and the Camorra, each using the other for favours and promises. The heads of the major clan families have become important power brokers in both local and national politics, each granting the other support, privileges and protection. Much of the economy in Naples is "black market" and as a consequence, a number of enterprises have moved elsewhere. According to the investigative journalist Roberto Saviano, *"in numbers, economic power and in ruthless violence, the network of Camorra clans dwarfs the Sicilian Mafia, the Ndrangheta, an organised crime group based in Calabria and southern Italy's other organised gangs."* Ever since he wrote a book about the Camorra 12 years ago naming the mobsters who he said destroyed his city, he has been under guard, changing houses constantly. It is not an organised crime network like the mafia - it is open to all. The "soldiers" are mainly criminals from the lower echelons of society who may well end up incarcerated or victims of violent death as a result of the lethal feuds between the armed rival clans. In recent years they have been forming alliances with Nigerian drug gangs and Albanian Mafia allowing them to traffic cocaine and women in sexual slavery, an activity that has now extended across the whole of Europe.

Innocent people are in danger of being shot accidentally from drive-by shootings between the cutthroat competing gangs so it is little wonder that many tourists shun Naples out of nervousness or even abject fear. And there we were, Marjie and I, in the midst of it all, wondering about the elegantly dressed man in the port who could sort out any problem for us. As soon as he said "I talk-a to my friend-a," we knew that our problems would be resolved and whatever we wanted or needed would be forthcoming – as long as we didn't upset him! There is a saying, "See Naples and die," which we thought could be appropriate to us if we crossed him. In fact, the correct sentence is from a proverb of unknown origin, *"Once one has seen the Italian city of Naples, one can die peacefully, since nothing else can match its beauty."* It was a truly intriguing place to be. We were having the time of our lives.

One night when we were fast asleep, we were woken by the sound of roaring engines. We went on deck and there we saw, in the dead of night, when all around was deathly still and quiet, a fleet of Riva speedboats whizzing up to the quay, where chains of men were rapidly unloading stashes of boxes from the boats into cars. The cars then screeched away at top speed only for more to arrive ready for the next fleet of Rivas to come racing in. The operation continued at breaknet speed for a good half hour then all went quiet as if nothing had taken place with not a car or a Riva to be seen. Of course, we never discovered what it was all about and knew better than to ask, as no doubt did anybody else who may have witnessed it and pretended they hadn't. (Rivas are boats built of the highest quality materials, with painstaking care for detail. Their woodwork, varnished to a high gloss finish, looks like glass. Status symbols of the rich, they are the height of luxury - fast, beautiful and renowned worldwide for style, elegance and perfection. Back in La Napoule the owner of our boat had one which he liked to use for short excursions, or for guests to ski behind.)

CHAPTER 14
CAMPANIA

Getting to know you

On Saturday 17th April, the owner arrived with his guests, comprising his sister and a couple of friends. I had a radio that was tuned in to the same frequency as his private aircraft so that I could listen to the pilot's conversation with the airport and know exactly where and when they would be landing. That way, I was able to be waiting for them at Naples airport in my smart uniform with a car, ready to whisk them to the boat with the least possible fuss. No sooner had they arrived on board than the owner said he needed to return to the airport for business reasons so we didn't see much of him at all and we were left to look after his guests. On Sunday, the owner still hadn't returned and his guests said they'd like to go to the island of Ischia for the day. I'd been relying on the owner to hand over a large sum of money for me to run the boat and as he was absent and not knowing how long it would be before he came back, or what expenses we'd accrue, I decided I'd better change some French francs into lire. The trouble was it was Sunday – not a day when banks would normally be open. I went to chat with our friend, who we referred to as Mafioso when he was out of earshot. He was standing on the quay talking to a group of spirited Italians.

"Wadda you want-a?" he asked in his usual polite and helpful manner.

"I need to change some money, is there anywhere I can do that on a Sunday?'

"I talk-a to my friend-a," he said and disappeared. Shortly afterwards he came back and gave me the name and address of a bank and instructions on how to get there.

"You knock on the door when you get-a there someone will let-a you in-a, he's-a waiting for you," he told me. And sure enough, when I got there, I tapped on the door and was taken through to an office where the money was exchanged. I was staggered and very impressed. He'd arranged for the bank manager to go to the bank and open up on a Sunday morning especially for me. Now that's what I call service! He surely must have had a lot of friends or maybe he just made them offers they couldn't refuse. Either way, we were glad he was looking after us and wondered what he would want in return. I knew that I would have to pay for the service and that a large tip would probably be expected when we left.

The weather was still unsettled when we motored out of Santa Lucia heading for the volcanic island of Ischia, the largest of the four Phlegraean islands, lying about 30 kilometres north of the Bay of Naples.

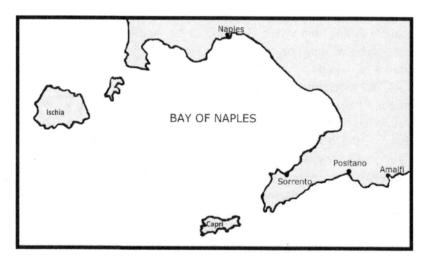

11. Ischia and the Bay of Naples

The islands are connected to the Phlegraean Field and form an archipelago in theBay of Naples. They are part of the 'Campanian Volcanic Arc', consisting of active, dormant and extinct volcanos in the southern Italian region of Campania. In fact, there is significant volcanic activity in the Tyrrhenian Sea itself due to its location over two tectonic plates. The sea consists of two basins, the Marsili Plain and the Valivov Plain that are located on each side of an underwater ridge, known as the Issel Bridge and there are numerous underwater mountains and volcanos. Ischia is a small, mountainous island just 10 kilometres from east to west and 7 kilometres north to south and is in an active volcanic field. The last eruption, in 1302, forced the population to flee to Baia, an ancient Roman city northwest of Naples, where they remained for four years. In 1883, an earthquake destroyed the villages of Casamicciola Terme in the north of the island and Lacco Ameno in the northwest. A 4.3 magnitude earthquake hit the island again in 2017, causing two fatalities, dozens of injured and 2600 left homeless as the huge tremor razed buildings to the ground across Italy.

There was grave concern at the time that it would trigger an eruption of a super volcano, that had been showing signs of reawakening and which lies just 40 kilometres away, underneath and to the east of the city of Naples, called "The big daddy of Vesuvius. It is a flat volcano because its magma chamber collapsed in on itself 39,000 years ago and gas has accumulated in the chamber. It is one of the most dangerous supervolcanos known. It is so immense that if it were to erupt, the result would be so catastrophic that it could wipe out much of life in Europe as we know it, sending firebombs and molten rocks as far away as Barcelona and Paris and the plume of smoke and ash would blot out the sun causing the earth's temperature to plummet. Monitoring it is difficult because it is underground and beneath the city of Naples and it has been showing activity since 1968. The ground has been rising, which has caused buildings and streets to collapse. It showed signs of activity two years before we arrived there and again in 1982 and 2016. Such news is not reassuring to anybody cruising in the area. However, Ischia's numerous thermal springs make it a popular tourist destination and wellness centre, especially among Germans. Angela Merkel is evidently a regular visitor and 5000 Germans live on the island. When we arrived in the port, the wind had increased, which made it difficult to manoeuvre and it had strengthened even more by the time lunch was over so we made our way back to Santa Lucia in a strong headwind. It was a stimulating trip.

Marjie and I dressed the vessel overall the next day in anticipation of the owner's arrival. Ships are dressed overall on special occasions. Each vessel carries a set of different coloured international code flags for signalling, square ones for each letter of the alphabet and pennants for numbers and substitutes, the latter are used to replicate characters to avoid carrying more than one set of flags. The flags can be used singly to display messages, for example, hoisting the letter "H", a flag that is half white and half red, displayed vertically, tells other craft that you have a pilot on board, 'Q', an all yellow flag, signals that the Captain is requesting 'free pratique', which means his ship is free from contagious diseases and he wishes permission to enter a foreign port. It is also displayed to request customs clearance. "O" signals man overboard and so on. When dressing overall, the flags are hoisted from the bow to the masthead and then down to the stern and there is a set order in which to arrange them to avoid spelling out improper messages or words. On most yachts I have skippered, I dressed overall for the first time the owner arrived and on his birthday if he happened to be on board at the time. I usually also had champagne ready for him and his guests, which was always an unexpected and pleasant surprise for them. They loved it. The owner arrived late afternoon and Marjie and I were intrigued by the change of behaviour in his guests. They were servile, fussing over him and they gave us the impression that they were anxious not to displease him. We knew that he had a widespread reputation on the Côte d'Azur as an unpleasant and difficult person so we were prepared for some trying times ahead.

The Amalfi coast

Tuesday, 20th April and it was time to leave. We said our goodbyes to Mafioso and I slipped a wad of notes into his waiting hand. We cast off, spent a considerable amount of time freeing our anchor that had become entangled with other moorings then motored to the fuel jetty to fill the tanks before setting off for Sorrento, on the southern side of the Bay of Naples. The tourist town of Sorrento marks the start of the Amalfi coast. It is perched on the top of cliffs with its multi-coloured houses tumbling down the hillside, separated from the busy marina below. Lord Byron, one of Britain's greatest poets, visited and inspired other literary masters to go there. Charles Dickens, Johann Goethe and Leo Tolstoy spent time in Sorrento and they undoubtedly stayed longer than we did. After we entered the port, we moored for a very short time for a quick reconnoitre and then we set off to Positano for lunch. The scenery was spectacular but we rode an uncomfortable swell and as we entered the port at Positano, it started to rain once more. I thought Italy was supposed to be a sunny country!

Positano is set in an enclave of the steep hills that form the beautiful, magnificent Amalfi coast. During the 15th and 17th centuries, Positano was a wealthy port but in the 19th century, the economy collapsed and approximately half of the population emigrated, mostly to America. It then became a poor fishing village until tourists became attracted to it in the 1950s, especially after John Steinbeck wrote in Harper's Bazaar in 1953, *"It is a dream place that isn't quite real when you are there and becomes beckoningly real after you have gone."* It has now grown to become an internationally recognised destination and we found it a delightful place to visit, with its colourful houses clinging to a vertiginous hillside - although we didn't stay as long as we'd have liked. When the owner, his sister and his guests had finished lunch they asked us to take them to Amalfi whilst they slept off the effects of an over-indulgent lunch. So far, the owner hadn't lived up to his awful reputation, in fact, he was very appreciative of everything we did and everybody was having a thoroughly good time. Unfortunately, it didn't stay that way!

Despite the rain, we couldn't help but admire the amazing Amalfi coast as we made our way to the next destination, the town of Amalfi itself. The steep coast, on the southern shore of the Sorrentine peninsula, between the Bay of Naples and the Bay of Salerno was listed as a UNESCO World Heritage site in 1997. There is very little agriculture except for the prolific cultivation of a special variety of elongated lemons called "Sfusato Amalfitani." They are double the size of other lemons, with thick, wrinkled skins, sweet, juicy flesh, very few pips and are used all along the coast for the production of the Italian liqueur Limoncello. Sorrento, Amalfi and the island of Capri all like to claim responsibility for the invention of this now very popular drink. It seems probable that its fame stems from the registering of a trademark in 1988 by Massimo Canale, whose uncle had opened a bar near Axel Munthe's villa in Anacapri during the years after WWII. He started a small production of Limoncello from his grandmother's recipe and registered it as 'Limoncello di Capri' and continued making it in increasing quantities to supply outlets further and further afield. It is, therefore, more likely that it is because of his enterprise that we have all heard about it, rather than the small and insignificant quantities enjoyed by the inhabitants of the Amalfi coast.

The small, remarkably pretty town of Amalfi is set at the mouth of a deep ravine at the foot of Mount Cerreto and is surrounded by dramatic cliffs. It became a major maritime power rivalling Pisa and Genoa after it freed itself from Byzantine vassalage in 839 and its success grew with the population rising to around 75,000 by the turn of that century. It remained independent until the Normans conquered it in 1073 and in 1131, it fell to Roger II of Sicily, then finally to the Pisans in 1135. Its prosperity declined after a major earthquake in 1343 caused part of the town and most of its inhabitants to disappear into the sea. It never recovered and as a consequence, today it is possible to walk from one side of the town to the other in 20 minutes. Marjie and I had a marvellous evening there in the enchanting port whilst the owner and his guests dined ashore. After our meal had been prepared, we set the table on the aft deck, opened a bottle of fine wine and gazed up at the lights of the town whilst we ate. It was good to be on our own and after the meal, we put on some soft music and danced until the exertion of the day caught up with us. I still have a vivid memory of that romantic evening. The next morning, after the breakfast plates had been washed up and the galley cleared for future action, we enjoyed ourselves looking around the lovely town. After lunch, we cast off and set a course for Capri on a reasonably calm, warm day whilst the owner and his guests slept.

Capri

Capri is a large limestone and sandstone rock with perpendicular cliffs that plunge down into the sea. It is actually two mountains joined by a ridge and is 7 kilometres long and 3 kilometres wide. The port is situated on the northern shore in a well-protected natural bay. It was extremely busy when we arrived, with ferries constantly going to and fro and I was uncertain where to go. The area nearest to the town appeared to be reserved for the ferries and other commercial craft so we found a place to moor in the marina, which is adjacent to the main port.

Unlike Naples, Capri escaped the ravages of WW2, as it was used as a recuperation centre for injured officers of both sides – first the

Germans and then the Allies. After the war, it prospered from tourism and new infrastructure was put in place. Water, which had always been in short supply, was piped from the mainland. The harbour was enlarged to accommodate larger, faster ferries and new hydrofoils were used to transport increasing numbers of tourists. We saw evidence of this influx, of which we were a part.

Although Capri was inhabited during the Neolithic and Bronze Ages, it was mainly developed by Augustus, the first Roman Emperor, who built villas, temples, aqueducts and gardens and used to visit often to live in his own version of paradise. When Augustus died in 14 AD, he was succeeded by Tiberius who moved permanently to Capri. He had become suspicious of the political manoeuvrings in Rome and feeling in danger, ran the Roman Empire from there until he died in 37 AD. His villa, the Villa Jovis, is in the North East of the island, high up and difficult to access and his quarters in it even more so. Because of its elevated remote position, Roman engineers constructed an intricate system for the collection of rainwater from the roofs and a large cistern that supplied it with fresh water.

Like many Mediterranean places, the island has had a colourful history, passing from one ruling body to another over the centuries. When the Western Roman Empire began to collapse in 476 AD, Capri became a province of Naples. In 1553, it became part of the Eastern Roman Empire after falling to the Turkish admiral Hayreddin Barbarossa and a short time later, to his ally, naval commander, Turgut Reis, known as "the drawn sword of Islam."

The stunning beauty of the island has attracted many famous people who have visited or owned property there. One of these was the writer Graham Greene, who bought a small house called 'Rosaio' at Anacapri in 1948; he visited it twice a year until his death in 1991 at the age of 86. He was made an honorary citizen of the town in 1978. With his disdain for tourism and travelling for pleasure, he once said: "It isn't really my kind of place". It was an unlikely location for him but he said, "On Capri, in four weeks I do the work of six months elsewhere."

Somerset Maugham, a frequent visitor, wrote a short story called "The Lotus Eater," about a British bank manager who went to Capri on holiday and fell in love with the island. He gave up his life in London to live there and swore to commit suicide when his money ran out but after years of languid island living, he lacked the courage to do it and spent his last days in poverty and deprivation. Tony Perrottet, in "The Lure of Capri" wrote, *"The character was based on Maugham's friend and lover, John Ellingham Brooks, who came to Capri as part of an exodus of homosexuals from England in the wake of Oscar Wilde's conviction, in 1895, for "acts of gross indecency." Brooks, however, escaped the fate of Maugham's character by marrying a Philadelphia heiress who, though she quickly divorced him, left Brooks an annuity that allowed him to spend out his days on Capri, playing the piano and walking his fox terrier."*

Another person who left his mark on Capri was the forward-thinking Swedish doctor and philanthropist Axel Munthe. He bought his property, a ruined house and chapel in 1887 and with the help of local residents, restored it into an amazing property now called Villa San Michele. The villa and its award-winning gardens were decorated with relics found on the island and also originating from elsewhere. It is sitting on top of a ledge to the northeast of Anacapri and has breathtaking views of the harbour, the Sorrentine peninsula and Mount Vesuvius. It was willed to the Swedish nation on his death in 1949 aged 91 and is today a museum and Swedish cultural institute, one of the most visited places on the island. The American author Henry James was one of many great cultural personalities who visited the villa. Afterwards, he called it *"a creation of the most fantastic beauty, poetry and inutility that I have ever seen clustered together."* He called it the most beautiful place in the world. Axel Munthe wrote a book about the property, called *The Story of San Michele*, an autobiographical account of his life and work. It was reputed to be the first 'bestseller' and was translated into 45 languages. It is still available today, 90 years later.

Gracie Fields, known as 'the Forces' sweetheart' for her work entertaining troops in WW2, also lived in Capri for the latter part of her life. Gracie was so popular that Hitler declared her an enemy of the Third Reich and Goebbels personally attacked her on the radio. A German propaganda magazine said of her work for the British war effort: "Gracie Fields has earned for England the equivalent of a hundred new Spitfires. She is adjudged a war industry, and should, therefore, be treated accordingly." The last straw came when she personally adapted one of her greatest hits, which in the new version concluded: *"They're going to string old Hitler from the very highest bow, of the biggest aspidistra in the world!"* Two days after she sang this at a concert in the French town of Arras, the Germans bombed the hotel where she and her husband had stayed and completely destroyed it, killing several occupants. On Capri, she lived in a property which had once been an English defence fort, complete with prison. She renovated it and named it 'La Canzone del Mare' – the song of the sea. It is still a popular beach club and restaurant, thanks to its privileged position set right into the cliffs. She died there in 1979 aged 81 and is buried in a non-Catholic cemetery on the island.

The town, which connects the two peaks, is 150 metres above sea level and a funicular railway takes four minutes to convey passengers from the port to the Piazzetta in the town centre but that evening, Marjie and I decided to climb to it via the Phoenician steps. Before we began we were tired from the nonstop work, navigating, cleaning, shopping, cooking, and everything else that was required to keep the guests happy. We didn't get very far before we realised the folly of our decision. There are 921 steps, the first few are easy but they get steeper and more arduous. Halfway up, I was stopped by two policemen. I have no idea why they stopped me and certainly no idea what they were saying or expected of me. Fatigued and gasping for breath, I stood nonplussed with a vacant stare and an idiotic grin on my face. Whatever they wanted to know, they didn't succeed and eventually gave up and left me standing on the steps, having reached the conclusion that I was an utter imbecile. It is a gruelling thirty minutes ascent at the best of times if you are physically fit and I advise against it if you are tired before you start, as we were. There is a funicular for the physically challenged and those of an imbecilic nature. The views at the top make it worthwhile, well, that's what we tried to convince ourselves. My heart went out to the inhabitants of the past who had to descend to collect water from the spring in Marina Grande and then cart it back up again and all the time hoping that they wouldn't be crushed to death by falling rocks. It is for that reason that the Bishops of Capri carved crosses on some of the steps to ask God to keep the rocks from falling. I wonder whether it worked or whether they succumbed themselves whilst doing it.

Thursday 22nd April, the weather was pleasant and the guests were enjoying Capri so much they decided to stay for the day and went ashore. Marjie and I effectively had the day free and being gluttons for punishment, made the insane decision to tackle the steep steps once more. To say that it is a bustling town is a massive distortion. When we made it, panting and wheezing to the famous Piazzetta in the town centre, it was so overcrowded that we saw nothing more than we had done the previous evening and everything was exceedingly expensive. Disappointed, we sat and sipped our cappucinos as slowly as we could to warrant the scandalous cost before we made our way back to the boat. *Vidal Sassoon said, "Capri on the Amalfi coast in Italy is my ultimate holiday destination."* Maybe it was less crowded and less expensive when he was there, or at a different time of year. Once everybody was back on board, we were instructed to set sail for the island of Ischia, whilst they enjoyed their customary afternoon siesta. Despite his reputation as a cantankerous employer, the owner had a good sense of humour and was actually a pleasure to have on board. They were having a fun-filled cruise but a chilling outcome was on the horizon.

Ischia

The port of Ischia, at the northeastern end of the island, is a natural basin surrounded by hills. It was once a lake that had formed in a volcanic crater after an earthquake. In 1853, an opening was made to join the lake to the sea and thus form a port. When we arrived for this second visit, the port was full. I had the engines on tick over as I turned the boat in circles, looking for an opening between two yachts. It didn't look promising and then I saw a small, very narrow space. A seaman was standing on the foredeck of each of the boats, looking at me as if to say "I dare you." There was no other possibility of a mooring, so dare or not I had to try. I positioned the boat by pushing one gear lever ahead and the other astern, spinning her around.

"Let go the anchor," I called to Marjie who was standing by on the foredeck. She looked at me in disbelief but released the brake and the anchor flew out as I pulled both levers into astern and we backed towards the small space between the two yachts.

"You'll never get in there!" the owner yelled. He and his guests hovered on the aft deck casting nervous glances at me, then at the impossibly small opening, then back at me. The crew members on the foredecks of the two yachts rushed to the pulpits, fenders in their hands. I remained calm. When we reached the bows of the other two yachts I called once more to Marjie.

"Hold it at that, come aft and get a rope on each of the foredecks." She wound up the anchor brake and ran to the aft deck where I was waiting for her. With a rope each side, held by the two surprised sailors on their foredecks, I instructed the owner, his guests and Marjie to push the boats apart whilst I motored astern little by little until we reached the quay, the two sailors jumped ashore and made fast our lines. I switched off the engines, went down from the flying bridge to the aft deck and helped Marjie put the gangplank into position.

"Bravo, bravo!" the two Italian sailors saluted me.

"I've never seen this boat taken through the eye of a needle before," the owner said. There were smiles all around that we'd found a place that had at first seemed impossible. The owner invited everybody, including Marjie and me to dine in a restaurant that evening.

And then it started to rain. By the evening it was torrential. Marjie and I went to find a taxi; walking huddled together under an umbrella and all we could find was a Piaggio Ape. Anybody who has visited Italy will be familiar with these three-wheeled vehicles that are based on Vespa scooters. They were developed after WWII when most Italians had no means of transport and no financial possibility to purchase a four-wheeled car. Corradino Ascanio, the inventor of the Vespa, (Italian for wasp), came up with the idea, which appealed to Enrico Piaggio, the Italian industrialist. They originally had a 50cc engine and were literally Vespa scooters with two wheels at the rear with a flatbed structure on the rear axle. At the time we were in Ischia, they were being produced with a 175cc engine and a cab for protection. They are called Ape, (Italian for bee) because of their work ethic. We went in one of them to choose a good restaurant and then back to the boat to collect the others followed by a second Ape. With four of us squashed into the tiny space of each Ape we were completely immobilised in the hot, steamy interior as we rattled along in the lashing rain to the restaurant. Endless flashes of lightning lit up the sky outside, followed by deafening claps of thunder. It was a horrendous storm. The restaurant roof started to leak and everybody had to move to avoid getting soaked. There was pandemonium inside as meals were abandoned, tables and chairs shoved clear of the leaks and the diners scattered to escape a soaking. The leaks got worse as the rain increased in intensity but we had an entertaining evening and a delicious meal. Back on board, curled up in our bunks, we listened as the storm continued throughout the night. The rain lashed down on the decks in a torrent, the thunder was deafening and the constant lightning flashes lit up our cabin through the portholes. When morning came, there was a violent wind and the heavy rain continued to lash the decks. The forecast was for the gale-force winds and rain to continue unabated so we were forced to spend another day in the well-protected port of Ischia.

12. The Pontine Islands

CHAPTER 15
THE PONTINE ISLANDS

Ventotene

Saturday 24th April, the wind decreased a little and the passengers were anxious to move on to Anzio. I plotted the course and started the engines. We took in the gangplank, cast off the stern ropes, hauled in the anchor and motored out of the harbour. When we cleared the safety of the port we were hit by a huge swell on the starboard beam and rolled and rolled. It was exceedingly uncomfortable and the passengers very quickly began to feel sick but didn't want to go back to Ischia after having spent two days there already in such miserable weather. We had barely started to cross the Gulf of Gaeta and they were at the limit of their endurance.

"What can we do, we can't tolerate this anymore?" the owner asked me.

"If I swing around to port and head west it will be more comfortable with the sea on our stern. It's only about 40 nautical miles to Ponza," I told him.

"We should go to Ponza, I'd love to go there it's supposed to be lovely," said his male guest.

"OK, let's go there," said the owner. I plotted the new course and swung the boat around. The motion was more tolerable but still very unpleasant as we rode up on one wave and then hurtled down into the trough at an amazing speed, then up we went again and back down again. I was fighting with the steering wheel to keep us on course as the wind and the sea pushed us onwards. The owner went to his cabin where he was violently sick as were the others, who vomited over the side. They were frightened and wanted it to end at any cost. The owner staggered up to the wheelhouse. He looked dreadful. His face was a deathly white.

"Is there anywhere else we can go, this is awful, I can't stand any more of it." he pleaded with me.

" It's not that much farther to Ponza, " I said.

"I don't care how far it is, isn't there anywhere nearer?" he implored me. I looked around and his guests were looking to me for reassurance and hope.

"There's a small island called Ventotene not far away, it's a prison island, we can go there if you want'" I said.

"Go there, go there, we've had enough," he said. There was a great sigh of relief from everybody and they suddenly found it possible to smile, even get excited at the prospect of some peace and quiet and for the motion to stop.

Ventotene is the remains of an ancient volcano. It is just 3 kilometres long, a mere 800 metres wide and its territory includes the small ancillary island of Santo Stefano, two kilometres to the east. The other islands are Palmarola, Zannoni, Gazi and Ponza, which is the largest and from which they get their collective name, the Pontine Islands, lying off the west coast of Italy. Ventotene has around 700 residents but was uninhabited for centuries due to its susceptibility to attacks from pirates. It was used as a prison island by the Romans and the unfortunate souls that were incarcerated there mostly starved to death. A prison camp had also been created on the nearby island of Santo Stefano by the French, which was later rebuilt by the leader of the Italian Fascist Party, Benito Mussolini. It was on Ventotene, however, that an Italian, Altiero Spinelli was sent by Mussolini's fascist government in 1927 for his communist and anti-fascist activities. After extensive studies, Spinelli became disillusioned with communism and was expelled from the Italian Communist Party for opposing Stalinism. He became a passionate supporter of supranationalism and federalism, believing it would unite individual states to the extent that it would be impossible to ever have another war in Europe. In 1941, together with another political prisoner, Eugenio Colorni, he secretly wrote the "Ventotene Manifesto." It was written on cigarette papers that were hidden under the false bottom of a tin box, which was smuggled to the mainland and circulated by the

Italian Resistance and other resistance movements. In it, he denounced the responsibility of nation-states for the horrors of war and promoted the idea of a federal Europe. After his release in 1943, he was an ardent supporter of a united Europe and played a leading role in its formation. He became a European Commissioner between 1970 and 1976 and a member of the European Parliament in 1976. In 1984, the Parliament adopted and approved a proposal by him for the establishment of the European Union, which was formally founded in 1992 with the signing of the Maastricht Treaty. In 2012, the European Union received the Nobel Peace Prize for "having contributed to the advancement of peace and reconciliation, democracy and human rights in Europe." Altiero Spinelli died in 1986 and was buried on Ventotene. The largest building of the European Parliament complex in Brussels is named after him. In August 2016, the Italian Prime Minister Matteo Renzi, the German Chancellor, Angela Merkel and French President François Mitterand laid a wreath at his tomb when they were there to discuss European policy following the United Kingdom's vote to leave the union. The Federalist Movement still holds regular meetings on the island.

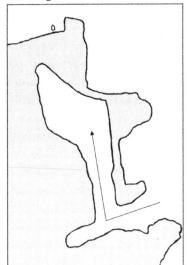

13. The harbour at Ventotene

To our passengers, despite the foul weather, the small island looked alluring as it came into view in the grey mist but it was to yield unpleasant memories.

"There's a tiny port that the Romans built, we should be able to get in there and get some protection," I said. Well, technically it wasn't the Romans who did the building, they'd used slaves to dig it out of the Tufa rock.

"I don't care who built it, I'm just glad they put it there," the owner replied. As we approached the entrance on the northeast corner of the island, I realised that it wasn't going to be easy. I saw the gap in the rock but the port itself was completely hidden. The heavy sea and the strong wind on our stern made it difficult to hold the course steady and I began to question my judgement in continuing through the very narrow passage. The waves were picking us up, raising us to the crests, which we surfed along for a while before we plummeted down, veering sideways as the next wave arrived. There was very little room to manoeuvre a boat of our size when we entered the cutting, which was just 30 metres wide. I reduced the engine revolutions. It didn't look good. There was no sign of a port, nothing but rocks all around us.

"Turn around, let's get out of here!" the owner cried. He was horrified.

"It's too late, I can't. We're committed," I told him. We were heading straight for the rocks at the end of the small, cutting – and then, to starboard, I saw the passageway to the small port. It was at a right angle to where we were headed – I would never have made it simply by swinging the wheel hard to starboard, which I did anyway - I pulled the starboard gear lever control into astern and with the port engine in ahead position I pushed the throttles forward to increase revolutions. The boat spun around rapidly. The owner and his guests stood on the aft deck transfixed, praying that we'd make it into the tiny port. Marjie and I were anxious too. It didn't look good. At that moment, the most incredible thing happened.

"Could we have a cup of tea please?" the owner's sister asked me. I was aghast. I couldn't believe my ears. Was she kidding? We were in a highly dangerous situation and she genuinely wanted Marjie to go below and make them a pot of tea. How very British!

"You'll have to wait, " I barked back at her as I struggled to keep control of the boat. Mercifully we did make it safely into the port. I've since read that somebody once said, "You take your life into your hands by berthing there." It is very shallow, the maximum depth is around 1.8 metres with rocky ledges on either side and there are underwater rocky ledges at the quays. The maximum size boat it can accommodate is 12 metres. With hindsight – I never should have attempted it. The only book I had available made no mention of the dangers or size restrictions. We were 18 metres with a draft of 1.5 metres but we'd made it. Then the trouble began.

The tiny port was filled with very small fishing boats with not enough space for us and hardly enough room to turn around but I spotted a possible place to moor just inside the entrance. Some fishermen gathered on the quay to watch and started shouting directions. I positioned the boat to where I thought would be a good spot to drop the anchor. In fact, it was the only possible spot and the lack of space severely limited me to manoeuvre the boat and lay out as much anchor chain as I would ordinarily have done.

"Let go!" I called to Marjie, standing by on the foredeck. She released the brake and the anchor chain rattled out as I pulled both levers into astern and backed up to the quay with difficulty because of the strong wind.

"Hold it," I called again to Marjie. She tightened up the brake and ran to the stern, where the highly energized fishermen leapt around keeping their small boats clear, all the while shouting in Italian to each other and to me. They took our stern ropes, attached them to the mooring rings and helped us put out the gangplank. We all breathed a sigh of relief – we were safe and protected from the elements. It wasn't to last!

Whether it was to calm their nerves from the fear and uncertainty they'd experienced or maybe it was just the typical English habit but the sister insisted that she have her pot of tea made. Marjie served it to them. We looked around at the pastel-coloured fishermen's houses built into the solid rock and that was the only opportunity we had to appreciate the pleasantness of the surroundings. There was a great deal of agitation taking place among the fishermen on the quay. They congregated at the foot of our gangplank and one of them clambered aboard.

"You go, you go," he said.

"Go where?" I asked.

"Go, go, not stay here." Then another of them came aboard.

"You go where ferry go," the other one said. I had no idea where the ferry went.

"Where?" I asked.

"Come, I go, show you, you not stay here, you go." I got the message loud and clear - they didn't want us. I wasn't looking forward to going back out again and neither was anybody else. Nobody wanted to start vomiting once more. I started the engines and left them idling in neutral. I raised the gangplank, let go the stern ropes and started to walk forward to check that the fenders were protecting us from hitting the wall on our starboard side whilst Marjie hauled in the anchor to pull us clear. I was aghast to see that we were going rapidly astern. The fisherman had taken control. He'd gone into the wheelhouse and pulled the control levers into astern and we were about to crash onto the quay. I flew into the wheelhouse, shoved him aside and rammed the levers into ahead, then pulled them back to neutral to bring us to a halt. We'd avoided hitting the quay by millimetres. Marjie turned and looked at me, startled, wondering what on earth had happened. When the anchor was heaved in, I motored back out of the port with the fisherman beside me, chattering in my ear in his limited English. He directed me to the new ferry terminal in a bay, around a headland and helped us moor up. The area was deserted and exposed because the seawall had crashed into the sea on a previous occasion and hadn't been completely repaired but it did offer us some protection from the swell. I decided not to put the gangplank out as nobody had any intention of going ashore in such an inhospitable place. Our Italian helper, for want of a more appropriate description, demanded 10,000 lire, which was about £6 back in 1976. (When cruising in Italy in those days, we always needed plenty of lire for handing out the expected and sometimes aggressively demanded tips and we always had to be prepared to bargain for everything. I can even remember bargaining over the price for aspirins in a chemist shop when Jill and I were in Italy.) The Italian pocketed his cash, said he'd return with bread, cheese and wine and left us.

Almost immediately afterwards, a large deputation of ranting, irate Italians marched down the hill towards us, accompanied by three uniformed policemen. When they arrived at the yacht they over-exaggerated their anger, shouting even louder than is normal for Italians. They grabbed our stern ropes, pulled the boat to the quay and two of the policemen jumped aboard. One of them was a particularly nasty character. He shoved his identity card in our faces and said that we'd broken the fishermen's mooring lines and they wanted 150 dollars. It was obvious that their unnecessary hollering and aggressive behaviour was meant to intimidate us. They succeeded. I tried to explain that it was the Italian fisherman who pulled the controls levers into the astern position if it was indeed that manoeuvre that had caused the damage and I doubted that any mooring lines had been broken. As far as I was concerned, they had seized an opportunity to take advantage of us. The situation turned nasty.

"What you want, you want money, I give you money," the owner said, pulling handfuls of dollars out of his pocket. Whilst the unpleasant outbursts were taking place, Marjie took temporary leave of her senses. She went to our cabin, picked up her camera and started taking pictures of the maniacal crowd. The men and particularly the police were furious.

"NO PICTURE, NO PICTURE!" yelled one of the policemen. The third policeman came aboard, demanded to see our identity papers and insisted that the film in the camera be destroyed.

"I didn't take any pictures," said Marjie in an unconvincing attempt to calm their fury. It didn't fool anybody. In fact, it made the policeman angrier. He made it perfectly clear that if the film wasn't taken out and thrown in the sea then he would confiscate and destroy the camera. Marjie had no choice, she removed the film and threw it in the sea. It was heartbreaking for her as it contained pictures of all the places we'd visited and would possibly never return to. The owner gave them the money they asked for and they stuffed it into their grubby little pockets.

"You come-a with us-a," the police threatened me, "bring-a ships-a papers and everybody's passaports-a." I collected up the documents he asked for and went ashore with them.

With one each side of me, they grabbed my arms.

"I'm coming with you," shouted the owner's guest. Nobody on board trusted either the police or the angry crowd. "Wait, wait," he called, "I don't think you should go with them alone." He jumped ashore and we were marched up the hill to the police station in the town above the old Roman port. I thought of the prison and all the poor souls who'd starved to death there – would I become another statistic, would I be incarcerated, never to be seen or heard of again? We were kept in the police station whilst they went through the painfully slow process of typing out details on reams of papers in quadruplicate. When they were satisfied that they'd punished us enough, they marched us back to the boat, a policeman on either side of us. We said our farewells and I vowed I would never, ever return to Ventotene.

Meanwhile, Marjie had retreated to our cabin in the focsle, upset that she'd lost the photographs that she'd taken of our voyage. The female guest went to her, invited her up on deck and poured her a large gin and tonic. The owner gave Marjie a kiss and cuddle to comfort her and had already told me after we left Ischia that he wished he'd met me ten years ago, so maybe he'd been difficult with other Skippers because he felt he had reason to be. I know that he was good with us and we enjoyed his company - not all of the time though, I have to say!

Marjie prepared lunch and before we'd finished, along came our Italian in his small motor launch, offering us cheese and wine at outrageous prices. The haggling began and after a lengthy discussion, the owner bought some of his wine and cheese and that was the first time I'd tasted provolone piccante, a sharp cheese that originates from Cassili, a little village near Vesuvius. I've been enjoying it ever since. As usual, after lunch, they slept and I decided that the weather had improved enough for us to cast off for Ponza. We were all so desperate to leave Ventotene, never to return and definitely didn't fancy spending the night there.

Ponza

It was a rough trip as we crashed our way through the waves, battered by the wind, but as we approached Ponza, the wind died down, the sea flattened out and the sky cleared. The sun shone enough for us to be dazzled by the sight of it setting on the horizon behind the island. The port, located at the southern end of the eastern shore, looked fabulous and inviting when we motored in. An array of different coloured houses curved around the picturesque harbour, with the main town perched on a cliff above. A couple of local fishermen beckoned us over to a vacant berth and helped us moor up and put out the gangplank. The owner had been violently seasick again and he stayed in his cabin for the rest of the evening. His sister and guests ate ashore. Marjie and I tidied up, ate our meal and collapsed into our bunks exhausted.

The next day, Sunday 25 April, the sun shone. It was a glorious day and we had time to explore the magical, magnificent island of Ponza, which according to local legends, was named after the Roman governor of Judea, Pontius Pilate, whose family owned a grotto on the island. Ponza is actually the above-water part of a much larger island called Tryrrhenia, which sank into the sea and is part of a caldera rim of an extinct volcano. It was heavily forested when it was first colonised by the Etruscans but now the trees have long since gone and the hills are terraced for the cultivation of grapes, figs and prickly pears. It was the Etruscans who created the blue grottos for which Ponza is well known. It is thought that they were created to breed marine life. The island is suspected of being the mythical island of Aeaea, home of Circe the goddess of magic, as described in Homer's Oddysey. After having been abandoned in the Middle Ages because of the constant raids by pirates and Saracens, Ponza was re-colonised by the Kingdom of Naples in the 18th century. In 1813 it was captured by the British during the Napoleonic wars but by the mid 19th century it became part of the Kingdom of Italy, now the Republic of Italy. Like Ventotene, it was also used as a penal colony by various regimes. Benito Mussolini sent his political opponents there and was imprisoned there himself after he was overthrown in 1943.

Apart from the fishing industry, the island now relies on tourism for its economy. I loved the little known, authentic, unspoilt fishermen's island from the moment we entered its deep, sheltered harbour, set in a bay of crystal clear water. Beyonce, Mariah Carey, Bruce Springsteen and Rihanna are among those privileged enough to know of its existence and in days past, it was also visited by Kirk and Michael Douglas, Burt Lancaster, Anthony Quinn, Gina Lollobrigida and Sophia Loren. It is only accessible by boat, there is no airport, no sumptuous hotels and its charm lies in its unpretentiousness and simple lifestyle. Marjie and I climbed to the town and walked to the other side of the island to admire the spectacular scenery. We finished up perched atop a cliff covered with pink mesembryanthemums and gazed down at the coastline and out to sea. It was a spellbinding experience. When we arrived back at the boat, Marjie prepared lunch for everybody and the owner decided he needed to be on the Italian mainland in case he had to leave for business.

Marjie's cooking abilities impressed me more and more each day. Like everything else she did, she excelled at it. Later in our lives, she was to gain quite a reputation for her expertise in the part of France where we chose to base ourselves. How lucky I am to be able to tuck into her delicious meals. What amazes me is that she hardly ever cooks the same thing twice, always inventing new recipes and never will buy anything that she thinks she can make herself. How could the owner and his guests not compliment her constantly and give her the praise she so well deserved? When they'd finished eating, we were asked to take them to Anzio. If they'd been able to foresee the dreadful consequences, they would never have wanted to go.

CHAPTER 16
THE ANZIO INCIDENT

A night to remember

We hoisted in the gangplank, weighed anchor and headed for Anzio. The passage was uneventful and it was a welcome change to have a reasonably calm sea and no rain or wind. Everybody was happy and looking forward to visiting the fishing port of Anzio on the coast of the Lazio region of Italy, where they'd wanted to go for the previous few days. We arrived at 18h00 and moored up in the exact same berth, opposite the harbour office, that Marjie and I were in on the trip out to Naples. A large crowd had gathered on the quay to watch us and not one person offered to take our mooring ropes. Marjie had to leap ashore and catch the ropes that I threw to her and attach them to the bollards so that I could make them fast. The owner offered to help put the gangplank out but not knowing what to do; he only hindered the operation. The quay was exceptionally high so the gangplank was at a very steep angle, so steep in fact, that we had to raise it off the quay when it wasn't being used to stop it rubbing. That evening they ate on board. When they'd finished, Marjie and I cleared away and tired from working so many hours, we climbed into our bunks and had a good night's sleep.

Monday, 26th April, the owner and his guests discussed plans for the rest of the trip during breakfast. He decided he wanted to leave and go to Rome and Florence. Nobody else wanted to go because they were anxious to cruise to Elba after Anzio so he agreed that he would go alone and meet up with us again in Viareggio on 29th April.

Throughout the trip, I'd been repacking and tightening the port stern gland in an unsuccessful attempt to prevent it from leaking. Nothing seemed to have any effect. I was at a loss as to what more I could do and was forever having to pump out the bilges. I was concerned because it was getting worse each day. The generator also hadn't been charging properly so I went ashore to find an electrical engineer to help out. I was beginning to think that maybe we hadn't really needed the new starting battery for it and that there was something else wrong. Marjie did what she usually did whenever we reached a new destination, which was to go ashore and buy food and wine for the six of us. After lunch, the owner ordered his taxi and set off for Rome, 51 kilometres north of Anzio, with much fussing and waving from his guests. When he'd left, his sister suggested that Marjie and I move into his stateroom, which we did.

Late that afternoon, the fishing boats started to return from their day's work and Marjie went off to buy a selection of the day's catch. I was feeling tired with a cold coming on so went to the owner's bed to rest for a while. In the early evening, the guests went ashore to dine. When they'd gone, Marjie cooked our meal and brought mine down to me but I wasn't hungry and was practically falling asleep. She was in the process of washing up whilst I slept when she heard the guests returning and went on deck to operate the gangplank. The angle was so steep, the owner's sister, the first in line to descend, hesitated. She didn't want to take the first step.

"Go on, it's perfectly safe," the others were encouraging her. Shaking slightly, still uncertain, she placed one foot on the gangplank and started to descend. To reassure her, Marjie stretched out her arms to help her aboard.

I was woken by an almighty crash and screams and shouts. I leapt out of bed and rushed up on deck. The gangplank docking socket on the deck had broken loose. The gangplank, with nothing to support it, swung inboard along the aft deck and the owner's sister was plunged into the icy cold water. The male guest, without thinking, jumped in after her. His wife was running backwards and forwards along the quay in a panic, screaming.

"Help, help, she can't swim. Help, help," followed by screams. Marjie grabbed a life ring and threw it to them but each time they tried to grab it, it drifted further and further away from them until eventually, both of them and the life ring had drifted out of sight beneath the dinghy that was slung in the davits at the stern. The panic-stricken wife on the quay was still screaming. I arrived amid the chaos, quickly took stock of what had happened and threw a rope towards the iron ladder that was set into the quay wall, assuming that's where they'd be heading and that if they couldn't make it, at least they'd be able to hold onto the rope. Without the gangplank in position, we couldn't get ashore.

Fishermen ran to help. One of them went down the ladder to try to grab the people in the water and others arrived rowing a dinghy. The wife on the quay was shouting at her husband who was floating motionless. The fishermen in the dinghy pulled the owner's sister out of the water. She sat bedraggled and in shock. Next, they pulled out the limp body of the man and laid him across her lap Marjie and I pulled on the stern lines and dragged the yacht back towards the quay. I held the boat in position and with lightning speed, Marjie leapt into the dinghy hanging on the davits and jumped ashore before the yacht sprung back from the quay again. The weight on the ropes was such that I could no longer hold them and I had to pull the boat back a second time, let go and then quickly jump ashore myself before the boat drifted away again. Marjie meanwhile had climbed down the ladder to get to the dinghy hoping to give CPR. The dinghy was already too crowded with fishermen and the two bodies so they pushed her away and she climbed back up to the quay.The dinghy was rowed to some steps about three metres away and Marjie ran to meet them. She was shocked when she saw the guest with his eyes open and staring as he lay across the owner's sister's lap. She could tell that he was already dead. The hysterical wife ran to me as soon as I'd jumped ashore and together we went to where the crowd had gathered by the steps.

The two soaked bodies were brought ashore and the wife of the dead man fell onto his body screaming and then began giving him the kiss of life. Marjie pounded on his chest.

"Turn him on his stomach," an English voice said. They turned him and the Englishman started to pump his back. There was chaos. People were shouting, screaming and running around and we were trying to ask them to call a doctor. I leapt back on board, grabbed two blankets, ran back to the owner's sister, wrapped one of them around her and gave the other one to the people with the lifeless body. A car sped towards us and screeched to a halt. The man was placed on the blanket and heaved onto the back seat of the car. Marjie and the Englishman climbed into the front and were whisked off to a hospital where a scruffy, unshaven individual greeted them and oversaw the transfer of our guest onto a trolley, which was wheeled away into a nearby room, where he was placed on a table. Marjie and the Englishman went back out to the foyer and sat on a wooden bench. Shortly afterwards the staff member who'd greeted them returned and pronounced that the man was dead. I was left to look after the two distraught ladies on the quay until an ambulance arrived. The owner's sister was placed on a stretcher and we were taken to the same hospital. When we arrived, she was placed in a separate room and put on a bed and I went and stayed with her. The dead man's wife went and sat with Marjie in the bare corridor. Marjie hadn't told her the earth-shattering news, preferring to wait, hoping that he wasn't dead after all and that they were resuscitating him. Eventually, a tired-looking, bespectacled man dressed in a white jacket came out of a door opposite to where they were sitting and broke the inevitable news to the wife. She was hysterical. Marjie tried to comfort her but she was inconsolable.

The owner's sister was shivering and non-stop rushing to the toilet. She was too distressed to be told of the death and was kept in overnight. I ordered a taxi and made two trips back to the yacht for her medicines and personal items. After that, Marjie and I took turns to support them, each in a separate room. The owner's sister was so cold that she was shaking uncontrollably. Marjie stood at the end of the bed and rubbed her feet then put them under her jumper in an attempt to warm them up. When I was with her, I cuddled her from time to time and in her confusion, she had the erroneous impression that I'd saved her life. How she reached that conclusion is a mystery. She asked several times if the friend who had jumped into the water was OK and Marjie and I were in the difficult situation of having to conceal the truth. The wife was in total shock and there was little we could do to comfort her.

Sometime later the police arrived and took Marjie and me to the station, leaving the Englishman with the dead man's wife. We made statements and answered a never-ending number of questions over and over again. In typical Italian fashion, mountains of paperwork had to be filled in in quadruplicate using an old typewriter. The dead man's wife and the Englishman, who we discovered was called Eddie and was on a boat called 'The Pool Fisher' moored at the end of our quay, arrived in another police car and when they'd made their statements we were all taken back to the port and our respective boats. It was 04h00 when they set us free and we were told that we would be picked up and taken back to the police station again at 08h00. Marjie made some coffee and afterwards, we all went to bed – the wife on the saloon settee and Marjie and I in the stateroom. None of us got much sleep and I'd forgotten all about being ill.

Bad cop – good cop

Well before 08h00, the police arrived, banging and shouting and whisked Marjie and me off once again to the station where they bombarded us with question after question. They were rude, aggressive and uncaring and we were tired from lack of sleep and hunger. They kept us there for three hours without any further developments having taken place since we were last there only a few hours before. One of them called the British consul in Rome and I made the dreaded call to the owner at his hotel in Florence.

"Hello, how is everything, is everybody having a good time?" he asked.

"Not really. I'm afraid I have some bad news," I said.

"What's wrong?"

" Last night your sister fell in the water and......"

"What! What are you telling me, that's dreadful, what happened, is she alright?" he demanded.

"Yes, she's alright, she's in hospital but ....."

"In hospital, what's wrong with her?"

"She's OK but there's more bad news. Your friend jumped in to save her and he had a heart attack. I'm afraid he's dead." I told him the full story and of the appalling way in which the police were treating us.

"I'll arrange to come to Anzio and don't worry about the police, I'm going to call the chief of police in Rome, I know him well. Leave it to me," he said.

Shortly after our telephone conversation, the hostile attitude of our captors changed totally. They became polite and even appeared sheepish and servile. They ceased questioning us and brought us coffee and croissants, then the police chief himself took us to the hospital to visit the owner's sister. What a difference it can make when one has friends of influence in high places – especially in Italy where the Camorra has a foothold! We were told by the doctor not to tell the sister about the death of the other guest, which was difficult because she kept asking so we had to invent ways of not answering directly. Marjie stayed with her a while longer whilst I went to arrange a hotel for the deceased man's wife, and the owner, who was on his way to Anzio from Florence. After that, we were taken to the morgue to identify the body, which meant more waiting around for the arrival of the officials – a sombre-looking pair if ever there was one. They had obviously chosen the right profession! Then we returned to the port and had lunch at a restaurant on the quay.

In the afternoon, I re-bedded the gangplank docking socket as best I could and put the gangplank back into use so that we could get ashore and back on board more easily but we used it with caution. The owner arrived at 15h30 with an interpreter from Florence. The undertakers arrived shortly afterwards and arrangements were made to fly the body to the U.K., after which, the owner went to visit his sister. Marjie packed everybody's suitcases so that they could all return home and then we tried unsuccessfully to get some much-needed sleep. In the evening the owner invited us all to eat in a restaurant. Considering the circumstances, the evening went as well as could be expected – everyone was trying to make the best of the situation. That night, back on board in the owner's stateroom, we fell into a deep, deep sleep.

At 09h30 the next day, 28th April, the owner came aboard with his pilot and his company director who'd flown out from the U.K. together on his private plane. They loaded up their cars with the suitcases and went to the hospital to collect his sister, promising to come back to say goodbye to us. When they came back, they went around handing out handfuls of dollars to everybody who'd helped us, including $100 to ourselves. Tearful and very fond farewells were said and then they drove off. We had lunch in a restaurant and went back to our bed to sleep some more, but with our minds going over everything that had happened it wasn't to be.

Bygone times

The weather worsened in the early hours of the morning. The sky became overcast and the wind howled so when we crawled out of bed after a sleepless night we decided to explore Anzio before the rain set in. Anzio was once part of Antium, the capital of the Volscians who were ancient Italic people in conflict with the Romans until they were ultimately defeated in 468 BC. The following year the Romans established a colony there. They built luxurious seaside villas, the remains of which still exist along the shores. The Roman Emperor Caligula was born there as was Nero, whose villa was the most famous. He also built a new harbour and the original moles still exist. Antium was deserted in the Middle Ages in favour of Nettuno, which is now a popular tourist destination and agricultural centre. The harbour was relocated further to the east at the end of the 17th century by Popes Innocent XII and Clement XI. The modern municipality of Anzio was founded in 1857 by Pope Pius IX when the boundaries of Nettuno were redrawn to accommodate the new town.

During WWII, the allied forces landed at Anzio and Nettuno as part of Operation Shingle, (code name for the Allied amphibious landings). A convoy of 243 allied ships left the Bay of Naples in the afternoon of 21st January 1944 and by midnight, 45,000 allied troops and vehicles had been landed on the beaches. Having encountered no resistance, Major-General John Lucas, instead of making headway inland, decided to wait until more troops arrived and by 28 January, 70,000 men had landed ashore. The delay enabled the German forces to establish a defensive barrier around the allied positions which they then began shelling. Pitched battles continued with each side gaining alternately. The stand-off and the worsening weather conditions brought the battle to a stalemate. By the 30th January, the Allies had 5,000 casualties. Winston Churchill was so unhappy with the operation he wrote to the supreme commander over operations in Italy, *"I expected to see a wildcat roaring into the mountains – and what do I find? A whale wallowing on the beachhead."* Major-General Lucas was replaced by Major-General Lucius Truscott on 22 February.

The allied landings at Anzio would have been a monumental disaster equalling that of Gallipoli in WWI had it not been for the breaching of the Gustave Line and the capture of Monte Cassino on

17th May. (The Gustave Line was a defence barrier completed by one of Nazi Germany's most competent commanding officers, Generalfieldmarschall, Albert Kesselring. It ran from the Adriatic to the Tyrrhenian Sea with Monte Cassino as its pivotal point due to its commanding surveillance location.) The Battle of Monte Cassino is also known as the Battle for Rome. It was taken at a high cost, resulting in 55,000 casualties for the Allies and around 20,000 for the Germans. Another assault on the line took place on 23 May and on that same day, Major General Lucian Truscott launched an attack on the surrounding German army, which was without an armoured division because Kesselring had sent it to reinforce the German army under attack at Monte Cassino. When the Germans retreated, Truscott and his seven divisions broke out of Anzio and was ordered to head towards Rome. Rome fell to the US forces on 04 June 1944, two days before the Normandy invasion. A film called Anzio, starring Robert Mitchum and other international stars, was made in 1968. It had mainly fictional characters but was based on the actual events of the battle.

We returned to the yacht and saw a great deal of activity taking place on the boat next to us. The fishermen, who had come from Ponza, were doubling up on their mooring lines.

"There's a tempest coming, you'd better double up your mooring ropes, it's going to be quite a storm," one of them said. We boarded and the kindly fishermen helped us secure our boat by attaching our bow lines to other vessels and extra stern lines to the quay. They certainly were earning the dollars they'd received from the owner. Feeling confident that everything was in place to see out the tempest, we went ashore once more to find a restaurant and enjoy an evening meal. As we started to walk along the quay, a car screeched to a stop beside us. The driver must have been watching and waiting for us.

"Where are you going?" a voice called. We looked at the driver. Our hearts sank, it was the chief of police.

"We're going to look for a restaurant," I replied.

"Get in," he instructed us. Feeling apprehensive, we climbed into the back of his car and he drove off, chatting with us as if we were old friends.

"I'll take you to a restaurant," he said and when we got there he told us to wait whilst he went to talk to the proprietor, whom he knew. "It's all arranged and I've ordered the wine for you." He shook our hands. "Enjoy your meal," he said and left. The meal was excellent and as for the wine, which he'd paid for, well, I can honestly say that it was one of the finest wines I have ever drunk. How sad that neither Marjie nor I can recall its name. Afterwards, back on board, we slept reasonably well despite the racket of the wailing wind, the creaking of the ropes and the slapping of the water against the hull as we were buffeted around. How grateful we felt towards the Ponza fishermen who'd helped make sure we were secure.

14. Leaving Porto Ercole

CHAPTER 17
HOMEWARD BOUND

Water, water everywhere

Marjie was in a deep sleep when I buzzed down to the stateroom on the intercom at 06h00 the next morning. "Let's go," I said from the wheelhouse. It didn't put her in a good mood being woken up so early in such an abrupt manner. The storm had eased enough for us to leave. It wasn't perfect weather but I was certain that the worst was over. I didn't want to hang around in case more storms came and I wanted to reach the next destination before nightfall. We'd both had enough of Anzio! It was such a pleasure to hear the roar of the engines starting up and to know that we'd soon be at sea once more. Marjie appeared bleary-eyed but soon woke up when she arrived on deck to be hit by the bracing wind. The troublesome gangplank was hauled aboard, the ropes were cast off, the anchor weighed and it felt good to motor out of the port of Anzio into the Tyrrhenian Sea and head north on our way back to France. The sky and the sea were a dull grey. The wind had decreased considerably but there was a huge swell and we were tossed around like a cork. It was very uncomfortable but we had no deadline so would able to stop where and when we chose. I set a course for Porto Ercole on the eastern side of the Monte Argentario promontory, the opposite side to Porto Santo Stefano, where we'd stayed on our way out to Naples. Both towns comprise the municipality of Monte Argentario, which is essentially a mountain connected to the mainland by two sand causeways known as Tomboli.

The name Monte Argentario is derived from the Italian word, argentarii, meaning money lenders because the family who had owned the mountain loaned money to the Romans to help finance the Punic wars. Porto Ercole was founded by the Etruscans and later conquered by the Romans who established the port. The walls and towers were built in the 15th century when it was annexed to the Sienna Republic and strengthened further during the wars between the French, who were Allies of Sienna, and the Spanish who were Allies of Florence. The Italian artist Caravaggio died there on 18th July 1610. He was a violent, short-tempered man and a fight in Rome had led to a death sentence for murder, which forced him to flee to Naples. The latest theory concerning the cause of his early death at 38, builds on his notoriously fierce temperament and a series of genetic clues that attribute the artist's death to an injury inflicted in one of his many street brawls. The fight, which triggered a staph infection, sepsis and finally death, reportedly occurred between one month and 15 days before the first signs of a fatal fever emerged. It is thought that he was found on Feniglia beach and taken to the church of Sant'Erasmo, which is situated in the old quarter of the town.

The trip was unpleasant because of the inclement weather and the rough sea but largely uneventful. The major problem was the leaking stern gland. I spent far too much time being thrown around in the stifling hot, noisy engine room checking it and constantly pumping out the bilges. I was mystified as to why I couldn't prevent it from leaking after having repacked it and tightened it so many times and was looking forward to some respite. It was a marvellous feeling when we saw Monte Argentario loom into view in the distance, by which time the sea had become much calmer. When we reached it, we motored into the old harbour of Porto Ercole to have a look but decided to explore the new marina Cala Galera in the northern bay instead. It was still under construction so wasn't mentioned on any of the navigation charts or in any books.

We tied up alongside the fuel jetty and ordered fuel, which we took on later that day and afterwards found a berth to moor for the night. It was good to be in a new, civilised port but the good feeling soon went when I discovered that the bilge pump was struggling and not pumping much water. I took it apart and saw that the impellor was damaged. Enquires for a replacement were unsuccessful. Nobody knew where I could get an identical one. I only had offers for replacing the whole pump and they couldn't say when it would arrive. I decided to wait until we reached Viareggio where I was certain I'd find the correct impellor. We took the opportunity to top up the fresh water tank but because the port was still under construction, the water distribution point wasn't

working properly and the only way to get the water to flow was to feed in 50 lire jetons that we bought from the port office. I put in several at once and the trickle of water that spurted out lasted no more than a minute - and we needed 800 litres! Marjie went to buy more jetons and we sat piling them in and getting nowhere so went to find an alternative solution. We were told to wait until the next day when it would be sorted out. In the evening, we had

15. Checking the engine

a meal and a good time at the yacht club with the crews from other yachts. We had such an enjoyable time we decided to stay another day. We launched the Dory, fitted the outboard motor and reconnoitred the bays and beaches, then went into the old harbour and visited the bustling, attractive town with its narrow streets. It was a relatively unknown place, frequented by the wealthy residents of Rome and apparently Vladimir Putin owns a property in the vicinity.

Saturday 1st May at 08h00 we cast off and followed a course to take us to Portoferraio in Elba. There was a strong northwesterly wind blowing and the sea was uncomfortable. At times, the strong gusts made me think twice about continuing as we rose and dipped, plunging our way through the waves that cascaded along the decks. The boat was excellent in a rough sea but that didn't help us when we were being thrown around and trying to maintain our balance. The nearer we got to the island of Elba, the calmer the sea became and by the time we motored slowly through the port entrance, it was completely calm. Two men on the quay grabbed our stern ropes and attached them to the mooring rings and then immediately asked us for 4000 lire. It was usual to tip frequently in Italy but that was the first time we'd been asked for a specific amount and they insisted on payment. Although it would only have translated to £2.79 at the time, it sounded a lot worse than it was. After a late lunch, we strolled ashore and in the evening had a meal in a very good trattoria frequented by locals. When we visit any new place, we mostly like to avoid tourist areas and seek out places that are popular with the locals. They are often cheaper but the main reason is that the food is more authentic and the atmosphere more fun. The cost, with wine, was 6,000 lire and for some inexplicable reason, the owner reduced the bill by 400 lire. We had such a good time in Portoferraio we stayed for another day to explore more of the island.

And the earth moved

When it was time to leave, we cast off after a large breakfast and set a course for Viareggio. It was a beautiful sunny day but as soon as we cleared the harbour, we hit a rough sea once more. There were lots of white caps and the wind was very strong so we took a battering until it started to quieten down when we were abreast of Livorno. I was constantly checking the leaking stern gland and the faulty bilge pump was hardly coping with the amount of water that was coming in so I was very relieved when we entered the port of Viareggio. It was filled to maximum capacity with yachts needing repairs. We dropped anchor and backed into the only space we could see, which was in a dirty corner, almost inaccessible and away from the other yachts. As soon as we'd finished making fast, I went to the boatyard to arrange for the repairs to the generator, the stern gland, the bilge pump and the fairlead that had been ripped off at Santo Stefano as well as the gangplank fitting. I was told we'd have to wait another two days before they could lift us out of the water and start the work, so I reserved a room in a hotel for the period that the boat would be in the hangar. Some of our friends from other yachts were staying at the same hotel.

I hadn't told Marjie how bad the leak was or about the volume of water that was pouring in and how the bilge pump was unable to cope because I didn't want to alarm her. When I returned to the boat, I did inform her in a matter of fact manner that we were lucky we hadn't sunk! Later that day we met up with friends, other Captains and Crews on yachts from La Napoule and other harbours in the South of France and had a good time socialising and swapping yarns. In the morning, we woke to discover that we were completely hemmed in by fishing boats. The whole area was filthy, noisy and smelly but the compensation was the free fish we were given by the friendly fishermen.

16. In the Picchiotti hangar

On Wednesday, we managed to extricate ourselves from the fishing boats that surrounded us and motored to the area where the travel lift was to hoist us out of the water. It took a long time for the operators to position the slings in the correct place around the hull but once it had been accomplished, the boat was lifted and taken into an enormous hangar that was filled with yachts. High in the air, the vessel was carried above all the other boats and gently set down and chocked up in a space that seemed just about big enough. It was very impressive to watch. I set to work organising the labour force and connected us to the electricity supply so that we'd have the refrigerators, lighting etc. working. In the evening we settled into the hotel, enjoyed soaking in a hot bath and had a meal in the restaurant with our friends. When we went to the boat early the following day, we were able to get lots of outstanding jobs finished. We hauled out the anchor chain and marked it every five metres with different coloured paint so that Marjie would know how much chain was out when we dropped the anchor. We repaired all manner of broken or damaged hinges, door handles, malfunctioning toilets, pumps etc. The boatyard labourers took out the port propeller shaft and discovered that it wasn't straight so when it rotated it made an elliptical movement at the stern gland, creating the leak that I hadn't been able to fix.

That evening, back at the hotel, we were joined by other crew members and had another enjoyable dinner accompanied by copious amounts of potent local wine. Towards the end of the evening, around 21h00, we thought we'd drunk too much when the floor moved, the table shook, glasses and crockery rattled and the hanging lamps swayed. The proprietor looked fearful. We found out the next morning that there had been a 6.5 magnitude earthquake in the Friuli region of Northeastern Italy. Seventy-five villages were affected, up to 978 people were killed, 2,800 were injured and 157,000 were left homeless. It was the most destructive type of earthquake, less than 20 kilometres below the surface with its epicentre south of Gemona, which was almost totally destroyed and where 326 people perished. A relief worker there said, "We don't have enough coffins." It was felt as far south as Rome and in Yugoslavia, Czechoslovakia, Belgium, Germany, Austria and Switzerland. We had been lucky and had been too inebriated at the time to realise what had happened. Around 500 aftershocks over a six month period destroyed already damaged buildings and caused others to collapse. Another 6.1 magnitude quake occurred on 15th September, which destroyed many of the buildings that had been restored and others to collapse anew. The aftershocks that followed the second quake resulted in 30,000 people leaving the area. *"Once you have been in an earthquake, you know, even if you survive without a scratch, that like a stroke in the heart, it remains in the earth's breast, horribly potential, always promising to return, with an even more devastating force." Salman Rushdie.*

On Friday, when the workmen tried to couple the straightened propellor shaft, they found that the engine was slightly out of alignment so it had to be nudged over in order for it to line up with the straightened shaft, which took another day and that gave us plenty of time to finish odd jobs. I rewired some electrical sockets and cleaned out the disgusting lazarette, which was a complete mess of ropes and cans. I replaced faulty hinges and a whole host of other bits and pieces and then we investigated the town further.

We stopped at a bus timetable and thought it would be fun to go to Florence on Sunday with two friends but when that day arrived, we woke up to the sound of heavy rain. Having made arrangements, we felt obliged to go, so to avoid getting soaked, ordered a taxi to take us to the bus station. Marjie got out and waited there whilst I continued on to the boat for an umbrella. When I got back our friends still hadn't appeared and the last bus had left for Florence so we decided to take the 11h00 bus for Pisa instead. It was still raining when we arrived but the weather improved later on and the sun came out. We enjoyed our day there and found a small restaurant in the centre to give ourselves sustenance for the climb up the famous tower in the afternoon.

Pisa was once a mighty maritime power. It reached its peak in the 11th century when it became one of Italy's four main maritime republics with a powerful fleet of merchant and naval ships. It remained a force to be reckoned with until its defeat by the Genoese in the Battle of Meloria, a small rocky islet off the coast of Tuscany, on 6th August 1284, which ended the long-standing rivalry between the two. During the next six years, the Genoese destroyed most of Porto Pisano and although it was rebuilt, Pisa never recovered. Education has been a contributing factor to Pisa's economy since the 14th century and it is well known for its elite university. Galileo Galilei was born there in 1564 and the earth has been revolving around the sun ever since. Pisa is, of course, also renowned for demonstrating to the world that you can't build tall towers on poor foundations. The leaning tower (Torre Pendente) was built in the Romanesque style to serve as the bell tower for the adjacent cathedral in the square of miracles, (Piazza dei Miracoli). Construction began in 1173 and after five years, when the second floor was reached, it started to lean due to inadequate footings on the marshy ground on one side. Surprisingly, this didn't ring any alarm bells and the building works continued. The tilt increased throughout its construction, which was completed in 1399 and for decades afterwards it continued, reaching 5.5°. Between 1990 and 2001, restoration work was carried out to stabilise it and it now leans at an angle of 3.99°. The tower is 55.86 metres on its lowest side and 56.67 metres on the highest side. We climbed to the top and puffed sighs of relief when we reached the last step, number 294. It was a strange sensation ascending a tilting building and on the side of the lean, it felt quite alarming. On our way back to the bus stop, we saw an onyx lamp for sale at a market stall. We'd seen the same one in Elba for 30,000 lire but in Pisa, it was 14,000 lire and after a little bargaining it came down to 12,000. We were pleased with ourselves and still have the lamp today.

Back at Viareggio, it was a pleasant evening and we enjoyed a glass of Asti Spumante in the hotel garden to finish off a fabulous day. The yacht was placed back in the water on Monday afternoon. We went for a sea trial with the engineers and electrician on board and everything seemed to work well. When we got back, we washed the boat down from stem to stern to remove the salt from the sea trial and the dirt that had accumulated from our time in the hangar with workmen coming and going. It felt good to be back on board – apart from concerns about the generator, which was still reluctant to start, despite the work I'd done on it myself and the work that the engineer had carried out.

Celebration

Friday 14th May, the weather forecast from Grasse Radio predicted 25–30 knots of wind and a rough sea. It didn't sound good! After a few moments of reflection, I took the decision to leave anyway and head for our home port of La Napoule. We'd had enough of Viareggio and were itching to be at sea once more so with the expectation of another battering from the sea and wind, we cast off. The weather conditions weren't as bad as the forecast had led us to believe and the further we motored away from Viareggio, the more the weather improved. It was a pleasant surprise to see the clouds evaporating away and the sea becoming calmer. The wind almost stopped completely, the sun shone and eventually, we had a brilliant, clear blue sky and a beautiful blue, calm sea. It was the first truly sunny day we'd had since we'd left France back in April and we made the most of it. We stripped off on the flying bridge and were very soon feeling in a holiday mood. It was a glorious sensation to be cruising at a respectable 15 knots in a stable boat, listening to the throb of the engines and feeling the heat of the sun on our naked bodies - and the stern gland no longer leaked! We'd had our share of being thrown around in rough seas; we were so relaxed that we hadn't paid too much attention to the navigation and were astonished to discover that we were abreast of Savona, much further on than we'd expected to be. The weather was perfect and as we were feeling jubilant, we continued onwards, filled with joy at the prospect of returning to France.

When we reached Menton, we discussed our options and decided to crack on to St-Jean-Cap-Ferrat, a small, well-sheltered marina on the eastern side of the lush, wooded, unspoilt peninsula of Cap Ferrat. It was only 45 minutes away and we knew there were restaurants close to the port. When we arrived, somebody on the quay took our stern ropes, attached them to the mooring rings and didn't expect money. It was the first time that had happened since we had left France and it was such a tremendous feeling to be back again in the country of liberty, equality and fraternity and the world's most popular tourist destination. We'd had a perfect, calm voyage and had allowed the automatic pilot to keep us on course whilst we savoured being in the open air in blazing sunshine, instead of being shut in the wheelhouse to shelter from rain and rough seas. We were filled with joy at the knowledge that the next day we'd be back in La Napoule. We opened a very good bottle of champagne, finished it off seated on the aft deck and later walked to a restaurant where we devoured a superb meal.

St-Jean-Cap-Ferrat was once a fishing village and the charming, tranquil, small town has kept its authenticity. The first settlers on Cap Ferrat were the Ligurians, followed by the Lombards in the 6th century. From the 8th century until the 11th century, it was occupied by the Saracens who used it as a pirating base. In the 12th century, together with Nice, it was given to the Dukes of Savoy. The French occupied it for a while during the 18th century and after Napoleon's abdication in 1814, it went to the Kingdom of Sardinia. In 1860, after it was again ceded to France, the wealthy began to build luxurious villas, the small fishing port was developed and by 1904, the commune of St-Jean-Cap-Ferrat came into being. King Leopold II of Belgium owned an estate there and in 1905, Béatrice Ephrussi de Rothschild built a Tuscan style palazzo in a beautiful, scenic spot that is now open to the public. Named as one of the pearls of the French Riviera, St-Jean-Cap Ferrat is known worldwide and the wealthy elite are drawn to it for its peaceful, unspoilt location, magnificent views, lush vegetation, rocky beaches and clear, blue water. We luxuriated in being there. In 2012, it was named as the most expensive residential location in the world after Monaco. Property prices have risen enormously in latter years, with the average price ranging from 44,000 – 60,000 € per square metre. One villa that was sold for 8,000,000 € in 1999, was resold eight years later for 83,000,000. We were in illustrious company; it has been visited and inhabited by royalty, heads of state, celebrities and all manner of the privileged and influential. Charlie Chaplin, Somerset Maugham, Jean Cocteau, Matisse, David Niven, Elizabeth Taylor, Richard Burton and Winston Churchill to name just a few. Andrew Lloyd Weber has property there as does a co-founder of Microsoft.

CHAPTER 18
A PIECE OF CAKE

One of the Triple Crown

The sun radiated down in an intense, clear blue sky when we woke the following morning. It felt and looked good. We leapt out of bed, had breakfast on the aft deck and cast off for our home port. There was a large swell on our port quarter, which made steering difficult but we were exultant, nothing could have dampened our spirits. The weather was perfect, the scenery and colours spectacular. There is something extraordinary about France and particularly the French Riviera, it has a unique, inviting smell. We were in heaven. *"The Mediterranean is in my DNA. I'm fine inland for about a week, but then I yearn for a limitless view of the sea, for the colours and smells of the Italian and French Rivieras."- Alain Ducasse.* We anchored between the Iles de Lerins to enjoy the rest of the day swimming, sunbathing, eating, drinking and appreciating how privileged we were to be in such an astonishingly beautiful place, doing what we wanted to do. What better job could there be? But our idyllic day had to end sometime, so we weighed anchor in the early evening and continued on to La Napoule where we finally moored up in our berth.

We had a fairly relaxing time for the next few weeks, meeting up and dining with friends, sampling the delicious food in the numerous restaurants in Cannes and other places and preparing the yacht for the owner's arrival in time for the Monaco Grand Prix on 30th May. I arranged to have an urgent overhaul of the starboard engine that had been causing trouble, have a new bilge pump fitted and the generator overhauled as it still wasn't working properly and hadn't done so since we had taken command of the boat, despite attempts to rectify the problem by both French and Italian engineers. The owner was due to arrive on Friday 28th May and an additional 12 guests had to be collected on the morning of the Grand Prix. The morning of his arrival, one of the guest electric toilets packed up and there was insufficient time to repair it. The toilets on yachts were a constant problem, mainly because people who used them didn't take sufficient care and it could be an unsavoury job fixing them – a shitty job in fact. No matter how many times Skippers explained to the owners and guests not to throw anything into the toilets, somebody almost always did. One of our friends was so furious one day after having spent a long time repairing one that he stormed into the saloon where the owner of the yacht and his guests were eating. He flung the offending object on the table in front of them. The cherry pip that he'd extracted from the toilet landed on the pristine table cloth to the horror and disgust of the group. I'm sure that there are many Skippers, Engineers and other crew members who would like to have the courage to do the same thing!

Dressed in our smart white uniforms, we listened in on the radio that was tuned to the plane's frequency and when the ground control instructed the pilot to land, I got in the company car and drove the 8 kilometres to Cannes-Mandelieu airport to meet the owner and his pilot. I dropped the owner off at his apartment, where he usually stayed, only coming to the boat to eat and for the cruising. The pilot made himself at home in the guest cabin with the non-functioning toilet and I explained that he would need to flush it using a saucepan that he could fill with water from the galley tap until I had time to repair it. Not what one would expect to have to do aboard a luxury private yacht! On Saturday, eight others arrived aboard and whilst sipping champagne, they discussed plans for the Grand Prix with the owner and then left shortly afterwards. The owner was anxious to impress his guests so Marjie went shopping to buy enough food and drink to prepare a sumptuous buffet for 14 people the following day - 16 including ourselves.

Sunday 30th May, the day of the Grand Prix. With the owner and the pilot aboard, we cast off and set course for the very attractive old port of Menton, where the 12 guests boarded and then we continued on to Monaco. With a surface area of just over 2 square kilometres and more than 38,000 residents (one third of whom are millionaires), the Principality of Monaco is the second smallest and the most densely populated sovereign state in the world, thanks to its tax laws. It is surrounded on three sides by France, with the fourth side facing the sea. Monaco is composed of four districts. Monaco Ville is the old city on a rocky promontory where the Prince's Palace, the Cathedral, the Oceanographic Museum and the Gardens are located. Monte Carlo is the principal residential and resort area, which includes the famous Casino and the Hotel de Paris. Fontvieille is the economical and industrial area and the Condamine district is where Port Hercules is located. The port has been used since ancient times and has anchorage space for 700 vessels under normal circumstances but on the days of the Grand Prix, almost every available centimetre of its 160,000 square metres is taken up by boats of every description. It is impossible to get in unless one has friends in high places. I'd contacted the port authorities two weeks beforehand to reserve a place but when we arrived, they refused to let us in. The number of yachts hoping to get a place in the port for the Grand Prix is staggering and only the wealthiest and most influential have any hope of succeeding. I argued with the authorities for a while and when it became clear that they weren't going to relent, the Brazilian diplomat that we had on board intervened and persuaded them to change their minds. We were allocated a perfect position among other sometimes enormous and outlandishly expensive yachts.

Everybody was excited and the atmosphere was electric as the tension built up for the 34th Monaco Grand Prix. The crowds lining the circuit were densely packed as was every apartment and hotel balcony. Grandstands had been erected around the harbour and they too were tightly packed with spectators. The yacht owners, guests and crews were eagerly awaiting the start of the Formula one race about to take place on one of the most dangerous tracks in the world of motor racing. The cars race through the narrow streets of Monaco, which includes Monte Carlo, the area of La Condamine and around the harbour. There are tight corners and a tunnel and if it were not already a Formula one Grand Prix, it would not be authorised today for safety reasons. The tunnel poses a unique challenge because the drivers enter from daylight into darkness then back into daylight necessitating the need to adjust their vision at the fastest point of the track. The triple Formula one champion,

Nelson Piquet, said of the Monaco Grand Prix, *"Like trying to cycle round your living room,"* and added, *"A win here was worth two anywhere else."* It is one of the three most famous races in the world that form the Triple Crown, the other two being the 24 Hours of Le Mans and the Indianapolis 500. The very air was charged in anticipation. I set up the TV so that it could be seen from the aft deck, enabling us to follow the cars after they'd roared around the harbour and out of sight. We were fortunate that it was a dry day. Marjie had prepared a grandiose buffet on the aft deck from which everybody helped themselves throughout the afternoon.

When the race began the noise was deafening. The powerful, tortured engines roared as the cars flashed past in what seemed to us like a mad frenzy; then they disappeared from sight only to reappear later and roar past again and again. They thundered around the 3.3 kilometres circuit 78 times to complete the race. The excitement everywhere was palpable. The thrills, the drama, the emotion, the energy was contagious. You could feel it in the air and it continued for lap after lap. And then - it stopped - and there was silence. The race was won by Nikki Lauder, driving a Ferrari 31212. He finished 11 seconds ahead of Jody Scheckter with Patrick Depailler in third place. There had been four accidents and one collision but for us spectators it had been a marvellous, successful, unforgettable day. Everybody on board was in high spirits when we eased our way out of the harbour and headed back to La Napoule, arriving at 20h30. The owner took his guests out to a restaurant and Marjie and I devoured what was left of the buffet on the aft deck with a diligent tasting of the half-empty wine bottles that we'd taken to the galley when tidying up the aft deck.

Lazy days

The owner had little inclination to go very far for the rest of our time aboard the Picchiotti. He was elderly, overweight, did no exercise at all and never walked anywhere, no matter how short the distance. I drove him everywhere. When he came to the South of France for his holidays, he slept in his apartment, located in a building next to the port, just 1400 metres away and I drove to collect him each morning and bring him to the boat where he always had the same time-consuming breakfast. He started with grapefruit, followed by a full English cooked breakfast, followed by toast and marmalade. Mostly after that, he climbed onto the coach roof cushions and slept until it was time for lunch, which was usually another long drawn out affair and when that was finished, he waddled along the deck to take up his position on the cushions once more until it was tea time. After tea, I'd drive him back to his apartment where he would rest from the overindulgences and the exhausting five-metre walks along the deck to and from the coachroof cushions. In the evening, I'd collect him once again and drive him to the yacht for the next marathon eating session, after which, I'd take him to his apartment for the night. The next morning, the whole rigmarole would be repeated and again the next day and again the next day and so on. His guests were often frustrated. The days were hot and sunny with clear blue skies, the sea beyond the harbour wall looked inviting and there were so many places to see.

"Shall we go out for the day?" they sometimes asked after breakfast.

"There's not much point now. It's nearly midday and it will soon be lunchtime. If we go out after lunch, by the time we get anywhere and drop the anchor, it'll be time to come back and we're already here," he'd reply. Eating and sleeping were his major occupations so his guests had to find ways to amuse themselves. The heat could be stifling and they longed to escape to a lovely creek where they could swim and feel the afternoon breeze, which we were largely protected from in the harbour. What he did like to do occasionally was go to the prestigious Carlton hotel for coffee after breakfast. Situated on the Croisette, the imposing hotel is renowned for its elegance and during the Cannes Film Festival it hosts many world-famous film stars and other celebrities. When it opened in 1911, it was the most salubrious hotel in Cannes and was frequented by the British and Russian aristocracy. The front façade, facing the Croisette, has distinctive cupolas on each corner, which allegedly resemble the breasts of La Belle Otero, the French Riviera's most famous courtesan in the run-up to WWI. She was extremely attractive with captivating dark eyes and was the most sought-after woman in the whole of Europe. The hotel's majestic former seventh-floor dining room was named La Belle Otero in her honour. The new restaurant is now at ground floor level with a magnificent outside terrace where we have occasionally dined ourselves. There is a second restaurant on the beach and the hotel has its own landing stage enabling yacht owners to arrive by boat and that's what our boss liked to do. Marjie and I would prepare the boat by stowing everything that was likely to move, disconnect the electricity cable and stow it, arrange a slip rope at the stern, start the engines, take in the gangplank, hoist the tender on the davits and secure it in place, let go the slip rope and the bow mooring and motor out of the harbour, taking in the fenders.

It took quite some time and all to travel a mere seven kilometres so that we could drop the anchor offshore from the Carlton Hotel, lower the tender into the water, hitch up the outboard motor, lower it onto the tender, lower the boarding ladder and take him ashore to the hotel landing stage so that he could be seen arriving in style by the hotel's guests. He took particular delight in it because he was known in the hotel and as he arrived, he would hold up a finger for each coffee he desired, depending on how many guests he had with him. It gave him such a thrill to be able to impress his guests and the throngs of people on the seafront. After coffee, the whole performance had to repeated in reverse; up with the boarding ladder and lash it in position, hoist the outboard and stow it, hoist and secure the tender, weigh anchor and head back to port, lower the fenders etc. until we were moored in our berth, then connect up the electricity. Once there we had to prepare lunch and wait on them. It was a lot of work for what must have been a very expensive cup of coffee! But he enjoyed it and he had a wonderful sense of humour, always cracking jokes. We certainly couldn't complain about being overworked but it was disappointing not to be cruising and seeing new places.

Nice 'n' easy

We came to understand why he'd gained a notorious reputation. He was never rude or nasty to Marjie and me but didn't hesitate to speak his mind to his guests, especially his regular lady companion who had once been his housekeeper until they'd indulged in a more intimate relationship. She wanted him to make her an honest woman by marrying her and he would have none of it, which caused friction. She fancied herself as an opera singer. What she didn't seem to realise was that no one else could see her potential. We were never quite prepared for the sudden high pitched shrieks that echoed throughout the boat from time to time. They could be quite alarming. Whatever we did with her had to, at some stage, involve her squawking. Once, when the owner was in the U.K. and we had her and her family on board, we thought it would be a good idea one evening to take the boat to a deserted bay when all the other boats had gone back into harbour for the night. It had to be deserted - if there had been any other boats there when we arrived, they would have very soon scarpered anyway. We motored across to a beach close to Théoule-sur-Mer, where Marjie and I had spent many a calm, romantic night together on the Dufour 35. We dropped anchor, lowered the tender and took them to the beach. It was such a beautiful, quiet night with a clear sky filled with millions of stars twinkling above. We collected some driftwood and lit a small fire to create a nice atmosphere. Behind and around us were the high cliffs and in front, the calm sea lapping gently on the shore with the Picchiotti lying at anchor a short distance away. We were the only people within a radius of several miles. They were special moments as we sat around the fire, quietly chatting, admiring the scenery.

"Let's play charades," somebody said and we all agreed. We organised ourselves into teams and had a fun time until it was her turn to mime. She took centre position facing us. We watched, waiting for her to begin. A piercing wail suddenly split the air as she began cavorting around; throwing her arms in the air and letting out dreadful screaming sounds. She clutched her breast, whimpered a little as the tempo and volume of the wails diminished and then we almost leapt out of our skins as she threw her arms wide and screeched out again as she tried, it seemed, to burst her lungs and vocal cords with an interpretation of what we supposed was an aria from some obscure opera because it didn't resemble anything that any of us had ever heard before.

"Stop, stop, you're supposed to mime. You have to keep quiet," her son explained to her. He jumped up and demonstrated how she was to mime silently so that we could guess what she was trying to tell us. She nodded that she understood. He came and sat with us and we waited for her to mime. Another terrifying sound caused us to jump as she screamed and wailed and cavorted along the beach. It was clearly not going to go according to plan so we had to implore her to stop scaring us and the wildlife and forget about charades.

Sometimes the owner liked to anchor between Ile St Honorat and Ile Ste Marguerite. It was one of the most popular anchorages; not far from shore, sheltered, shallow, beautiful and safe. The smell of the pines and herbs and the noise of the cicadas added to the attraction, but it was always swarming with other anchored yachts and people swimming. When one of our guests went for a dip, he was taken with the clarity of the water.

"I can see the bottom," he cried.

"What did you say?" the owner called from where he was sunbathing on the flybridge. The guest looked up and repeated, "I can see the bottom." and then he spluttered and had trouble staying afloat. The owner had whipped down his shorts and exposed his large, naked bottom over the safety rail. It was not a pretty sight!

One afternoon, when we were moored in our berth at La Napoule, the owner decided he'd like to go for tea in the Royal Hotel in Sanremo. He loved that because just like in the Carlton Hotel on the Croisette in Cannes, the staff knew him. The pilot was instructed to make the necessary plans to take him and his guests, including Marjie, to Sanremo's nearest airport, which was at Albenga, (the city of a hundred spires). From there they took taxis to travel the 62 kilometres to Sanremo. It must have been one of the most expensive cups of tea ever! The grandiose five-star Royal Hotel is situated on a hill overlooking the sea a short distance from the town centre. It was opened in 1872 at the time the Russian aristocracy had made Sanremo their winter resort and it has retained its Belle Epoche charm. The owner, his guests and Marjie drank their tea in the fabulous subtropical garden, with its abundance of palm trees and magnificent heated seawater pool to the sound of a full orchestra playing. I stayed aboard the yacht and prepared an evening meal for when they returned. On the flight back, the pilot handed Marjie the controls for a while. She wasn't having any effect as they continued flying calmly and evenly with nothing happening so decided to see what happened if she moved the stick forward a bit. The nose went down and they started descending. It was then that the pilot said, "O.K. I'll take over now".

From time to time, friends, business acquaintances or family members of the owner would use the yacht for a holiday and the atmosphere was more relaxed than when the owner himself was on board. The boat was used more then because they were keen to visit well-known places and swim in sheltered creeks. It was surprising how impractical some of them were, having had an easy, pampered life without having to do very much for themselves. The owner's sister stayed in his apartment once and we had a telephone call from her complaining that the bedside lamp wasn't working.

"Was it working when you arrived?" I asked.

"No," she replied, "I don't know how it works."

"There's a switch halfway along the flex. Try pressing the button on that."

"I've done that and it still doesn't work."

"Is it plugged in?" I asked.

"Oh, I don't know."

"Well, follow the lead and see if it's attached to the socket," I said. There was a pause for a while.

"No, I don't think so, it's lying on the floor," was her response.

"OK, put the plug into the socket," I said.

"How do I do that?" she asked

"There's a socket in the wall, just push the plug into the socket."

"Oh goodness me, I couldn't do that, I don't understand anything technical."

"Nothing can happen, just plug it in."

" Oh no, I couldn't do that, that's far too technical, you'll have to come and do it for me." I had to get in the car, drive to the apartment block, park the car in the underground car park, take the lift to the apartment, plug in the lamp and switch it on for her and then drive back to the boat. Unbelievable but true!

All that jazz

We did do some cruising with the owner but nothing that we hadn't done before, just the usual places, St Tropez, the Iles d'Hyères and other coastal harbours. When the owner wasn't using the boat, we carried out general maintenance where and when required and generally enjoyed ourselves in every way possible. It was a fabulous life we had, eating out in restaurants, water skiing, swimming and using the Dory and outboard motor or the Riva to go off to small deserted creeks where we had picnics in total privacy on the beaches or on small rocky islands. We had the company car to travel around and explore the South of France and we discovered for the first time, the "Grande Parade du Jazz," arguably the largest, most esteemed jazz festival in Europe. It had been held in July since 1948 and was set in the Jardins de Cimiez, where there is a Roman amphitheatre that served as one of the three stages. It started at 17h00 and continued till midnight with 200 musicians playing throughout the eight-day festival. It was, without doubt, the most fantastic musical experience of my life. It was immensely popular so parking in the surrounding streets was always difficult. When we got out of the car and heard the jazz blasting out in the distance, the excitement was so great, I found it difficult not to run there. When we arrived, making a decision was almost impossible. There could be Miles Davis on one stage, Herbie Hancock on another and Earl Hines on the third. To complicate decision making even further, the artists changed every hour or two so they overlapped. To have to choose between such famous artists as Stan Getz, Jimmy Smith, Count Basie, Sarah Vaughan, Milt Jackson, B.B. King, Dizzy Gillespie, Wynton Marsalis, Buddy Rich, Lionel Hampton and so on was extremely difficult. The list of performers was endless. We visited year after year and there can hardly be any of the "Jazz Giants" that we haven't seen. The area was vast and there was an open-air restaurant serving Creole food prepared by chefs flown in from New Orleans. We ate and mingled with the performers. Oh, such wonderful memories! Harold Jones, a well-known and respected drummer, said of jazz, *"They call it music but it's just this side of magic."* Sadly, in 1994, it became more pop-oriented so we stopped going.

In the winter months, after the first falls of snow at the end of November, we went skiing in the Maritime Alps in France and sometimes to Limone in the Piedmont region of Italy. Limone is one of the oldest ski resorts in Italy. There are 80 kilometres of trails and we once had a dreadful experience having no choice but to ski down in a whiteout when all the lifts had been closed down. It was a scary feeling being unable to see where we were going whilst moving at a fair speed. It took us a long time to find our way to the base of the resort and what a relief when we arrived. There seemed to be no system for the authorities to keep track of who was left on the slopes and we could well have been found the following morning, two frozen lumps of nameless humanity.

CHAPTER 19
THE GOOD FAT CAT

Accidents legislate

The owner was very pleased with us and asked if we would stay with him the following year and then we discovered that he wasn't quite as nice as we thought he was. We suggested he increase our salary and he wasn't happy. We had a long drawn out discussion over a period of some weeks. We were adamant that the salary we were receiving didn't compare to what other Captains and Cooks were paid and all we were asking was to be brought up to the same level. Our boss did reluctantly agree to pay us what we'd asked for but his attitude towards us changed from then on.

Shortly before Christmas that first year, we were asked to dismantle the troublesome generator and load each section into the back of the car and take it to the U.K. to be repaired. At the same time, the car was to be serviced. The managing director implied that we could take our time on the return journey without actually saying so. He wanted to justify selling the boat because it was a drain on the company finances so we had an agreeable journey home, stopping twice at hotels and enjoyed relaxing evening meals. We stayed in the U.K. for our four weeks holiday, making use of our Netley Abbey apartment. We visited Marjie's family and mine and enjoyed meeting up with our friends, Pat and Ian and George, who'd sold his Arpège and was reduced to being the owner of just one yacht. When the time came to return to the

South of France, we collected the car and the sections of generator and had another relaxing drive through France. Once back in La Napoule, we had to reassemble the generator and install it in position in the engine room.

In the spring of 1977, because of the insecurity of yachting, never knowing if or when a boat would be sold, we started to look for a small house or apartment to buy so that we would always have a base to call our own. We found a suitable property on a new development on the Costa Brava and we'd made plans to view it with an English company who'd offered to pay our expenses if we purchased it. We made an appointment for a viewing to take place after the boat had been prepared for the coming season. I made arrangements for the boat to be slipped at the Chantier Naval de l'Estérel at Port Pierre-Canto in Cannes. The boatyard had been instructed to clean and antifoul the underwater section and replace the sacrificial zinc anodes, which protect the submerged metal parts of a vessel by inhibiting corrosion. Propellers are normally made of bronze and the propeller shafts, stainless steel. When the two different metals are submerged in seawater, they act like a battery with a current flowing between them causing one of the metals to give up electrons; this is referred to as galvanic corrosion, which affects all other metal parts such as rudders and rudder struts. By introducing a third metal, zinc, which corrodes and releases electrons much faster than the other metals, the corrosion on the other metals is neutralised. Marjie and I wanted to work on the topsides, which meant erecting metal trestles. I collected two of them, placed them in position and started to adjust the height of the horizontal bars to support planks of wood that we could stand on. I raised the bar to the correct height on one side and secured it in position. When I raised the other side of the bar, the fastening that I'd just secured gave way and the horizontal T shaped bar crashed down like a giant pair of heavy, rusty scissors, and sliced through the web between my forefinger and thumb, almost severing the thumb. Holding my hand to stem the flow of blood as much as possible, I rushed to Marjie who was on the other side of the boat.

"Can you do anything with this?" I asked her, releasing my grip to show her the gaping wound. She was horrified.

"We've got to get you to hospital straight away," she said and called to the yard manager, told him what had happened and showed him my hand - by which time I was feeling faint and nauseous. He agreed that I had to be taken immediately to the Brousaille Hospital in Cannes, which I knew only too well having spent more than a week there after my sailing accident in 1975. Marjie drove me and by the time we got there it was past midday and in France, virtually everything stops at midday until 14h00. Nothing is allowed to interfere with the French lunch break! By midday, they are always ravenous because they generally have an early breakfast, consisting of nothing more than a croissant dipped in their coffee before each bite. As a consequence, by midday their blood sugar level is low and they need to eat.

There were very few hospital staff members around and I was sent to a room to wait for somebody to treat me. Twenty minutes later, two young, quite scruffy individuals came in and sat beside me. They were students and one of them had brought his sandwich with him. They looked at my hand, chatted between themselves about what they thought they should do and then set to work sewing it back together. First, my hand was injected and then a few bites were taken out of the sandwich before they came and sat down, sewing away, chatting and eating. At the end of the operation, I was bandaged up and sent on my way, with an appointment made to call back to have the stitches removed. It's not surprising that the hand became very badly infected and I had different antibiotic treatments over the course of a couple of months of hospital visits and wondered at times if it would ever heal properly. I avoid all medication whenever possible and especially antibiotics. As a teenager, I'd come to the conclusion that I had to take responsibility for my own health and avoid doctors and their methods of treating illnesses so it was particularly upsetting for me to have to take not one but three different antibiotics. The accident scuppered any ideas about buying a property in Spain – fortunately! Sometimes things happen that push us in a different direction and although we don't realise it at the time it often works out for the best. Nothing is accidental! *"Man never legislates, but destinies and accidents, happening in all sorts of ways, legislate in all sorts of ways."* - Plato

Altruism

When the work was finished on the boat and it was placed back in the water, we motored back to La Napoule and shortly afterwards received a letter from my friend Bob in Majorca. He'd separated from his wife and needed a shoulder to cry on so we invited him to come and stay with us. A week later, a tired-looking, well used Land Rover pulled up at the bottom of the gangplank and out stepped Bob with a small suitcase in his hand.

"Good to see you, Bob. Bring the rest of your luggage, you can use the guest cabin," I said.

"Luggage? This is it, it's all I've got left," he replied as he walked up to join us on the aft deck. We sat down and he explained what had happened. His business in Palma had been in financial difficulty so as a last resort, he signed up in the merchant navy, leaving his wife and a friend to keep the business running with the money he sent them. When he left the merchant navy and went home to Palma, he discovered that his wife and friend had become romantically involved and had managed to swindle him out of the business and of virtually everything that he possessed. He had nowhere to go, very little money and his only belongings were his Land Rover and the contents of the small case that he'd carried aboard. After ten years in the yachting industry, that was how he'd finished up. I have not seen his ex-wife since I'd holidayed with them in Majorca so haven't had the opportunity to hear her side of the story. He stayed with us for two weeks and when the time came for him to move on, we gave him the keys to our apartment in Netley Abbey and told him he could stay there rent-free for as long as he liked. We felt sad to see him heading off all alone. I knew only too well how it felt to be cheated on by an unfaithful wife.

We followed the same routine at La Napoule as in the previous year except that early in the season, whilst the owner was lying on a beach in Hawaii, he had a heart attack and from that moment on he hardly used the boat again. It was put up for sale and in the meantime offered for charter. We had a two-week charter with a Swiss banker and his family. They arrived at the bottom of the gangplank in a cream coloured Rolls Royce. He was tall with thinning silver hair and had piercing pale blue eyes. He was expensively dressed in a fine silk blue and white striped shirt, blue shorts to match and soft white leather moccasins. His wife had a pleasant, attractive face, wavy auburn hair and kind, smiling eyes. She wore a loose-fitting cotton dress and gold sandals. Both of them were deeply tanned. They had a property in Port La Galère, a newly constructed development close to Théoule-sur-Mer and a short distance from La Napoule. They came aboard and the banker introduced himself and his wife to us explaining that they wouldn't be sleeping on the boat. We were to collect him and his guests from Port La Galère each morning, take them somewhere for the day, give them a simple lunch and return them again each evening to Port La Galère. He handed over 500 francs, equivalent to the average weekly wage in the U.K. at the time.

"Buy yourselves some swimwear," he said. He then gave us a further wad of cash to buy food for the following day. His wife suggested that we buy a cooked chicken and some salad ingredients for four people and then they left us. When we picked them up the following day we learned that he had a good knowledge of the coast and knew where he wanted to go and they'd brought a large quantity of food and wine. At the end of the day, when we dropped him off at La Galère, I asked him what he wanted us to do with the food and wine we'd bought that they hadn't needed.

"Oh, you can have it or throw it away," he said.

The next day, we bought more food as we'd been instructed to do but once again it wasn't needed. When they boarded, he told us where he wanted to go and we took him to a beautiful, small creek at the foot of the Estérel Mountains where there was a hotel perched at the top of the cliff. We dropped anchor and took them ashore in the Dory and they took the private cable car to the hotel/restaurant where they dined and enjoyed the fantastic view. Marjie and I spent our spare time swimming in the crystal clear blue sea in the well-protected creek. When we returned to La Galère, he gave us another 500 francs.

"This is for you to go to a nice restaurant this evening," he said. We thanked him and went back to La Napoule. By the time we'd tidied everything away and washed the salt from the boat we were too tired to go to a restaurant so ate the food that hadn't been eaten at lunchtime. Whilst we were sitting enjoying our meal with a good bottle of wine that the charterer had left on board for us, the Rolls Royce drove up and stopped at the bottom of the gangplank. The charterer climbed on board and rushed down to his cabin saying that he'd forgotten something, then left. The next day when we went on our day trip he came up to me.

"So you didn't go to a restaurant last night?" he said.

"No, we felt a bit tired," I replied.

"Here's another 500 francs, make sure you go out tonight," he said. Not bad - he'd only been with us for three days and he'd already given us the equivalent of three weeks average U.K. wage.

The next day we were due to go to St Tropez. There was a fresh wind on the port quarter which got stronger the further we went. The sea was quite choppy but not uncomfortable so everybody was happy. I knew that the nearer we got to St Tropez the worse it would get and that on the return journey we would be crashing around in a rough sea. I said as much to the charterer to warn him so that his guests wouldn't suffer unnecessarily. He didn't believe me, in fact, he scoffed at the idea.

"Well, I thought I should let you know so that you would be aware of the situation," I informed him.

"No, it's a lovely day and the sea is perfectly OK," he said.

"Well, we'll continue, but the sea is behind us and not affecting us too much at the moment. It will be entirely different on the return trip when we're heading into it."

"Oh, no, it will be alright, " he insisted. I knew that he was wrong and that we would be in for a pounding when the wind increased and we headed back.

"I'm only telling you because I don't want anybody to suffer on the return journey and have their day ruined. It might be better to find a sheltered bay somewhere else for the day." He stared at me, unsure of how to respond.

"Look, I tell you what, why don't I turn around into the wind for a short while now to give you an idea of what it will be like coming back, because it isn't too rough at the moment." He gave a faint smile as he continued to stare at me. "At least then you'll have an idea what to expect." I could see that he still didn't believe me.

"All right," he agreed, smiling as if to humour me. I spun the steering wheel to port and we heeled over slightly to starboard as we turned and the sea came onto our beam. Then it started, the bow rose into the air and as we crashed down again with salt spray flying over the bow and along the decks. I eased the throttles back to make the movement more comfortable. The looks of shock on the faces of the charterers told me all that I needed to know. They held onto whatever was convenient to hold themselves steady. They stared at each other.

"What's going on?" his wife asked as she made her way towards us. The banker said nothing.

"I'm just giving you an idea of what the return journey will be like so you can decide if you want to continue on to St Tropez," I told her.

"Well, we don't want to continue, I can tell you that now," she said, looking at her husband with steely defiance. The guests made their way to the wheelhouse looking a little distressed.

"We're going back," she told them.

"I agree, you were absolutely right Captain, thank you, take us back." The banker confirmed.

"I can find a sheltered spot for the day somewhere else," I suggested.

"No, it's getting too rough, take us back to La Galère and we'll try again tomorrow," he said. I pushed the throttles forward and we crashed our way through the waves to his home port. He never questioned my judgement again after that and from then on we had an excellent relationship of mutual respect.

The following day, we cast off from La Napoule and moored up alongside the quay in La Galère so that they could board easily. The unpleasant weather of the previous day was no more. The sky had cleared to an intense blue, the wind had dropped completely and the heat from the sun was fierce.

"Good morning, Captain, we want to go to St Tropez for lunch," he instructed. When they had all boarded, I started the engines, called to Marjie to cast off the mooring ropes and we motored out of the harbour and set off for St Tropez once again. When we arrived, there weren't many free berths available and I knew that to have any hope at all of being allocated one would cost him dearly. The harbour master was well known for expecting and receiving excessively large backhanders and our charterer knew as much since he'd been there before. I motored towards the main quay, Jean Jaurès where everybody wanted to be. It was lined with restaurants, bars and shops and there were only two vacant berths. Sure enough, the harbour master was waiting and watching us with his greedy little eyes in eager anticipation. He must have recognised our charterer because he waved us in, which would have been a virtual impossibility under normal circumstances. It could also have been that he recognised me as I'd been there many times previously and, out of necessity, had always tipped handsomely. I spun the boat around and backed up to the quay. As soon as we'd made fast and lowered the gangplank, the charterer jumped ashore and surreptitiously placed a 500 franc note into the money-grabbing mitt that was outstretched as if to shake hands.

That was the way the charter continued for the two week period. He was a generous man and wise because by giving us the first 500 francs before we'd even done anything, he'd secured excellent service from us for the duration. *"The value of a man resides in what he gives and not in what he is capable of receiving."* - *Albert Einstein.*

CHAPTER 20
HEAVEN'S CALL

A foot on the ground

Throughout all that had been going on, we had never stopped looking for a property that could give us more security and a place to go to at weekends. Having both been through a traumatic divorce, we had little spare cash and were still paying off the mortgage on the Netley Abbey apartment as well as the rates, so had just 45,000 French francs, which was the equivalent of £4,500. (Bob had offered to pay the rates in return for us letting him use the apartment but we didn't accept because we knew he was short of money.) Almost every estate agent we had visited or phoned thought we wanted to rent when we told them how much we had to spend but eventually we found a perfect apartment in Seillans, one of the picturesque, medieval Provençal hill villages in the Var department forty minutes drive from La Napoule. It was a perfect getaway. The village, perched on a hill, overlooked a plain between the Alps and the Estérel mountains and was and still is recognised as one of the prettiest villages in France. The steep cobblestoned centre was only accessible on foot and at its summit was a castle and a 13th century church. There were a couple of small squares, a bar, a post office, and five restaurants. The surrounding countryside consisted of forest, olive groves and vineyards. The apartment was small with one bedroom and had been occupied by an elderly man. It looked quite presentable with his furniture and belongings inside and we fell in love with it and bought it without any hesitation. We signed the contract to purchase, called a 'Compromis', in August and the sale was completed in December. When we took possession and were given the keys, we went inside and felt sickened as we saw the full reality of what we'd bought. It was filthy, with mice running around inside and needed an enormous amount of work to renovate it.

"Oh dear, what have we done?" I said to Marjie who stood and stared at the mess. She looked at me and I could see that she felt exactly as I felt, disheartened, more accurately, we felt sick. That evening we had been invited to have dinner with some friends in Antibes, which was just as well. It cheered us up to talk about it, especially as they were also renovating an old house in the centre of town.

We'd committed ourselves so had no choice but to tackle the renovation. From that moment on, we devoted a lot of our spare time to renovating and stayed there, camping out in the mess whilst we worked. We knocked down walls, built a new kitchen and bathroom area, ripped down the ceiling and exposed the oak beams, installed up to date electrical and plumbing systems, had a new front door made and built a fireplace. When it was finished, much later, we couldn't have been more pleased. We loved our little "Pied à Terre" and it fulfilled all that we had expected of it. Whenever we approached the village we always appreciated the complete contrast to the coast that we'd just left. The slight smell of musty plaster hit our nostrils as we opened the door, and we knew we were home.

An emotional time

After we'd spent a long weekend laying tiles in the apartment, we returned to the boat on the evening of 9th January so that we could buy more renovating equipment the following day. We called at the Port Captain's office for mail and were handed a telegram. Not usually a pleasant experience, so we opened it with some foreboding. It was from a German who'd heard that we were a reliable and conscientious couple who could shortly be out of work when the boat was sold and had asked us to contact him. We never did find out who had recommended us to him. It was a wonderful way to end a day that had been miserable and hard work. Our spirits lifted and we celebrated by eating out in a restaurant. The following day, Tuesday 10th January, we woke feeling good that we had a prospect so soon of another job. We went shopping once more to buy lights and mirrors for the apartment and in the afternoon returned to the boat. Whilst we were unloading a few items, a port employee brought another telegram. "He must be keen," we thought, expecting it to be from the German. The words leapt off the page. My heart pounded and I felt weak. "DAD DIED TWO DAYS AGO," it read. I almost collapsed from the shock as I walked up the gangplank. We weren't particularly close, dad and I, but the impact of those five words shook me to the core. The euphoria of the previous day was no more. There is an old Yiddish proverb that says "Man plans and God laughs," and there are a number of biblical references to that idea, one of which is *Proverbs 27: 1. "Do not boast about tomorrow, for you do not know what a day will bring."*

We made arrangements to leave the boat, packed our suitcases and loaded them into the Ford Granada, which had to be taken back anyway for its annual service. We folded the rear seats down and placed a sleeping bag in the back, locked the boat and left late that night to drive to the U.K.. We drove all through the night, taking turns driving whilst the other slept in the back of the car. It was a long, tiring and at times dangerous journey because the weather was so appalling. There was thick, almost freezing fog, which remained for the entire journey once we had left Lyon behind us. When we stopped at a café for a rest and breakfast the following morning, we still had a long way to go and knew that because the journey had taken so long and we'd missed the early ferry, we would have to wait in Le Havre for the overnight one.

That evening, after we'd driven onto the ferry, we familiarised ourselves with the layout of the boat and found our respective four-berth couchette cabins. (Males and females were separated). The cabins were open and had four bunks with vinyl-covered mattresses, each one with a blanket. In the bar, we saw a yacht Captain that I knew with his partner and chatted to them for a while before we went to our bunks, hoping to get a good night's sleep. We heard and felt the ferry leaving the port and once we were in the English Channel, were surprised how rough it was but we were so tired that we slept well. All went according to plan until I woke in the night for a pee. The ferry was rolling around far more than I could ever have imagined for a vessel so large. Our cabins didn't have a toilet compartment so I got out of my bunk to search for one. I walked along the passageway, well I didn't exactly walk, I staggered from side to side crashing into the partitions as I was thrown around and more alarmingly, I was ankle-deep in water that was sloshing around on the floor. When I reached the bar area, it was deserted and upturned chairs were scattered across the floor. Broken glasses and bottles were everywhere and the floor was awash with water surging back and forth as the ferry rolled frighteningly from side to side. Two people appeared, it was my Skipper friend and his companion.

"What's happening?" I asked him.

"There's a force 10 gale and windows have smashed. We think the wheelhouse windows have broken too. People have been injured, some fell off their chairs. We're turning around and going back to Le Havre," he told me.

"Where are the staff and crew?" I asked.

"There aren't many around. They're sick, injured or frightened. We have a couple of friends in the crew and we've been helping them because they're so short-staffed," he said. I made my way to the flooded toilet area, then back to our cabin and climbed into my bunk and slept in spite of the diabolical rolling of the ferry.

"Wake up, we're there." It was Marjie shaking me "We've arrived and the engines have stopped," she said.

"No, we're back in Le Havre. We had to turn around and come back because the weather was so bad," I told her. "We'll be stuck here now until things improve." Then I told her what had happened whilst she'd slept. She didn't believe me.

"What are you talking about, it's seven-o clock and we've just docked." I insisted with my story until she realised I was telling the truth. We'd been travelling through the rough seas all night long only to finish up at exactly the same place that we'd started from. I climbed out of my bunk and we both made our way to the restaurant area, walking through the debris that still lay where it had been thrown by the dreadful rolling and crashing in the savage wind and sea. Breakfast was being offered to all the passengers for free but there were very few takers; the restaurant was virtually deserted. My friend was there with his companion behind the counter helping to serve breakfast and there were a few people eating, but that was about it. The friend went into more detail about what had happened and explained that some passengers had

had to be hospitalised and repairs would have to be carried out to the ferry before we could set off again.

Much later that day, we cast off once again and although the conditions were terrible, made it safely across the English channel. We were eager to set foot on dry land and get to our apartment, which was available because Bob was away delivering a yacht to France. Throughout the month of January that year, the U.K. suffered from severe weather as a series of deep depressions moved across the British Isles. The worst days were the 11th and 12th of January, the very days that we crossed the channel. A deepening depression had moved southeast across Britain with ferocious northerly gales that caused extensive damage across the south and the east of England. There was a tidal surge in the North Sea, heavy seas breached sea defences and rivers burst their banks. The floods and gales caused considerable damage inland, seaside piers were irreparably damaged and there were a number of deaths at sea. Whirlwinds overturned cars and blew people off their feet in Hull and Newmarket. It wasn't a good time to be there but it was as it was and once we were settled into our apartment we soon forgot about the appalling weather and focused on getting to Gravesend so that I could see dad before he was buried.

The palace of eternity

On the 13th, we drove to Gravesend and stayed with mum who was distraught at the loss of dad. Her sister, my Aunt Ethel, was staying at the same time. She had travelled down from Liverpool where mum had been born and where she had met and married dad. We were not and never had been a close family. When I started working on the Thames steam tugs at age 15, it was usual for me to work 140 hours a week and when I wasn't working I was dating girls, partying and staying out late. I had been deeply scarred by dad's drunkenness during my infancy. He'd received a substantial amount of money as compensation following a disastrous accident at work that had left him disabled and had spent it all on booze. As a result, there were frequent arguments between mum and dad and the memories of those days had such a profound impact on me that I never wanted to be at home. I loved them both of course but the underlying unhappiness in the house was something I chose to avoid. There was never any physical contact between dad and myself that I can recall and I found it difficult to have a conversation with him. He was a closed man, never revealing anything about himself and through all his suffering in his later years, I never once heard him complain or ask for help. He never really said much at all so nobody could ever know his innermost thoughts. That night as I lay in bed, I swear I heard his voice coming from downstairs and I thought about how he would always offer to clean my shoes for me before I went out. It seems ridiculous that I should have thought of such an insignificant thing when there was so much happening.

Marjie and I went to the undertakers the next day. We were met by a tall, slim, well dressed, kindly man who led us into the room where dad lay in his coffin. I looked down at him expecting to see him looking serene and at peace. He was lying with his mouth open. I stood and stared for a long, long time as a whole range of different emotions arose and melded together. He looked so frail and wasted, not at all as I remembered him. We'd had a difficult relationship at times but at heart, he was a kind, gentle man. He didn't react to negativity, conflict or aggression. Mostly he would say nothing and allow the other person to work themselves into a frenzy if they chose to, whilst remaining calm himself. I've inherited that trait. I do not allow myself to become a victim of inner turmoil, which ultimately manifests itself physically. It's regrettable that during my very young years, dad and I went along a path that damaged our relationship. I understand now why he probably took to drinking. He'd suffered so much in his life and was stuck in an unhappy marriage but I was too young to understand at the time that it happened. I knew only that he was hardly ever home and when he was, he was drunk and arguments were endless between him and mum, who neither drank nor smoked. When his compensation money had been squandered and no more remained, his true, kind, gentle, forgiving character was revealed. I examined every minutest detail of his drawn, sunken face and tried to imagine the pain, sorrow and disappointment he'd suffered. It was deeply etched in every pore of his slender frame.

He'd started work at 14, had very little schooling and consequently was not erudite. He'd survived the first world war and in the second world war, he was down in the bowels of a ship, shovelling coal into the furnaces when a torpedo struck. I try to imagine the fear, panic and carnage that must have taken place. First the explosion, then the cries and screams as the vessel listed, with water pouring in and everybody rushing to escape. Whether he finished up in the sea or managed to get into a boat I'll never know because he refused to ever talk about it. He survived only for the same thing to happen a second time on a different vessel. He never overcame the loss of his closest friend in the war, which had a lifelong effect on him. A few years after the war, he was again shovelling coal, this time into the furnaces at the Gravesend gasworks where he worked. The furnace exploded. The blast of red hot coals and molten metal catapulted onto him, severely burning him and scarring him for life, physically and mentally. He lay in the hospital bandaged from head to toe for such a long time, he was a stranger to me when he finally came home. He'd lost an eye, had umpteen skin grafts and never worked again. As if that wasn't enough to cope with, he spent the rest of his life in a discordant relationship, suffering from emphysema and dependant on having an oxygen cylinder by his side in his later years. The French poet and novelist Victor Hugo said, *"It is by suffering that human beings become angels."* Dad had earned his place with the angels.

I was aware of Marjie standing patiently beside me as the different emotions whirled in my mind. I allowed my brain to process what was happening internally and when my mind was calm, I found myself attuned to an overwhelming feeling of love. I did something then that I'd never done before, I reached down and stroked his hair. It was much finer than I'd realised and I felt a strange sensation when I caressed him because there had never been any physicality between us before. I wished it could have been different. I continued stroking and looking at him. His death had killed something inside of me too for his blood runs through me, so in some way, he will always be with me. What I did next, I sadly would never have done whilst he was still alive, I bent down and kissed him for the very first and the very last time. I took one more final look, turned and left dad to take his deserved place among the angels in the palace of eternity. I still think of him a great deal and he has sometimes visited me in my dreams. I miss and love him dearly.

Weep not for me though I have gone
Into that gentle night
Grieve if you will, but not for long
Upon my soul's sweet flight
I am at peace, my soul's at rest
There is no need for tears
For with your love I was so blessed
For all those many years

There is no pain, I suffer not
The fear is now all gone
Put now these things out of your thoughts
In your memory, I live on

Remember not my fight for breath
Remember not my strife
Please do not dwell upon my death
But celebrate my life.
(unknown author)

After the funeral, mum's sister returned to Liverpool and Marjie and I stayed with her until we felt that we could do no more for her. My sister Val and her husband Doug were living in Rochester at the time and were able to visit her regularly to help her adjust to her loss. We drove to Nuneaton to stay awhile with Marjie's parents and as Bob had left our home in Netley Abbey we'd decided to let it so drove back there, contacted an agent, gave him a set of keys and left him to it. A couple of days later the phone rang. It was the German who'd sent us the telegram the day before we received the one about dad. He wanted to meet us in Cologne and we agreed. He made the arrangements for our flights and when we arrived we were met by one of his chauffeurs who took us on a guided tour of Cologne. In the early afternoon, we were driven to meet the German and his wife and over lunch, where sausages featured quite heavily, discussed the details of employment. He offered us a higher than average salary to take command of a large motor yacht that he was having built in Viareggio. We came to an agreement and he promised to send us a contract. After lunch, the chauffeur took us back to the airport. It had been an agreeable and constructive day. When we arrived back at Netley Abbey, we slept well. The next day,

190

we arranged to have the car serviced and when that was done, we stayed in Netley Abbey and enjoyed meeting up with our friends until it was time to head off back to the Picchiotti. We loaded up the car with as many of our belongings as we could, locked the apartment and set off for the journey back to France, arriving at 01h00 on 6th February.

CHAPTER 21
WIN SOME LOSE SOME

A little knowledge

On 4th March, the German called us and reiterated that he would soon be sending us the contract of employment. We were thrilled. However, two weeks went by and we'd received nothing. We began to have doubts and sure enough, after the third week, we received a letter explaining that he'd found somebody else. We found out later that the influential owner of the boatyard where the yacht was being built had persuaded the German to employ one of his acquaintances. Ah well, "Que sera sera". At the beginning of the season, in June 1978, the Picchiotti and the owner's apartment were sold. It was bought by a Norwegian who had his own Norwegian Skipper so we made it known to anybody who was interested that we would be looking for another command. The owner flew down to finalise the sale and to settle other outstanding matters and I went to the airport to meet him and Dennis. I loaded their luggage into the boot of the car and took them to the Hotel Sofitel, where we'd stayed when we'd first arrived to take command of the Pichiotti. I parked outside, unloaded the luggage and underneath it all was a crumpled lump of material.

"What's this?" I said, picking it up.

"Aaargh, that's my hat!" the owner bellowed. He snatched it from my hand, threw it into the gutter and jumped up and down on it yelling, "My daughter bought me that for my birthday. Look at it. Look at it." He picked it up and threw it down again. "It's ruined. It's ruined." He stamped on it again then picked it up and pommelled it, trying in vain to return it to whatever shape it may have originally been. I tried so hard not to laugh. For Dennis it was too much, he couldn't contain himself any longer and exploded into laughter. Seeing him doubled up whilst the owner punched away at his hat, I gave up the fight and burst into laughter myself. We just couldn't help it. The owner was incandescent and red with rage. That was my last memory of him and we never saw him again. When the sale was concluded the agency gave us a percentage of the sale price, which was the standard procedure if the owner hadn't done so himself. Somebody was sent from the U.K. to drive the Ford Granada back and we bought ourselves a second hand, bright yellow Renault 8, a small rear-engined family car. They were manufactured between 1962 and 1973 and we paid a very low price for it in 1978. They are now a collector's item and are selling for 10,000€!

We'd become friendly with a Captain who knew the sales representative for Jongert yachts and he recommended Marjie and me to take command of a brand new 18-metre ketch that had just arrived at La Napoule from the Jongert shipyard at Wieringerferf where it had been built in the Netherlands. We were given the job on his recommendation without being interviewed or without ever having met the owner. We went aboard to meet the German Captain who had sailed the yacht from the Netherlands to La Napoule. He'd been employed as the yacht's permanent Captain but was leaving. We should have listened to his reasons for leaving more attentively. At that time though, we were too enamoured to be taking command of what was considered to be one of the finest, most luxurious and best-equipped steel sailing yachts in the world. What a magnificent vessel she was. She had a clipper bow, windows on the stern and was powered by a Mercedes diesel engine. Owned by a super-rich German, she had every top end, state of the art gadget imaginable. No expense had been spared and she had been built and fitted out to the highest possible standards. I could not have been happier and nothing the Captain said could dampen my spirits. He told me how he'd found it impossible to continue because the owner, his wife and friends knew absolutely nothing about sailing and their demands were sometimes laughable in their naivete. When he tried to explain to them why he couldn't do as they asked, the atmosphere became tense and unpleasant. Among many other tales, he told me how the owner's wife demanded that he hoist the spinnaker single-handed in the Bay of Biscay and couldn't understand why he refused. The fact that he'd decided to leave the instant he arrived in France should have set alarm bells ringing but I needed to find out for myself - and I certainly did!

17. The Jongert at anchor

Shortly after we took over from him, we also took delivery of a hydrofoil that had been built in Russia and shipped to us. The owner wanted it as an extra plaything and as far as I know, we were the only yacht to have one and wherever we went it attracted a lot of attention. It was not finished to a high standard, in fact, it was of a very basic metal construction but terrific fun to drive. When the owner wasn't around and we had plenty of free time, Marjie and I used it a great deal. Once we'd gained enough speed, the struts beneath the hull raised the vessel out of the water reducing the drag and we positively flew. It was good to ski behind. The hydrofoil was too large to take with us when we went cruising so we also had a smaller speedboat that we could hoist on the davits. The owner had a private jet, which was too big to use Cannes-Mandelieu airport; instead, he had to land at Nice whenever he came to use the boat. It was a small airport with just one terminal then but these days it has been extended by claiming land from the sea. Nice Côte d'Azur Airport is situated at the end of the Promenade des

Anglais and is now the third busiest in France. Taking off and landing there opens up an impressive view of the coastline and the Maritime Alps and in 2014, it took first place as the most beautiful airport approach in the world, beating 200 other entrants. By 2018 it had lost its crown but was still ranked in the top three.

With the owner and his guests on board, we cruised the length of the west coast of Corsica and the east coast of Sardinia down to the capital of Sardinia, Cagliari, in the south. We called into as many ports as possible and each time we arrived, the owner ordered a taxi to take us all to the best restaurant in the area. We couldn't fault his generosity. Whenever we stayed in any port for more than one day, if he didn't invite us to dine with him and his guests, he would give us money to eat in a restaurant, even if we were in prohibitively extravagant places such as Porto Cervo. We ate superb meals and drank splendid wines. However, due to his ignorance of maritime matters, he became irritated when things went wrong or if it wasn't possible to do exactly as he asked. At Porto Cervo, the generator was playing up and before we could switch on and have a supply of electricity, I had to spend time in the engine room trying to get it started.

"What is the matter?" he demanded, "The generator is new - why isn't it working?"

"Well, I won't know what's wrong until I've checked it out and then I'll be able to tell you more," I told him. It took me a half-hour to fix it and get it running again and he was furious that he'd had to wait for electricity. His attitude didn't get it fixed any quicker; the reverse in fact, as it made the situation more stressful for me and I was less likely to come up with any useful ideas as to what was causing the problem.

Once, we were entering an attractive bay in northern Sardinia where he had friends anchored on their motor yacht close to the beach. He wanted them to take photographs of us under full sail. The wind was in the right direction and we were running under foresail, main and mizzen. I handed the helm to one of his guests and instructed him what to do so that Marjie and I could hoist the spinnaker. I asked another guest to help us, explaining exactly what to do as nobody had sailed before.

18. Under full sail

The spinnaker on an 18-metre sailboat is quite a handful to cope with. When the genoa was dropped, the spinnaker was hoisted. It filled with wind and looked incredible. Next, we hoisted the mizzen staysail and what a majestic sight we must have been! The huge spinnaker and mizzen staysail were both the same bright red and black horizontal stripes and with the main and mizzen full, we were hammering along towards the beach at a breath-taking rate. As we raced along, drawing ever closer to his friends, I had to calculate the amount of time required to lower the spinnaker and mizzen staysail, hoist the genoa again and then rush back to the wheelhouse in time to sail around his friend's motor yacht, bearing in mind that it had a much shallower draught than we did and was anchored very close to the beach. The shoreline zoomed frighteningly close. I handed the helm to the same guest as before and instructed him what to do. Marjie and I went on deck and working as fast as we possibly could, lowered the mizzen staysail and spinnaker before I ran back to the wheelhouse, leaving Marjie to explain to the guests how to hoist the genoa and free off the main and mizzen sheets, as I swung the vessel around to starboard to sail around the anchored yacht. When we'd accomplished all that, the owner was quick to voice his disappointment.

"Why didn't you sail round him with the spinnaker still up?" he said. I tried to explain how I couldn't just continue heading to the beach under full sail with the wind on our stern and that we needed time to drop the spinnaker and mizzen staysail and hoist the genoa before we ran aground. I told him that we couldn't turn into the wind with the spinnaker and mizzen staysail set as they were sails that could only be used with the wind on the stern. I emphasised the fact that Marjie and I were the only ones on board who knew how to sail and we couldn't rely on anybody else if the situation became difficult. He understood none of it and neither did he understand why I couldn't race up to within a few metres of the beach, stop the boat dead in its tracks and then drop the spinnaker, mizzen staysail, main and mizzen. He was not happy and I understood why the previous Skipper had left as soon as he'd reached a port and was able to get off. One of the guests who spoke fluent English was a little kinder and more understanding. His English was so good that it was impossible to detect any accent; in fact, he could have passed for an Englishman. He spoke of things in England that we had long since forgotten ourselves, like the radio programme 'Workers Playtime', a British radio programme that ran from 1940 till 1964. It was a touring show broadcast live from factory canteens all over Britain as a morale booster for British workers during WWII. The Minister of Labour and National Service, Ernest Bevin, occasionally appeared on the shows to praise the workers and exhort them to make even greater efforts. It made us wonder what our charming English speaking German guest was doing in the U.K. during the war!

The best was yet to come

The situation wasn't helped by the owner's wife having a drink problem. She was as ignorant as he was when it came to yachts and sailing or anything else to do with boating. One day in northern Sardinia on a windless afternoon, we were anchored in a beautiful bay surrounded by high mountains when she asked if I would take her water skiing. We were the only vessel anchored in the sparkling clear blue water with a striking golden beach a short distance away. I lowered the speedboat and she leapt into the sea. I threw her the ski rope and slowly motored a safe distance from her. Because the water skis on her feet were buoyant and she was inebriated, she had trouble positioning herself. She thrashed around in the water trying to control the floating skis, turning in circles and finished up with several coils of the equally buoyant ski rope around her neck.

"Go, go," she hollered. If I'd pushed the throttle to maximum, I've no idea what the result would have been. She'd probably have been decapitated.

"You need to free the rope from around your neck," I called to her.

"No, no – go, go," she cried, getting annoyed. I waited.

"GO! GO!" she screamed at me. I motored slowly towards her and began to unravel the coils of rope from around her neck.

"Why don't you go?" she slurred.

"We have to get the rope clear from your neck," I said and between her drunken yells, I did free the rope and motored away from her again.

Go, Go," she yelled again. I took up the slack on the rope and pushed the speedboat throttle to maximum. I don't quite know what happened but she never managed to get up on the skis. I saw a crumpled figure spinning all over the place as she was being pulled through the water. After several attempts, she realised that it wasn't going to happen.

Our next stop after Porto Cervo was Arbatax, a small town set on the peninsular of Cape Bellavista, halfway down the east coast. There is a small port that had originally been founded by fishermen from Ponza. North of the town is a striking white sandy beach and an attractive bay to the south. Red porphyry rocks rise from the sea with a dramatic mountain range as a backdrop. When we arrived and had moored to the quay, the owner, true to form, sought a taxi to take his guests, Marjie and me to the best restaurant in the region. The taxi driver took us to a new development away from the old town and the owner then invited the taxi driver to join us. The meal wasn't up to the standard that we had become accustomed to - it was mainly pasta but it was enjoyable. Afterwards, we were stunned when the taxi driver paid the bill! Back on the yacht, however, he hung around for the rest of the day hoping for some sort of reward. What he had in mind became obvious when he sat down next to one of the women and placed his hand on her bare leg. He didn't get anything other than an exceptionally large tip.

Cagliari, overlooking the beautiful Golfo degli Angeli, (The Bay of Angels) was the next stop. It is Sardinia's largest city and is the island's capital. It lies on an area of flat land between hills and has a well-protected harbour. It was a Phoenecian colony during the 8th and 7th centuries BC and in the 6th century BC, it fell to the Carthaginians. They held it until they were conquered by the Romans in 238 BC during the first of the three Punic Wars between ancient Carthage and the Roman Republic. When the Western Roman Empire fell, Cagliari along with the rest of Sardinia was taken over by eastern Germanic tribes known as the Vandals. The Vandals held it for a brief period after which it became a province of the Byzantine Empire In the Middle Ages, Cagliari became the capital of one of four independent Kingdoms of Sardinia. The Pisans took control from the 11th until the 14th century after which the Spanish conquered the island and it became one of the numerous Kingdoms that formed the Spanish Empire.

Charles II of Spain had suffered from ill health since birth and when he died childless in 1700, he was the last of the Spanish Hapsburg Kings. His closest relatives were the Austrian Hapsburgs and the French Bourbons and if either had inherited the entire Spanish empire the balance of power in Europe would have drastically changed. Consequently, his succession led to a war that involved most of the European powers, including the House of Savoy, a dynasty originating in the Alpine region between France and Italy, which eventually grew to include most of Italy. As a reward for siding with the Hapsburgs, the House of Savoy was given the Crown of Sicily, which they later exchanged for Sardinia. When Italy was unified in 1861, Sardinia became part of the Kingdom of Italy.

During WWII, in February 1943, Cagliari suffered heavy bombing by the Allies, which damaged 80% of the buildings. On 3rd September of the same year, after the armistice was signed between the Allies and the Kingdom of Italy, the Germans took control of Cagliari and Sardinia but soon retreated to reinforce their positions in mainland Italy and the American Army took control.

We didn't stay there long. After one night we returned to Arbatax where we spent another night before we sailed north to the city of Olbia, situated in a large bay in north eastern Sardinia. It is the economic centre of that part of the island and it is where the owner had arranged for his private jet to be waiting, ready to take him home, bringing his sister and niece out at the same time. After a long, tiring sail up the eastern coast, it was dark well before we reached Olbia. When we were clear of the northern tip of Isola Tavolara, which lies a few kilometres off the coast, I turned on a westerly course and we were looking forward to catching the first glimpse of the welcoming five-second duration flash of the Isola della Bocca lighthouse. It is located on a small islet at the southern entrance to the outer port and the flash is supposed to be visible for a distance of 15 nautical miles but as we sailed closer we saw nothing. I couldn't understand what was wrong. It was pitch black and I couldn't see where we were supposed to go. Not only could we not see the flash of the lighthouse, but we could see no leading lights of any description.

I continued on the course I'd set, hoping that sooner or later one of us would pick up the loom of the light but it never appeared. Olbia is a busy transit port but we saw no activity. Confused, I continued onwards in the dark. According to my calculations, we should have already spotted the lighthouse but still, we saw nothing. I was relieved when I saw the lights of a few fishing boats approaching us. The fishermen were very friendly and as far as any of us could tell, they were explaining that there was a strike and no lights were working. At least that's how we understood it, although it seemed unlikely; but in any case, there were certainly no lights visible anywhere. They led us in and when we'd moored up, the owner bought some spiny lobsters from them.

When we'd finally moored up alongside the commercial quay, the owner brought out a bottle of schnapps. We were all very tired and pleased to have arrived and the schnapps was much appreciated. Marjie cooked the lobsters, which we enjoyed with some excellent bottles of Moselle wine that the owner had brought with him from Germany. We stayed overnight and the following morning his sister and his niece arrived for the journey back to southern France. Before the owner and his guests left, leaving only his sister and niece on board, he gave me an enormous wad of cash, which he'd been doing throughout the trip, never once having counted how much he'd given me. I don't know if he ever had any idea or even cared how much he gave me but I kept meticulous accounts anyway. It would have been very easy to have had a more relaxed attitude though.

"I want you to take my sister to all of those wonderful restaurants that we've been to and make sure she has a good time," he said. Well, he couldn't have said anything better!

It was too late to leave that day so we spent another night in Olbia. As with Cagliari, it was first developed by the Phoenicians in the 7th century BC. They were followed by the Carthaginians, who constructed walls and towers around the settlement. Next came the Romans, who built paved roads, thermal baths, a forum and an aqueduct making Olbia the largest city on Sardinia's east coast. In 450 AD, the marauding Vandals attacked and burned the Roman fleet, (in 1999, 24 shipwrecks were discovered.) When Olbia recovered and became part of the Byzantine Empire, it was known as Phausania. Later, when it was ruled by one of the four independent states of Sardinia, it was known as Città. The name was changed yet again to Terranova when the Pisans founded a colony there and that name remained until 1939 when Mussolini's Italian fascists decided to call it Olbia. There are interesting ruins remaining from the Carthaginian and Roman occupations and other touristic sites but we never had the opportunity to see any of them. We left the next day and headed for Porto Cervo; after all, we had been instructed to revisit all the wonderful restaurants. From there we went to Bonifacio and other ports along the west coast of Corsica before finishing up at Calvi in readiness for the crossing back to La Napoule.

On the way to Calvi we were under full sail but the nearer we got, the more the wind lessened until we were wallowing in calm conditions with the sails flapping uselessly just a few miles from our destination. I started the engine and left the yacht to drift whilst Marjie and I lowered and stowed the sails. As soon as that was done, we went to the wheelhouse, spun the wheel to take us on the final leg of the journey and pushed the throttle lever to cruising speed. The next instant, in the blink of an eye, a violent Mistral hit us. We were flabbergasted that it happened so quickly and would not have believed it possible that such a strong wind could suddenly appear out of nowhere. The scary experience has stayed with us. How fortunate that we'd dropped and stowed the sails when we did. When we reached Calvi we anchored and had to wait for three days for the Mistral to abate before we could set course for La Napoule.

19. On the deck of the Jongert

CHAPTER 22
THE END IS NIGH

Stormbound

We made one more trip to Corsica and Sardinia with friends of the owner. It was the end of the season and the weather had deteriorated in the final few days of the cruise. A Mistral had been forecast so the guests flew back to Germany from Ajaccio, leaving Marjie and me to make our way back to France on our own. When the unbelievably violent Mistral struck we were stormbound for more than a week, the longest period that I have ever been in a port awaiting favourable weather. The Mistral or "Maestrale" as the Corsicans and Italians call it, can reach 150 kilometres an hour, creating huge, dangerous seas. Nobody would want to be caught out in one and it would be foolish indeed to leave the safety of a harbour for an extended voyage whilst a Mistral was blowing. I once did just that when I was Captain of the "Passing Fancy" and vowed I would never do so again. So we stayed where we were. The English poet William Cowper wrote, *"God moves in mysterious ways, His wonders to perform. He plants his footsteps in the sea, and rides upon the storm."* Be that as it may - we stayed in port!

We got to know Ajaccio pretty well whilst we waited for the Mistral to die down. The town, the largest on the island, is the capital of Corsica. It is situated in a sheltered position on the northern shore of the Gulf of Ajaccio with wooded hills to the north that surround the charming old port, with its brightly coloured fishing boats and yachts of all types and sizes. The port was named after one of the town's favourite sons, the singer and actor Tino

Rossi (1907 – 1983) who appeared in 25 films and recorded hundreds of songs, including one called Ajaccio. His villa there is now open to the public in the summer.

Being a part of the daily life in Ajaccio was a pleasure despite the howling wind and the constant clanging of rigging on the masts. It is thought that the first settlement and port were established around the 2nd century AD by the Romans when there was considerable prosperity in the Mediterranean Sea. This is borne out by recent underwater archaeological discoveries. The earliest written record of a settlement was in 601 AD by Pope Gregory the Great, who was Pope of the Catholic Church from 590 – 604 AD. After the Roman and early Christian presence, the town, like most other Corsican coastal settlements fell into decline and virtually disappeared after the 8th century. It was rebuilt by the Genoese in the 15th century as they sought to enlarge their influence on the south of the island. The town quickly expanded and was inhabited virtually exclusively by the Genoese until eventually the Corsicans were allowed in and became citizens of the Republic of Genoa.

The French, the Ottomans and the exiled Corsicans invaded Corsica in 1553 and took almost complete control of the strategically important island from the Genoese who'd ruled it since 1492. The Genoese launched a successful counter-attack and governed until 1755 when Pasquale Paoli proclaimed the Corsican Republic and took over most of the island. As Paoli was establishing his control, the Genoese sold the sovereignty of Corsica to the French behind his back. The secret treaty was made public in 1768 and France proceeded to take over the island. They formally annexed it in 1780 and Paoli went into exile.

Napoleon Bonaparte was born in Ajaccio in 1769. At the age of 10, he studied at the Military College of Brienne in France for five years and later at the Military School of Paris before taking up a position as Second Lieutenant in the artillery regiment of La Fère in Valence. When the French revolution broke out in 1789, he became a member of the Jacobin Club, the most famous of several revolutionary organisations and in 1792, returned to Corsica as Lieutenant-Colonel in the Corsican National Guard.

Paoli had already returned to Corsica in 1790 after it had been integrated with France. He had been pardoned, elected President of the Executive Council and had become a conservative, favouring an alliance with Great Britain, where he had been welcomed with open arms during his exile. He sent Napoleon on his first military service, an expedition to attack the northern Sardinian island of Maddalena, under his nephew, who had received secret orders to make sure the expedition failed. Napoleon found out about this and wasn't too pleased; when he returned to Paris in 1793, he managed to get Paoli denounced. A warrant was issued for Paoli's arrest and Napoleon was sent to Corsica to take the citadel of Ajaccio from the Royalists who had held it since the beginning of the Revolution in 1789. He was defeated by the Paolists and the Royalists and went on the run with his family. He was taken by friends on a ship to Toulon and later moved to Marseille.

On January 21 1793 the French king, Louis XVI had been accused of treason and sent to the guillotine. That period, after the creation of the French First Republic, was named 'The Terror' after numerous massacres and public executions and Paris was rocked with revolt. However, in the South there were a lot of pro royalist people who were horrified as to what was happening in the North. Toulon was a very important naval base and to help them protect it the Royalists handed over the port to an Anglo Spanish fleet under the command of Vice-Admiral Lord Hood. The Revolutionary forces surrounded the port on 8th September and the "Siege of Toulon" began. Napoleon was made a Colonel and using heavy artillery, retook Toulon on 18th December. Following his success, he was made a Brigadier-General and thus began his meteoric rise to fame. He became First Consul and Emperor, spreading his revolution throughout Europe. In 1811, he made Ajaccio the capital of the department of Corsica and it has remained so ever since, despite very strong feelings still of Corsican Nationalism.

Ajaccio is an economic, commercial and administrative centre of Corsica that relies nowadays on tourism and fishing for much of its economy. There is an airport, the Ajaccio Napoleon Bonaparte Airport, which had started its life as a grass landing strip in the second world war and now hosts international companies offering flights to many destinations. The port, where we found ourselves stormbound, now has an almost daily ferry service to Marseille, Toulon, Nice, Livorno and Sardinia, and cruise ships are also regular visitors.

Grab the meat

It was clear that the boats that sought shelter from the wild, brutal wind had taken a battering. One motor yacht arrived with the aft deck awning torn to shreds and no doubt other damage that wasn't evident to us, but the most memorable was a yacht that arrived next to us with torn sails that were badly stowed and ropes hanging loose. The crew were shouting at each other and it almost became physical as they tried several times, unsuccessfully, to back up to the quay. Each one had a different view as to how they should achieve it and with nobody in control, they ran backwards and forwards yelling with a great deal of arm waving and jumping up and down, which attracted a lot of attention. It was difficult not to laugh at their crazy antics. I ran down our gangplank and went to help them by taking their stern ropes. I pushed my way through the gathering crowd that had assembled to watch the spectacle. Each time the boat came close to the quay, the crew on the aft deck threw the ropes towards me but they were consistently way off target. The ropes landed in the water and the yacht drifted away again.

"Hurry up, my tea's getting cold," I said. It was said half-jokingly but I was seriously concerned about the state of my tea. If I'd known of the hell that they'd been through, I wouldn't have said that! When they finally managed to moor up, they weren't sure how to put out the gangplank; that too took a long time and involved a lot of argument, by which time I'd given up any hopes of enjoying my cup of tea. When things had settled down and the entertainment had ended, the crowd dispersed and some of the unshaven, dirty, miserable crew scrambled ashore. They looked as if they hadn't slept in a long time.

"Where have you come from?" I asked one of them.

"Marseille."

"Where are you heading for?" I asked.

"America," he replied.

"America! You're a little off course aren't you?" I said. Considering that America is on the other side of the Atlantic and they'd finished up almost in Italy, I was dumbfounded.

"Shortly after we left, the navigator got seasick and he was the only one who knew how to use the electronic navigating system," he told me.

208

"Where was your first port of call supposed to be then? You do realise that you're in Corsica now, don't you?"

"We were hoping to make Majorca but without a navigator, we had to try and get there on our own. We'd no idea where we were."

"When did you leave Marseille?" I asked him.

"Three days ago," he told me.

"You've been out there in this wind for three days and after all that you finish up here in Corsica, miles off course?"

"We don't care where we are as long as we're safe," he said. He was dishevelled and his red, bloodshot eyes stared out from a pale, drawn face.

"Why didn't you drop the anchor when you backed in just now, it would have held your bow in position and made it easier for you to manoeuvre," I said.

"We don't have an anchor any more. When we first saw land, we motored into what we thought would be a sheltered place and dropped the anchor but the end of the chain wasn't attached and the whole lot disappeared over the side." The crew member I was talking to was an Englishman who'd been employed by the American owners and it distinctly had not worked out for either of them. He went on to tell me of the endless disasters that had happened. When they were rolling around violently in the huge seas, the tender on the davits had broken loose from its lashings and when they tried to stop it flying around and fasten it again, it became too difficult for them to control. It eventually broke loose completely and disappeared into the sea. They were ravenous because they'd run out of food and they hadn't slept for more than 24 hours - and so it went on. The female cook was sent ashore to buy food and the shaken girl looked a sorry sight as she stumbled down the gangplank. After three days of being thrown around, she swayed along the quay towards the town.

I felt sorry for the Englishman so invited him aboard the Jongert for something to eat and drink. I also wanted to know more about what had happened. He leapt at the opportunity of escaping the chaos and the arguments. He must have thought that Marjie and I owned the Jongert and kept calling me "Sir" as he was telling us in more detail of the terrifying three days they'd had. Then we heard a loud crack, a splash and screams and shouts. We rushed up on deck. Their gangplank had collapsed when the cook had tried to return on board with the shopping and she was floundering in the water. One of the Americans grabbed a boat hook. We heard the others shouting "Get the food. Get the food." Meanwhile, the cook was thrashing around trying to find something to hold onto. Nobody was concerned about whether she drowned or not as long as they saved the bags of food.

"Help me!, Help me!" she screamed but they ignored her. The boat hook struck a bag and as it was hauled up, it split and the food fell out. We saw a couple of steaks drifting away.

"Grab the meat," somebody shouted. We rushed to help the girl but some other horrified onlookers got there before us and pulled her to safety. She stood on the quay in a state of shock. When the Americans had rescued what was left of the food they finally turned their attention towards the wet, distressed girl who had used the gangplank of the yacht on the other side of them to get on board. They started arguing again and then disappeared inside, clutching the shopping that they'd salvaged. Our Englishman went back to his own boat and Marjie and I returned to the Jongert.

Here we go again!

Seven days after we'd first arrived in Ajaccio the weather forecast was for the wind to drop to a more acceptable level. We knew that even if the wind strength decreased dramatically we would still be in for a very rough crossing to La Napoule but knew also that the closer we got to France, the more comfortable it would be. I'd calculated that it would take us about 12 hours to complete the journey if we were able to cruise at a reasonable speed, which was unlikely in the rough sea. It wasn't something that filled us with pleasure but we had to get back. We had become fed up with the owner's attitude. When he made known his disapproval at the amount of time we'd spent in Ajaccio it was the last straw for us but no matter how annoyed he was I was not going to be bullied into casting off and going to sea in a Mistral; I'd had my fill of sailing in Mistrals and knew how potentially dangerous they could be. Bob had once delivered a motor yacht from Calvi to Cannes in a rough northwesterly and the yacht took such a horrendous pounding that the wheelhouse roof lifted off.

I laid off the course to take us directly to La Napoule. I checked the engine and everything topside making sure we were ready for sea. Marjie checked below decks. When we were both satisfied that

210

it was safe to go, I started the engine. We had no intention of hoisting the sails in such a rough sea - we just wanted to get back to our home port as quickly as possible. We set our slip rope and pulled in and stowed the gangplank. Marjie went to the foredeck. I let go the slip rope and pulled it in then went to the wheelhouse.

"Heave away," I called out to Marjie. She pressed the button of the electric windlass and hauled in the anchor. When it was stowed, she pulled in and stowed the fenders and came into the wheelhouse to join me. We were off, come what may. *"We must free ourselves of the hope that the sea will ever rest. We must learn to sail in high winds," - Aristotle Onassis*. We motored out of the harbour and headed west towards the four Sanguinaires Islands, (Blood Islands) 15 kilometres away that form an archipelago lying just off the Pointe de la Parata. Blood Islands sounds rather disturbing but the name is given them because they are composed of dark red porphyry rock and we knew that once we had rounded them and set course for La Napoule we would be hit by the full force of the wind and sea. We were not mistaken!

To say that the journey home was uncomfortable would be an understatement. We were thrown around all over the place. "Here we go again," we said to each other. So many times had we endured strong winds and rough seas around Corsica, we came to expect it.

"Only 12 hours to go," I said to Marjie and the look she gave me indicated that she didn't think it was funny. I felt so proud of her as I watched her expertly steering the yacht through those awful seas and I couldn't help thinking how privileged I was to be with such a truly wonderful girl. We set watches initially of two hours on and two hours off, each of us holding the course as best we could whilst the other one tried to rest. Neither was easy. The one steering struggled to hold the course as the bow was lifted high up on the crests of the huge waves before it plunged back down again and the waves broke over the bows sending vast volumes of water along the decks as it rose up once more into the next wave. At least we had the shelter of the wheelhouse.

And so it went on hour after hour all through the day and part of the night, crashing and banging our way through the waves. We fought with the steering wheel to hold the course and ate and drank whenever and wherever possible. The propeller rumbled, churning the water as it drove us forward, driven by the powerful, reliable Mercedes diesel engine thumping comfortingly beneath our feet. During the daylight hours, the sky was crystal clear, a brilliant, intense blue and the night sky was so clear that the sight of the endless stars was breathtaking. The moon was a huge glowing sphere that lit up the sea. If it hadn't been so rough and we hadn't been thrown around all over the place, it would have been an enchanting night. As we suspected, the closer we got to France the less the wind howled and the smaller the waves became and by the time we arrived, closing in on the coastline, we spotted the warm, glowing welcoming lights of the towns and eventually the flashing lights off the entrance to La Napoule. We were exhausted and delighted as always to be back in France.

Not long after we'd arrived, the owner came to La Napoule. He was dissatisfied that we'd stayed so long in Ajaccio and we were dissatisfied with him. And so another job came to an end. It was the end of the season anyway and he was probably delighted that he wouldn't have the expense of keeping us on through the winter. We had our car and we had our charming, fully renovated apartment in the enchanting, mediaeval provençal hill village. It didn't seem so bad - so with our wages stuffed in our pockets, we set off for a new adventure inland.

CHAPTER 23
HOME SWEET HOME

A yearning for learning

We were over the moon with the apartment and loved the tranquil village life and the stunning views. There were a number of retirees, mainly American and English and we were soon in demand to do odd jobs for them; carpentry, plumbing, upholstery, gardening, building, painting and decorating, catering. We did it all and had a wonderful time meeting people and socialising. It was such a contrast to yachting. A week after we'd catered for a wedding, we received a phone call from one of the guests who owned a well-known chain of clothing shops in the U.K.. He complimented us on our catering skills and asked if we could visit him and sort out his central heating system as it wasn't working and since he had family staying with him, he wanted a warm house. He welcomed us cordially when we arrived. I left Marjie talking to him whilst I went into the boiler room to see what was wrong with the heating system. Nothing was working. I noticed a green button with "start" written on it. I pressed the button, the boiler burst into life and the water started to circulate through the radiators.

"It's working and you should have a warm house soon," I said.

"Oh, that's wonderful, thank you so much," he said and then he asked us if we would be prepared to work for him on a permanent basis.

"We don't use the house much and we'd like you to stay as resident caretakers. We will pay you well and you would have your own accommodation in our grounds, separate from our house," he told us and then went on to offer us a number of enticements, hoping we'd accept. Marjie and I didn't need to discuss it.

"Thank you, we're flattered, it's a good offer but we prefer to wait for another opportunity on a yacht," I answered. It would have been a hard to resist offer for somebody but it wasn't what we wanted.

We worked when we felt like it and with so much spare time we were able to concentrate on subjects that interested us. We joined 'The Good Book Guide' in the U.K.. Before the days of the internet, its monthly brochure was a godsend to expats who had no access to books in English. We regularly had boxes of books sent out from them. The Guide first started about 1978 but finally went into liquidation in 2001, unable to keep up with internet rivals like Amazon; its own attempt to join them was underfunded and they were unable to compete. We joined associations and research groups and immersed ourselves in spiritual matters, meditation, yoga, philosophy and the more we read, the wider our field of interests expanded. With so many options available to us nowadays in our multicultural society, we can broaden our knowledge by reading, listening, contemplating and looking at other beliefs to find what rings true. Rigid religious doctrines based on power and profit are being called into question and are no longer the only choice nowadays. Science, quantum physics, eastern philosophies and other concepts are all there to be discovered.

We explored them all, including the esoteric subjects, in our search for an understanding of the universe and our role in it. Without studying all that is out there, how can we know which fits best? We immersed ourselves in astrology and investigated numerology, I Ching, tarot, palmistry, reincarnation and anything else that we thought was interesting and may have validity. I became particularly engrossed in quantum physics, the workings of the brain and participated in organised research projects on dreams and meditation. I've had extraordinarily vivid dreams since childhood and as I investigated them, I began to understand them more and developed the ability to program my dreams for information, occasionally having precognitive dreams, a source of information which has helped many famous inventors to get inspiration for their projects. In my case, I haven't invented anything, but have had ideas or help in many other ways, including financially. The following dream is just one example and it came to me after I'd pondered on the implications of the "Block Universe Theory" that suggests time is not linear as we believe it to be. Our perception of time is that it runs from past to present to future but according to the Block Universe Theory, the past, present and future exist simultaneously spread out in different parts of space-time. According to Einstein, nothing can travel faster than light (186,000 miles per second) and at the speed of light, time ceases to exist. The light from a star may take 500,000 light-years to reach us but if we could hitch a ride on a photon of light on that star, our journey to planet earth would be instantaneous - so time as we perceive it is an illusion. For a quantum physicist, past, present and future information would be found in the zero-point field; for those following a spiritual path, the knowledge lies in universal consciousness and for religious people it may be God.

"I have dreamt all my life, dreams that have stayed with me ever after, and changed my ideas; they have gone through me; like wine through water, and altered the colour of my mind. And this is one I'm going to tell it – but take care not to smile at any part of it." – Emily Brontë, Wuthering Heights.

Before sleeping one night, I programmed a dream to clarify the Block Universe concept and what follows is the result. At the time I programmed the dream, Marjie and I had signed a contract to buy a house in another village close to Seillans and had paid a deposit of 10% of the purchase price to secure the deal. When the time arrived for the balance to be paid and we had to transfer pounds sterling into French francs, I had the dream in which I heard a voice telling me to wait until the exchange rate reached a certain level. (When I say voice, it was more a "knowing". There are no words to adequately describe exactly how I received the knowledge.) The rate given me seemed unlikely at the time but I had enough faith to wait so I stalled the signing of the contract. The vendor became more angry with each passing week but I waited and waited, listening to the radio each day for the latest currency exchange rates as they rose little by little. Then one day, I was driving through Cannes and the magic figure was announced. I pulled into a parking slot, contacted my bank and instructed them to transfer the funds immediately. The following day, the exchange rate began to drop again and as far as I am aware, never reached the same level again. The odds of that happening by chance are remote indeed. Not only did I receive information from the future but I also profited financially. How did that happen? Where did the voice come from? Where do we go when we dream? Perhaps we journey to a different dimension of space-time. The prophet Mohammad talks of seven heavens, *"Allah has created the seven heavens, one above the other."* - *K 71:15* and the concept of seven heavens is also taught in Hinduism and Judaism. There could be many other dimensions as yet undetected and unimagined. For the mathematical consistency of string theory or M theory, 10 to 26 other space-time dimensions are required.

Eastern philosophies have as their principle, "Thou art That," which means that we are made of the same "substance" as God. This is known as Pantheism, (reality is identical with divinity.) Some Gnostic groups (early Christians,) believed in Pantheism and their teachings were symbolic, with deep spiritual meanings learned by initiates. St Paul is thought to have been a Gnostic and his early writings are Gnostic; he writes in Ephesians 4:6, *"one God and Father of all, who is over all and through all and in all."* My supposition is that modern Christianity is a one dimensional interpretation of Gnosticism, where symbolic teachings have been taken literally by those who never learned the intended inner meanings and have introduced division through their doctrine of a personal God as a separate entity from ourselves, living in a faraway place called heaven. Hindus, pre-Christians, ancient Egyptians, Greeks, Stoics, Taoists and in more recent times, Albert Einstein, Carl Sagan, Carl Jung, Nikola Tesla, Friedrich Nietzsche and many others believed in Pantheism. It was taught by Plato and St Augustine. It is as old as philosophy itself and is often considered the final truth of philosophy. God is in all things. His reality permeates this universe and all other, as yet undiscovered universes. His divine presence is everywhere, in every star, mountain, river, plant, animal and human. He is the universe and to seek Him we need to look within ourselves. The Astrophysicist Bernard Haisch, in his book, "The Purpose Guided Universe" theorises that God has become the Universe to experience his potential. He quotes, *"Advances are made by answering questions. Discoveries are made by questioning answers."* The profound implication is that we are all connected and every action and every thought we have affects every other person or thing in the universe. Quantum physics provides scientific evidence of Pantheism. It hypothesises that the universe is a hologram where each part contains the whole. At a fundamental level, we are charged particles connected to all other charged particles through quantum entanglement, sharing information instantly, unlimited by distance. All information since the beginning of the universe and all probabilities are stored in the quantum field. It is consciousness that collapses the waves of probability and brings about what we call reality, which is actually an illusion. Some scientists tell us that a chemical process in the brain produces consciousness, according to quantum physics however, it is consciousness that creates everything and in Buddhism and other ancient philosophies it is all that exists.

Our concept of reality is produced by the brain. When we look at an object, light is reflected from it onto the lens, which directs it onto the retina. From there, it is transformed into electrical impulses that travel to the visual cortex at the rear of the brain. The brain then creates a three-dimensional image from the information received, yet as each person's eyes are different, we don't all see the same thing. There is also an infinitesimally small time-lapse between looking and seeing, as electromagnetic impulses travel at a speed of about 300 miles an hour.

Light is less than 1% of the electromagnetic spectrum, having a wavelength of 400-700 nanometres and going from red to violet. That is all we humans can see, although other creatures' worlds appear different to our own. For example, snakes can see infra-red, birds and bees can see ultra-violet and cats and dogs can hear sounds that we can't. However, the other 99% of the electromagnetic spectrum does affect us and our world, sometimes beneficially and sometimes detrimentally, even though we have no awareness of it. Science now tells us that atoms, the basic units of matter, are 99.99999% empty space and that the smallest known sub-atomic particle is in an indeterminate state – or multiple states at the same time, so that all that can be predicted is probability. The world that we think is real, isn't real – a concept familiar to eastern philosophies, and now backed up by quantum theory. However, long before quantum theory, Hindus believed in the existence of a sub-atomic particle so small that it can never be measured. It is a spark of spirit. It is conscious and consciousness pervading the universe. It is Krishna consciousness and to know the Supreme Being Lord Krishna, (God, Allah, Spirit?) we must first know ourselves. (Bhagavad- Gita 15:15)

Hindus and Buddhists believe that we need to go through every possible experience over countless lifetimes (reincarnation.) Somebody once asked the Buddha how long it would take and the Buddha replied, "as long as it takes to wear away the Himalayas with a silk cloth." Since time is an illusion and the subatomic level is one of all probabilities, maybe the universe is splitting into infinite copies of itself, with us living out every possible outcome of every possible event right now. The idea of infinite worlds is not new; it goes back as far as the 3rd century BC. The earliest recorded example was at the time of Greek Atomism which proposed that the physical world is composed of fundamental indivisible components known as atoms. In the Koran, Allah states that he is the "Lord of all worlds." The multiverse has been hypothesised by cosmologists, physicists, astronomers and philosophers. I hence have difficulty accepting that with all our imperfections, we have just one lifetime to get things right.

All of this, of course, is a threat to the authority and revenue of the Vatican. In 1600, Giordano Bruno, an Italian Dominican Friar, philosopher, mathematician and cosmological theorist, proposed that the stars were distant suns with their own planets that may contain life. That alone would have been sufficient to warrant him being tortured or incarcerated by the church but it wasn't for that reason that he met his fate. What did for him was his preaching about a transcendent and infinite God and questioning the literality of Catholic beliefs of eternal damnation, the trinity, the divinity of Jesus and the virginity of Mary. The church, which preaches tolerance, compassion, love and forgiveness, had him lashed to the stake and burned alive. These days, some members of the church hierarchy themselves question those same beliefs as do more and more of the general population, who also call into question the fancy ceremonies, elaborate costumes and obscene wealth of the church, which were anathema to Jesus. We do not need authoritative figures - we can seek and find the divine within ourselves; it is the very core of our being and Pantheism is proffering the answers. *"For indeed the Kingdom of God is within you." – Luke 17:20-21.* After many years of searching and debate, I have found a path that fits for me. Others may choose different paths and those choices should be tolerated and respected by us all because we are all where we need to be at this moment in time.

We explored Gnosticism and the so-called "Secret Gospels" that differ in some ways from the New Testament texts. The Gospel of Thomas, discovered in the Nag Hammadi library in 1945, was probably the earliest known Christian writing; then there is the secret Gospel of Mark, the Secret Revelation of John and the Gospel of Mary. They all contain "secret information" and special knowledge passed on by Jesus to his closest disciples and have not been included in the accepted version of the New Testament. However, there is also a reference to the secret knowledge of the Gnostics in the New Testament; in 1 Corinthians 2; 6-8, Paul writes of *"God's secret wisdom that has been hidden"* that was given to *"the mature,"* the implication being that there is a secret knowledge passed on only to those initiated into the great mysteries. There is also an esoteric version of Judaism called the Kaballah, which teaches the hidden mystical meanings of the Torah that was preached by Jesus. He frequently stated to his disciples that the true interpretations could only be given to them - to others He must speak in parables. From His Sermon on the Mount, *"Do not give what is holy to the dogs, nor cast your pearls before swine, lest they trample them under their feet, and turn and tear you to pieces"* *Mathew 7: 6.* We re-read the Bible and the history of Christianity, of the conflicts that existed in the 2nd century and how the Orthodox Christian Church authorities claimed Gnosticism and other sects to be heretical and suppressed or destroyed their mystic texts. In the Koran, the prophet Mohammad also talks of *"a hidden book that none but the purified may touch, a sending down from the Lord of all being."* (K 56: 76-79). Many Muslims take this teaching literally, believing that they must wash their hands before they touch the Koran. Sufis are Muslims who played a major role in the spread of Islam and believe that there is a mystical and metaphysical meaning in the Koran, just as there is in the Bible. Mohammad believed that the book, in the mind of God, had been given to Jews and Christians but that it had been tampered with and some common people, unaware of the hidden meaning, share *"only fancies and mere conjectures."*

We went to Bible study classes but found them disappointing. I became frustrated that the people present were unprepared to discuss different interpretations of the Bible, the universe and consciousness. There is so much that we don't understand and maybe never will. None of us can claim to know the absolute truth but we can all profit from sincerely searching for it. I suspected that the members of the bible study group were afraid to open their minds and expand their consciousnesses because their own deeply held beliefs may be challenged and partly because they feared the influences of malevolent entities like the devil and demons. I once tried to talk to a devout Catholic friend about messages obtained from dreams and the response was "How do you know it's not the devil talking?" I would highlight that it's not only the Catholic faith that thinks that way but other religious faiths too. The devil, demons and eternal damnation, in my opinion, are a creation of the human intellect; probably conceived to scare the daylights out of people to make sure they attended church to contribute to its coffers and expand its power. They are not a part of my belief system. If energy and power are given to an imagined fear, the fear becomes a reality that dwells in the heart and creates darkness where love and light should be and that which is feared will be perceived to exist everywhere. We always have a choice and a belief is a choice that affects our other choices. We can choose to conquer fear or we can choose to allow the fear to conquer us. *"The only thing we have to fear is fear itself." – Franklin D Roosevelt.*

Fear is used as a controlling mechanism to brainwash others and to satisfy the ego and lust for power of whoever instils the fear, whether it be an institution like the church or an individual. We are each responsible for our own actions and the consequences thereof and the power of suggestion is very real and should never be underestimated. When I had my kinesiology and psychotherapy practise in York in the 1990s, a man came to me in distress, seeking my help because he had been told that certain behaviours he had were caused by demons. Somebody had convinced him that mythical entities were controlling him, which had filled him with fear. Employing neuro-linguistic programming (NLP), I helped him to recognise that he and not imaginary forces was responsible for his behaviours and that he could take control and make the appropriate changes. When he'd accepted responsibility, I facilitated him to choose alternative behaviours using the indescribable, awesome power of the most evolved system on the planet that he himself possessed - his brain. The unwanted behaviours were replaced with more acceptable ones and he left satisfied with his new choices of behaviour, free of the anguish that had been implanted in him and secure in the knowledge that the ability to bring about change lay within himself. Accepting responsibility for our actions and behaviours can bring about profound changes and set us free. *"May your choices reflect your hopes, not your fears." Nelson Mandela.*

Somebody once said, "The more spiritual I become, the less religious I become." That is exactly how Marjie and I felt. I readily accept, however, that others feel differently and I respect their choices.

In touch with nature

We bought so many books and continued to expand our knowledge. We studied natural healing methods, some of them from antiquity and delved into the study of nutrition. As we learned more we began to search for nutritious food for free. We picked and ate chickweed, dandelions, alexanders, wall pennywort, clover, plantain, nettles and many others. We bought freshly ground flour from a local wheat producer to bake our own bread and the more we learned the more we wanted to learn. We bought books on and studied, reflexology, homoeopathy, massage, crystal healing, hypnosis, Bach remedies, osteopathy, psychology, iridology, radiesthesia and anything else that caught our attention. Our thirst for knowledge was insatiable and we each gravitated more to our own specialised subjects; Marjie became more immersed in herbalism and nutrition and I concentrated more on studying the brain and quantum physics that seemed to provide many answers for me. And it all started after we read a small paperback book called "Living better on less," by Patrick Rivers.

We had everything we needed and were very happy. We loved our little apartment and the village lifestyle and were making new friends. We went on long walks in the marvellous Provençal countryside where the views were spectacular, the colours vibrant, the smells heady. We were free to go regularly to the Grande Parade du Jazz in Nice. We were enjoying ourselves so much that we were in no hurry to go sailing again. Until something unexpected happened in June 1979.

CHAPTER 24
THE CALL OF THE SEA

Old friends

"Ello 'ow are ya?" I heard when I picked up the phone.

"Is that you Keith?" I asked.

"Yer, we're in Antibes. Ah've bought a new boat and we'd like ta see ya" he said.

"That would be great, what do you suggest?"

"Why don't you come down tomorrow," he replied.

"Sounds like a good idea, we've got nothing else on that can't wait."

"Ten-o clock and we'll go out for a trip an' 'ave lunch on the boat somewhere."

"OK see you then," I confirmed.

"Wow, that was a surprise," I said to Marjie and told her what had happened.

At ten-o clock, we arrived at Keith's new yacht, which was moored in Port Vauban, Antibes. It was a 58 ft Hatteras, a twin-engined, fibreglass motor yacht.

"Morning, come aboard," he said. It was good to see him and Anne once again. We brought each other up to date on what we'd been doing in the four years since we were last together. Keith explained that he'd bought the Hatteras in partnership with a friend and had a Skipper and his wife as crew but wasn't happy with the way things were going. I understood why he was unhappy. The boat was in a disgusting state. There were oil drums stacked along the aft deck, ropes lying around instead of being neatly coiled up, oilskins and other clothing scattered around the wheelhouse, the decks were filthy and the yacht was covered in salt. It saddened me to see such a nice yacht so neglected. He asked me where he thought we should go for lunch and I suggested that we drop anchor between the ever-popular Iles de Lerins. It was almost always calm there, the water was shallow and it was a good place to swim. Keith instructed the Skipper to cast off. Marije and I had anchored there many times before so I asked the Skipper if he was happy for me to suggest an area to drop anchor as he had no local knowledge, having never been in the Med before. He agreed and on the journey to the islands, he and I talked about the relationship he had with Keith and how he felt about being on the Hatteras in Antibes. He complained about how he considered it absurd that the yacht should be kept tidy and have cushions to sunbathe on and flowers on the table.

"Boats are meant to be at sea," he stated vehemently.

"Well, they're also to be enjoyed," I reasoned. We were never going to agree so I said no more and we had an enjoyable afternoon with Keith and Anne. At the end of the day, we thanked them both and agreed to meet again later in the season. We also thanked the resentful Skipper and his wife before we left for home.

A week went by. The phone rang. I answered it.

"How would you like to come and be my Skipper?" It was Keith.

"What's happened?" I asked.

"My Skipper's leaving. It isn't working out and he's going," he said. I wasn't surprised.

"Let me discuss it with Marjie. Can you call me back tomorrow?"

"Yes, all right," he agreed. We didn't want to leave our idyllic existence in the village, we had many friends and we were free to do what we liked when we liked. Every day was a blessing and we couldn't have been happier. We still hadn't decided when Keith phoned the next day and I explained that we appreciated his offer but we were settled into a wonderful lifestyle that many people could only ever dream of. He pleaded with me.

"Oh, please," he said and I knew then that I couldn't say no to him. He had been a good friend to me.

"OK, when do you want us to call by and see you?"

"Can you start as soon as possible?"

"Meaning when exactly?"

"Tomorrow if you like."

"How does your Skipper feel about that?" I enquired. I didn't want to be involved in anything unpleasant and certainly didn't want to be responsible for anybody becoming unemployed.

"It's his idea. He doesn't like it down here and wants to go home and anyway, we're not getting on together."

"OK, if that's what everybody wants, we can be there tomorrow," I assured him.

20. The Hatteras

We locked up our apartment and left to join Keith the next day. The Skipper and his wife had a lot of personal belongings to take back with them so we unloaded our bags from our Renault 8 and sold it to them. They left the same day and as soon as they'd disappeared from sight we started to tidy up. I went into the filthy engine room and thoroughly cleaned everywhere, then took the ten-gallon drums of engine oil from the aft deck and stowed them in the engine room. Marjie cleaned everything everywhere below decks, especially the greasy galley. Keith and Anne returned to the U.K. after a couple of days and left us free to continue getting the boat in order and I employed a day worker to help us. We washed the layers of salt off the boat, scrubbed the decks and cleaned the whole boat topside. We used the tender to clean and polish the hull. We varnished the woodwork and oiled the decks with teak oil. It was two weeks of hard work and we felt pleased with what we'd achieved. When everything was ship-shape, Keith and Anne came back to Antibes, we'd stocked up with food and bought a large bouquet of flowers and a vase to set them in on the aft deck table. They were astonished at the transformation. Keith was so impressed, he called the co-owner and insisted he come to Antibes to see how things should be.

Nothing lasts

The remainder of the season went well. We had some good cruising, at times with Keith and Anne, other times with his co-owner and sometimes with their friends or business acquaintances that they'd loaned the boat to. They were all good company, easy to please and we laughed so much when we were all together, it felt as if we were on a permanent holiday. At the end of the season, they decided to sell the boat and Keith had devised an extremely generous commission arrangement for Marjie and me. The sooner we sold the boat and the higher the sale price, the more we would be given and it decreased as time went on or if the sale price dropped but either way it was a good deal for us. I informed the agencies that the boat was on the market and in an effort to avoid having to pay them their commission, I placed a 'For Sale' sign on the stern, hoping to conclude a sale myself.

By the time we'd finished painting the engine room and cleaning, polishing and making everything look as good as new, the yacht looked fantastic. She was 58 ft long with a 16 ft beam. The enclosed wheelhouse had every navigational aid, radar, ship-to-shore radiotelephone, VHF set, echo sounder etc. Steps led down to a spacious, luxurious saloon. Aft of the saloon, down further steps, were two double cabins with a shared toilet and shower room, then further on a stateroom with its own toilet and shower. Forward of the saloon, there was a full-width galley which had a dishwasher, an ice maker, a large fridge-freezer, an electric cooker and oven, a microwave oven and a small washing machine. Our cabin with toilet and shower room was forward of the galley. In the engine room were twin V8 Detroit Diesel engines, each 450hp, giving a cruising speed of 14 knots and there was an 18-kilowatt generator. We had inlets enabling us to connect directly to the shore water and electricity supplies. There was central heating and airconditioning throughout. We had a large flybridge with an electric davit to hoist the tender and stow it at the aft end. The aft deck had sliding windows along half the length. We were ready and waiting to make a sale but could never have envisioned the shock and devastation of what happened next

Death and destruction

On 16th October, at around 14h00, we were sitting on the aft deck relaxing after lunch when suddenly the yacht rose up above the quay, straining the mooring ropes to breaking point. Alarmed, we ran to the stern to throw fenders over to prevent the transom smashing into the quay wall. All the other boats also rose up; some of them collided with each other, and others crashed into the quay. Yacht crews rushed around as they tried to prevent their yachts from suffering damage. Then we plunged down lower than we were originally and again we rose up higher than the quay before finally settling back down to where we were supposed to be. Some sailboats with counter sterns sustained damage when they crashed back down again with the sterns crashing on the quay, where they remained. It was mayhem, nobody could understand what had happened. We thought there must have been an earthquake that had created the tidal wave.

At the time, work was being carried out to claim land from the sea to extend Nice airport and build a seawall to protect a future commercial harbour at the end of the airport's runway. It was supposedly the largest public construction site in Europe. A convoy of lorries transported thousands of tons of ballast each day to be poured into the sea. Nice airport is situated at the delta of the River Var and the continental shelf on which the construction was taking place is narrow, steep and consists principally of clay. Torrential rain had been falling for 15 days so the River Var was swollen and it is thought that the vast volume of water washed away part of the foundations, first of the airport extension and then the seawall. The colossal structure collapsed in seconds, sending 40 million tons of ballast crashing into the sea taking 11 construction workers with it. Two of them clung onto debris and stayed afloat until they were rescued two hours later, six perished, their bodies later recovered and the other three were never found. The resulting tsunami was two and a half to three metres high and travelled at a speed of 546 kilometres an hour. It reached as far as the Ile du Levant, 91 kilometres away in less than ten minutes. In the other direction, it was felt as far away as Menton. The worst-hit area was La Salis, a mere 1.5 km from where we were in Antibes harbour, where the height of the tsunami reached three and a half metres and an 80-year-old man was killed. The killer wave surged inland for 150 metres causing death, widespread damage and chaos. The intensity of the tsunami was such that the surging undercurrent stretched and cut two underwater communication cables between France and Corsica. The cables lay at a depth of more than 2,000 metres and were 80 and 110 kilometres from the coast. Our berth was at the inner section of the marina so we were reasonably protected and escaped unharmed but many yachts moored in the outer section of the port were left badly damaged.

The good guys

Having read our books on self-sufficiency, we had a yearning to live off the land ourselves and wanted to buy enough land to be able to grow our own fruit and veg. Since changing our diet and way of life, minor ailments had disappeared and a miraculous change had taken place for Marjie. She'd suffered terribly from rhinitis - at least that is what it had been diagnosed as - for three years and had had two operations on her nose, which only made the problem worse. So like me, she avoided the orthodox medical approach as much as possible. The so-called rhinitis cleared up completely on our new regimen and she was also able to throw away glasses that she'd needed for close work. It was indisputable to us that diet has a major impact on health.

We visited local estate agents and told them that we were looking for a ruin on a sufficient amount of land to achieve our goal of self-sufficiency. We called past the agents every week to see if they'd found anything for us. The answer was always no, until one day an agent that we knew and had visited several times, presented us with a wad of details of some properties he had. We waded through them, finding nothing that was applicable.

"Well I do have this one, but I don't suppose it's what you're looking for," he said. It had been for sale for a long time and nobody had shown any interest so he'd forgotten all about it. The pretty stone ruin on 3 acres of land was exactly what we wanted and had been there all the time! We signed the 'compromis' and put the apartment up for sale.

We bought a Renault 4 van, which was Renault's answer to the ever popular 1948 Citroën 2cv. A number of features of the 2cv were incorporated into the R4 such as soft springs to absorb bumps on poorly maintained roads. The Renault 4 cars and vans were hugely successful. They were of a very basic design with sliding windows and were popular among all walks of life. From when they were first introduced in 1961 until 1994, over eight million were produced. The amazing little van served us well for 13 years and was indispensable when we had our self-sufficient smallholding later on. It gave us the freedom to transport furniture and other cumbersome items such as goats and bales of straw and allowed us to spend weekends in the apartment and occasional weekdays skiing in the Maritime Alps. We were very happy and even happier when in November, a gentleman and his wife hailed us from the quay and told us they would like to look at the boat with a view to buying it. After he'd completed his inspection he made an offer, which I refused because I didn't want to have a reduced commission. We haggled a little more until we arrived at a price that we both agreed was acceptable. He asked if we would stay on with him as permanent crew, we agreed on a salary, shook hands on the deal and then he invited us to join him and his wife for lunch in a restaurant. He left to make contact with Keith and confirm the deal. When everything was concluded, Keith sent a cheque to our bank and he didn't bother to come to Antibes to remove any items which meant that we profited from several cases of whisky, cases of wine and anything else that he said he didn't want.

The new owner was very easy going and we became more like friends than employer/employee. He spent a lot of money fitting the Hatteras out to his own specification. Expensive new aft deck furniture, plastic screens around the aft deck that could be rolled up in good weather and pulled down and zipped up in inclement weather. He bought a small tender that could be used with either an outboard motor or sail so I was able to teach him how to sail. He had a bar built on the aft deck, refurbished the interior and anything I asked for he agreed to and was generous with money for running the boat. We always ate together on the aft deck or in restaurants. He bought a car that was for our personal use as well as his own and we took him on drives to show him and his wife the inland areas of the Côte d'Azur. On one of our excursions inland, we took him to where our apartment was and he was so dazzled by the lovely, picturesque village and the situation of our home that he immediately wanted to buy it, but since we were employer/employee, he considered maybe it would be inappropriate. We sold it not long afterwards however for the full asking price. Shortly after that, the tenants left our apartment in

Netley Abbey and the agent informed us that some of the furniture needed replacing. We didn't want to be bothered with it so instructed him to sell the apartment and everything that was in it, which he did.

We didn't go on any long cruises with the Hatteras because the owner's wife preferred to stay close to the coast. She was happy to visit local ports and neither of them was keen to leave harbour if there was any possibility of foul weather. He negotiated to buy his own mooring to avoid paying rent to somebody else. The prices were extortionate considering that the berths were only on a 24-year lease. The deal was that he would have to pay cash to get a good price and the cash would be sent to me when he returned to the U.K., which placed a huge responsibility on me. I was concerned about carrying around such an enormous amount of money. To give an idea, the price of the same berth today would be around £85,000. When the money arrived, an appointment was made with the bank manager and together we sat and counted out the cash. I then stuffed it into a plastic supermarket bag and carried it through the streets of Antibes to the port, where I gladly handed it over to the middle man who had negotiated the deal with our boss. The season went well until 19th June when we were hit with another shock.

More heartache

Marjie's sister, Jill, contacted us to say that their mother had died. She'd been suffering from rheumatoid arthritis for many years and the prolonged high doses of cortisone that she'd been prescribed had taken its toll. The end result was a massive stomach haemorrhage. We contacted the owner of the boat to tell him that we would be leaving for the U.K. to attend the funeral and set off to be with Marjie's dad who was devastated. Before the service and burial, we took him to the funeral parlour so that he could have one final look at the woman he'd spent the best part of his life with. The door was open at the entrance to the room where she lay. The coffin lid was standing on end with her name visible on a plaque. It was more than he could bear. He collapsed and as he slumped forward I grabbed hold of him and held him upright until he'd recovered enough to slowly make his way to say his farewell to his departed wife. After the funeral, he travelled to Barnham with

Marjie's sister to spend time with her and her family. Marjie and I returned to Antibes and Marjie began researching extensively into the causes of arthritis, the effects of it and how to cure it using natural methods. Having watched her mother slowly deteriorate over the years, she had become so horrified by the disastrous side effects of the large doses of cortisone that she was determined to find a more efficient treatment. We had convincing, first-hand knowledge of the benefits to be had from a correct diet. It was obvious to us that if there is a chemical imbalance in the body, which is what a lot of dis-ease is, then nutrition must play a major role. Every single part of the body is nourished by the bloodstream and the blood transports to the cells the results of what we eat and drink. She began with books by Adelle Davis, bought on the same trip to England; "Let's get well" and "Let's eat right to get fit." We don't necessarily agree now with everything that she wrote but it was a start. Each time Marjie bought new books, we tried the diets ourselves. She now has many books and is still researching nutrition 40 years later.

Bonuses

Keith came to see us in July and told us he wanted to buy a property in the South of France so we accompanied him on his search, advising him, translating for him and helping him in every other way until he decided to buy a recently built, two-bedroom apartment in Marina Baie des Anges, in the commune of Villeneuve Loubet. It is a complex of four pyramid-shaped buildings, representing white waves that form a semi-circle surrounding a harbour. The construction, comprising 15,000 homes and a shopping centre, began in 1968 and was completed 25 years later. The harbour can accommodate 530 yachts from 6 - 35 metres in length. Keith fell in love with it. He told us he intended to buy a small motor yacht that he could drive himself and liked the idea of being able to sit on his balcony and look down at his yacht lying in its berth. After he'd bought the apartment, Marjie and I went with him to buy everything that was needed to furnish it and then he bought a Ford Fiesta that he could leave in his garage whilst he was in the U.K.. When it was finished he flew his wife down and she was so overwhelmed with what we'd accomplished, she cried.

In the meantime, the Hatteras was put up for sale once more. The owner's wife wasn't keen on going to sea and was especially nervous each time they came to the South of France. Our boss was the only one-eyed pilot in the U.K. at the time and flew his own small private plane. That could have been the main reason that tranquilisers featured heavily for her throughout the flight. When the season came to an end, the owner, who had recently had a house built in Sarasota, Florida, told us that he was going to send us on holiday there for two weeks to show his appreciation for all that we'd done for him and his wife and he booked our return flights from Heathrow with Delta Airlines for 13th November.

Marjie's dad was coping as well as could be expected, living on his own after 41 years of marriage. He'd always had an urge to travel but had never had the opportunity to do so and we paid for him to come and stay with us on the yacht before we went to Florida. His kindly neighbour, Colin, drove him to the airport and stayed with him until boarding time. Colin was always there for him and called by each day to make sure that he was OK. Marjie's dad had never flown before and was awestruck. On the plane, not having been abroad before, he stood in the aisle confused. The air stewardess came up to him and told him to sit down.

"I don't understand, I only speak English," he said

"I'm speaking to you in English, I am English," she replied.

We met him when he arrived and drove him to the yacht. He was overwhelmed. He stood on the deck on a bright, sunny day looking up at the planes in disbelief as they flew overhead on the flights to and from Nice airport. One day we took him back to the airport so that he could see the planes landing and taking off.

He'd never had a shower fitted in his house so that was a new experience for him. It hadn't occurred to us that anybody would not know what to do. He confided to us afterwards that when he saw the water gushing down, he put his peaked cap on before stepping under it! We also took him to Italy for the day to visit the Friday market at Ventimiglia and have lunch. He was amazed. The huge and popular market stretches along the palm-fringed seafront. It was a lovely, satisfying feeling to see him enjoying himself so much and learning new things such as having a genuine plate of spaghetti instead of that which came in tins, which was common in those days in the U.K.. When it was placed in front of him, he had no idea how to tackle it and we had to demonstrate how to eat it.

Nowadays, of course, things are different. Those were the days when we didn't have to worry about drinking and driving so it was normal to have at least one bottle of wine with a meal so we ordered a litre. He wasn't used to drinking wine and got a little bit carried away, guzzling more of it than he maybe should have. Later, after the meal, when we were walking around the market, he started to sway.

"This sun is strong, it's making me feel dizzy," he said. We had a sneaking suspicion that the wine might have had more to do with it than the sun!

He stayed with us for two weeks. We took him to all the tourist spots, St Tropez, Monte Carlo, Cannes, Nice etc. and we took him to see the ruin that we'd bought. He was the sort of person who had never taken a risk in his life, always working hard, being precise and careful and tending his allotment in what little spare time he had and was aghast when he saw what we'd bought.

21. It'll be nice when it's done!

There were just about four stone walls, parts of which had collapsed into the single 30-square-metre room, half a roof, which was about to collapse, no windows and a dilapidated door that was jammed shut. It had been abandoned for so long that the three acres of land were completely overgrown. He didn't say anything, just stared in unmitigated disbelief and it was obvious from his expression that he thought we were completely insane. He must have had genuine concerns about me and what on earth Marjie was doing associating with a lunatic but didn't say anything, he didn't need to, his face clearly registered the alarm he felt. Shortly before we were due to fly to Florida, we drove back to the U.K. in the boss's car with Marjie's dad in the back, which added to his pleasure. Not only had he flown for the first time, he'd stayed aboard a luxury motor yacht on the French Riviera, visited Italy where he ate spaghetti and got tipsy, splashed around in a shower with his cap on, travelled the length of France in a car and to top it all, crossed the channel on a ferry. He wasn't the most expressive of men but it was obvious that it had been an unforgettable adventure for him and it had given us an enormous amount of pleasure to have been able to make it possible for him. We made sure that he got on the train to Nuneaton where he was met by the ever-reliable Colin.

CHAPTER 25
GOOD TIMES BAD TIMES

Honeymoon

Marjie and I drove to Gravesend to spend a couple of days with my mum. We'd agreed that after five years together we should get married before we went on the transatlantic journey. The arrangements had been made at Gravesend Registry office for the 12th November. We hadn't told anybody about our plan so nobody that we knew was present. When we were asked by the registrar where our witnesses were we had to confess that there weren't any.

"Well, I can't marry you if there are no witnesses present," he told us.

"I'll see if I can find somebody outside who would be willing to help us," I said and off I went. I first stopped a young lady.

" Excuse me, I wonder if I could ask you a favour, I'm about to get married and we have no witnesses, would you be kind enough to help us out if you have a couple of minutes to spare?" She agreed without any hesitation.

"Oh, of course, I'd be delighted," she said.

"Thank you so much," I said and took her through to the office.

" I hope you don't mind waiting whilst I find a second person," I said. She agreed, in fact, she seemed to be enjoying herself. I left her with Marjie and the patient registrar and went out to find a second willing person. I saw a young man approaching and I repeated the same request to him.

"Yes, just give me a few minutes and I'll be right back," he said and he disappeared into the distance. I waited for ten minutes. "He's not going to come back," I thought to myself. And then I saw him approaching with a lovely bouquet of flowers that he presented to Marjie when we arrived in the registry office. It was such a marvellous gesture and it's unfortunate that we didn't get the opportunity to repay him somehow but he rushed off as soon as we left the office as husband and wife. Such thoughtful acts of kindness reveal the love and compassion in a person's heart and that young man's goodness has had a lasting effect on Marjie and me. St Francis of Assisi said, *"For it is in giving that we receive"* and I have no doubt that the universal law of cause and effect will have rewarded him in abundance.

The next day, we flew to Florida where we were met by our boss and his wife. They took us to his extravagant house on the Mexican Gulf coast and spent the next couple of days showing us around. He introduced us to people he'd struck up relationships with, took us on a mini cruise in his launch that was moored close by and we dined in his favourite restaurants. He hired a car for us for the two weeks that we were there and gave us more than enough cash to spend as we wished and then they returned to the U.K.. The house was incredible. It was huge and had everything that a multimillionaire could wish for. We relaxed for a couple of days and just enjoyed being in such a fabulous place. We could walk straight from our bedroom into the pool outside. After we'd had our fill of Sarasota, we toured Florida in the car, travelling down the west coast to the Everglades and up the east coast visiting all the tourist attractions, such as the Kennedy Space Centre, Disney World etc. We stayed in motels and wined and dined with no expense spared. With plenty of money still remaining, we closed up the house and flew back to Heathrow where our generous boss met us and took us to stay in his vast country estate for a night. It was there that we arranged to terminate the relationship at the end of the year. We had already discussed it prior to our trip to Florida but we hadn't set a final date.

Karma?

Before heading home to Antibes, we set off the next day to spend some time in Barnham, West Sussex with Marjie's sister, Jill, her husband Ron and their three children, Nick, Rachel and John. If we'd known what was to happen, we never would have gone there. We made ourselves at home for the final week of our one month holiday and on the third day, Jill and Ron invited us to go to Chichester with them for a coffee. We had an enjoyable day out and when we returned to their house something didn't seem right. It didn't take long to realise we'd been burgled. Jill and Ron had lost valuable items, Marjie and I had lost our camera and all the photographs we'd taken of what was effectively our honeymoon, all of our cash had gone and I had lost an expensive briefcase containing all of the books, charts, documents, homework and case histories that I'd completed for a diploma course in astrology. The police didn't seem interested although they visited and searched for fingerprints but not much else - so Ron was eager to do the detective work himself. It was easy to ascertain the entry point because a downstairs window was broken. When the burglar entered he dropped down onto a sheet on tiptoes with his muddy boots on. He slipped, so that by the time his heel landed, the remaining footprint was almost 20 inches long. This made it longer than the largest shoe size ever recorded, which was size 36 and belonged to a certain Robert Wadlow, an American also known as the 'Alton Giant' who was 8ft 11 inches tall. Ron spent the next few days outside the house looking for a giant with excessively long feet. Regardless of their size, he suspected every person who passed and asked them where they were going. Needless to say some of them told him where he should be going and he failed to apprehend the culprit

The burglar was caught at a later date when one of the medals he'd stolen was seen for sale but as is often the case, it was no consolation to any of us since we were not compensated and the only item that was returned was the empty camera that was damaged. It was a disappointing return to the U.K.. Things didn't get any better when we returned to Antibes. In fact, they got worse.

To cheer ourselves up after the burglary and to celebrate the sale of both the French village and Netley Abbey apartments and the purchase of the ruin on three acres of land, we rented an apartment at Isola 2000 for a two-week skiing holiday. A lot of our affairs were stored with a friend who lived on the outskirts of the village and the rest we'd loaded into our Renault 4 van together with our skiing equipment. We also had a small folding table and chairs, a camping cooker, battery radio, sleeping bags and everything else we thought we might need since we'd have nowhere to stay other than in the van once we'd left the Hatteras.

Cap 3000 is a commercial centre close to Nice airport. When it opened in 1969, it was ahead of its time and was the first such commercial centre in France, inspired by American shopping malls. The two-storey building had a cinema, 50 shops and cafés and restaurants. It has since been extended three times and the car park has doubled in size to accommodate the vast number of visitors. We went there regularly along with many other expats to see English language movies each week and that's where we went one night in convoy with a few friends, each in our own cars - in our case, our van. After a few drinks in the bar, we took our seats and enjoyed the movie. When we came out we made arrangements to meet on a friend's boat for a final drink to finish off the evening. We walked with one of our friends to where we'd parked. The van wasn't where we thought we'd left it so we looked elsewhere. Still no van. We looked all around the car park and it was nowhere to be seen and then it dawned on us. Somebody had stolen it and we'd lost almost everything we had. Thankfully, the friend we were with took us back to the boat. We contacted the local gendarmerie and they weren't very helpful. We had to get a document from them for insurance purposes and each time we went there, the nasty, rude, irritable and exceedingly unpleasant gendarme that was handling our case went out of his way to let us know he didn't care in the least about the theft of the van. When I contacted him by phone, he hung up on me. Having booked our apartment in Isola 2000 and having lost our means of transport and all of our skiing equipment, things didn't look promising. As word of our predicament spread it wasn't long before an Australian couple called out to us from the quay one day and offered to take us to the ski resort in their car. We had never seen them before and we were grateful for their kind offer, which of course we accepted. It was an encounter that contributed to a complete change in our lives a few years later. With our transport to the resort arranged, we bought new skis, clothing, goggles, gloves, hats and boots.

Isola 2000 is located in the Maritime Alps next to the Mercantour National Park. We'd skied there before as well as at Auron, Valberg and Greoliéres-Les-Neiges, all of them approximately just a one and a half hours drive from Antibes. The area had been part of the Kingdom of Piedmont Sardinia until the unification of Italy in 1861 when it became part of the Province of Cuneo. Following the end of WWII, when the treaty of Paris was signed between the Allies and Italy on 19th February 1947, Italy lost its colonial empire, its borders with other countries were modified and the mostly uninhabited Alpine area around Isola 2000 was given to France. In the late 1960s, an Alpine skier, Peter Boumphrey, discovered the area on a map of the French Alps and had the idea of building a ski resort close to the small village of Isola, which is situated at an altitude of 875 metres and to which the land belonged. The mayor offered no objection. The land had no agricultural value and since the inhabitants of the village were leaving for the cities, he saw it as an opportunity for development. Access to the resort area was via a narrow dirt road that suffered from constant avalanches in the winter and rockfalls in the summer so the construction of an alternative route was considered but the Mayor insisted that access passed through his village. Improvements were made to the existing track but it still presented difficulties and we've suffered a few minor mishaps on our various trips there. The resort opened in December 1971 with accommodation for 6,000 people and much additional development has taken place since then. At 2,000 metres, it is one of the highest resorts in the Alps. It has 120 kilometres of pistes and a microclimate that ensures plenty of snow and plenty of sunshine.

We had a wonderful holiday. The skiing there was superb with a lot of snow having fallen, making the resort approach road impassable for a few days after we got there. The mornings were cold and icy with the snow frozen until the sun came out so sometimes we took the chair lift instead of the téléski to make the ascent easier and more comfortable. The chairlifts are on a non-stop continuous circuit so when they reach the top you have to push yourself off and ski away quickly as the chair spins around and heads back down. With all the extra snow it meant that we had to be quick off the mark at the top to ski clear of the chair before it spun around and clobbered us. Marjie, whose history with téléskis and chairlifts up to that point hadn't exactly been bathed in glory, found this out the hard way. She hesitated a bit too long after stepping off and the chair walloped her on the back of the head with a mighty crack and sent her flying. It took her a while to recover from the shock and when I inspected the place she was rubbing I saw that she was cut. This warranted a bit of extra attention, which was duly administered, and then we skied off down the slope. Once at the bottom we got in the queue to repeat the experience.

This time when we got to the top, Marjie was understandably a bit apprehensive, and missed the pivotal moment of exit – the few seconds where you have to go for it. She didn't go for it and the next thing I saw was the view of her still sitting in the chair disappearing back down the slope. After this hard won experience she thought she'd got the hang of it and stayed on the seat for the trip back up. Now it was the ascent that caused the problem, as half way up she dropped her sticks over the side and looked down to see them resting comfortably on the snow below, surrounded by rocks and bushes. It was left to me to ski down the hard way to retrieve them without my sticks as I gallantly gave mine to her. So you could say the holiday had its ups and downs as far as Marjie was concerned, although it was left to me to have a real accident a few days later. This resulted in me receiving a lot of fuss and attention for several days, so wasn't all bad. It happened three days before we were due to leave.

The sky was crystal clear, brilliant blue, not a cloud to be seen and the winter sun was hot in the thin mountain air. Marjie went off to tackle one of the eleven red runs and I grabbed the téléski to take me to the top of one of the three black runs. For those who are unfamiliar with skiing terms, black runs are for advanced skiers, red runs are for intermediate skiers, blue runs are for beginners and green runs, or nursery slopes are for learners. I grabbed hold of the passing téléski, was yanked off the ground by the sudden speed of it, landed back down again with my skis pointed uphill and was dragged to the top of the slope. There were more than two metres of snow after the heavy snowfall and the view from the top of the slope was breath-taking as I gazed across the snow-covered mountain peaks and way into the distance. I felt exhilarated and tingled with excitement. I looked down the slope eager to set off, pointed my skis downhill, pushed off with my sticks and sped away.

The swishing sound as I traversed through the snow, navigating my way around the moguls at breakneck speed was music to my ears and then it happened. I took off, somersaulted through the air, landed with a mighty bump and started to roll down the slope. The binding on my left ski released as it was designed to do in such circumstances. The ski broke free and still attached to my leg by its strap, it spun around and the sharp metal cutting edge sliced into my shin. I lay down in the snow to recover. My leg was hurting and I had no other choice than to get up, refasten my ski and make my way down the piste to the resort as quickly as possible. At the bottom I found Marjie and she helped me limp my way to the doctor.

What happened next was not very pleasant. The time it took me to painfully ski down the piste had allowed my bloodstained ski pants to stick to the gaping wound. Removing them ripped the flapping piece of triangular shaped flesh further away from my shin, which made the wound worse (and made my eyes water!). After injections, the loose flesh was sewn back in position and I was sent on my way with a packet of painkillers but it didn't end there. That evening in the restaurant, my leg pounded and the pain was intense. When we removed my trousers and the dressing back in the apartment, the wound was foaming. I had an uncomfortable night and the next day we returned to the doctor. He had to remove the stitches, pull the flap of flesh away again, clean out the foaming mess and sew it back together once more. I spent the last few days limping around in pain but it gave me an opportunity to get to know the Australian couple better. He had a coin-operated pool table business. The tables were placed in bars and clubs along the Côte d'Azur and he made quite a good living from it with very little work involved. On the final day of the holiday, he and his wife drove us back to the yacht and we remained friends until he left the South of France, when he played an important role in our lives.

A friend in need

When the time came for us to leave the Hatteras, we had nowhere to go and once again Keith came to the rescue. He was grateful for all that we'd done for him and offered us the use of both his apartment in Marina Baie des Anges plus his car and he volunteered to pay all the expenses. It was a wonderful gesture, very much appreciated and demonstrated what a true friend he was. We moved into his lavish apartment and the very least we could do was to offer to keep his small motor yacht in good condition. Keith came to stay a couple of times and as always when we were with him, we had a hilarious time. He took us to restaurants and we had day trips on his boat. We met new people in the Marina Baie des Anges and made new friends. Most yacht owners are always ready to sell their craft if the price was attractive enough and Keith was no exception so he put his in the hands of an agent at an inflated price just in case a buyer happened to be looking for such a vessel - and that was how we met Brian and Eileen. They contacted us to arrange a viewing of Keith's boat on behalf of somebody they knew. Brian had been Captain of a motor yacht himself and his wife Eileen had been his crew/cook. They were in a similar situation to ourselves; looking for a new command because the yacht they had been employed on had been sold, so we had much to talk about. Their contact didn't buy Keith's boat but we saw a great deal of them after that. We became close friends, so close in fact, that nowadays we consider them as family members.

We had a good time whilst in Keith's apartment. We made occasional trips to Italy and on one of them bought an expensive set of three leather suitcases to store our clothes and personal items that we'd taken off the Hatteras. We went away for a day skiing from time to time and had meals in restaurants with Brian and Eileen. Our stolen van was recovered empty and very badly damaged. The insurance company paid to have it repaired and when it was ready, because we had use of Keith's car, we drove it to a friend's house where we left it until we next needed it.

What about le Milieu?

Yachting could be an unstable profession. During the five years that Marjie and I had been working on yachts together, the boats had been sold four times. We had a burning desire to create our self-sufficient, organic smallholding so we discussed how we would be able to achieve it. The cruising season in the Mediterranean was short, the yachts being used on average only six to eight weeks each year and we were paid generously throughout the whole year. How else could we make the same amount of money by doing very little work which compared with crewing yachts professionally? I believe that opportunities are presented to us constantly throughout our lives and we are asked to make a choice. We cannot avoid making choices, some entail risks but with faith and courage, we have the possibility to change and improve our lives. At the time that we were pondering on the options available to us, along came our Australian friend and told us he wanted to sell his pool table business. We discussed the practicalities of Marjie and me taking over from him. We had the cash from the sale of our apartment in Netley Abbey, we were unemployed and we almost had a home. It sounded as if it could be a good idea. The pool tables were sited in bars and clubs along the Côte d'Azur, from Menton on the Italian border to St Tropez and inland and he also had a pool room in Antibes. Theoretically, once they were sited there was very little to do except collect the money from time to time. That part of it sounded good! We were aware of the existence of organised crime (Le Milieu) along the Côte d'Azur and of their penchant for the slot machine business and the easy pickings to be had so we had some concerns but it was time to try something new and we agreed to buy his business anyway. Our concerns were later justified when a bomb was planted in a bar in Nice and exploded causing a huge amount of damage and fatalities and the pool table that survived the blast had to be removed hastily. On another occasion, a bar owner in Antibes, where we had two money-making pool tables, was gunned down in his car one evening but that is all too much to include in this book.

A couple of weeks after we'd agreed to buy the business Keith called and asked if we would be interested in taking command of a recently built 60ft schooner that one of his friends had bought and wanted it sailed from the U.K. to Antibes. We hesitated for half a second. Of course, we would - it was a dream come true! We hadn't cruised much for the past three years and the thought of sailing again set our hearts racing. There was no need for an interview, Keith had recommended us and that was sufficient for his friend. We postponed buying the pool tables until the end of the season, which was no hardship for the Australian because his income soared in the summer season when he sited the tables in campsites. When the time came for us to vacate Keith's place permanently, we packed our suitcases with as much of our belongings as we could and put them in storage in Keith's underground store. The next day we took the remainder of our belongings down to the store. It was

243

empty! Everything that was in there had been stolen. It turned out that the very people who were employed to maintain security in the complex and prevent burglaries were the ones that were responsible. They'd been helping themselves from all of the underground stores. Nothing was ever returned.

CHAPTER 26
WE MEET AGAIN

On the move

Our flights from Nice to Heathrow were booked and paid for by our new boss for mid-April 1981. It was a typical sunny Mediterranean day when we left and we were looking forward to another sailing adventure. I watched Marjie board the plane before me and thought how lucky I was to have her with me. I knew that at any moment, wherever, whenever, whatever we were involved in, if I put forward a suggestion that we move to another country or change our lifestyle to do something completely different, she'd consider it and probably end up being as enthusiastic about it as myself. That was just as well because I tend to do things on the spur of the moment and like to try something new every six or seven years. I was a risk-taker, confident that everything would work out well and not many women would have been comfortable with that. Marjie was exceptional. She was indeed my soul mate.

We took our seats and relaxed until we landed at Heathrow in the pouring rain. Our boss had a car waiting for us and we were driven to a large, beautifully equipped house that he owned and kept especially for the use of his guests. After we'd settled in, we went to find a restaurant and had a good meal. The next day we met him. He was a small man with a kind, smiling face, clean-shaven, stocky and wearing a smart silver/grey suit. Grey seems to be the standard dress for British businessmen and the darker the better, which is such a contrast to the colourful, tanned, continental businessmen.

His suit colour was a pretty good match to his hair colour. He gave us a tour of his factory that was close by and over lunch told us about himself and of his plans for the schooner. He wanted us to set sail in June and in the meantime, we'd be living aboard a Grandbanks 49 motor yacht that he also owned and which was moored on the River Hamble. It sounded good. We stayed one more night in the house and the following day were driven by one of his employees to Port Hamble and given a considerable amount of cash for expenses. It was still raining. We got the keys from the harbour office and installed ourselves in our comfortable new home.

We had several weeks before we were due to set sail for the Mediterranean but there was plenty to do before then. We had to sail the Grandbanks to Lymington and then go to Poole in Dorset, where the schooner was moored and sail her from there to Lymington. At Lymington, she was to be lifted out of the water for general maintenance and antifouling before we fitted her out for the sea passage but in the meantime, we enjoyed being in Hamble once more and meeting up with old friends. We needed crew to help us sail the schooner to Antibes and I could think of nobody more capable and more enjoyable to be with than my previous crewman on my delivery trips, our friend Ian and his lovely, vivacious, attractive wife Pat. When I asked them if they would be available and willing to join us, they agreed and were as delighted and excited to accompany us as we were to have them with us. I knew that whatever the outcome, it would not be a dull trip with them aboard.

When the time came for us to take the Grandbanks from Port Hamble to Lymington, the owner, his wife and a couple of guests joined us. There was a gale forecast with a possibility of the wind increasing to force 10. I didn't know how the Grandbanks would handle in those conditions as she had a high superstructure which would create a lot of windage. However, I did know the area well and wasn't too worried. Southampton Water and the Solent, the strait that separates the Isle of Wight from the mainland, were fairly protected and Lymington was only 15 nautical miles away. I started the engines and we cast off. It was a breezy trip with salt spray flying everywhere so everybody huddled inside until we entered Lymington marina. It was a relief to see somebody standing on the pontoon to show me where to go and to help us moor up. When we left the shelter of the wheelhouse to put out the fenders we felt the full force of the wind and rain on our faces and we were being blown away from the pontoon. I went back inside, took the wheel and motored slowly towards the pontoon, bow first. Marjie threw the rope and the harbour master fastened it to the mooring post. I turned the wheel to starboard and called to Marjie to allow some slack as I motored forward.

"Make fast!" I called when the rope was leading aft, then, using it as a spring, continued slowly motoring until the stern had swung around alongside the pontoon so that Marjie could throw the stern line to the harbour master and make it fast. She then hurried to the bow to throw out another rope as a bow line. When we were securely moored, we all sat and had a picnic lunch together, with the wind still howling and the rigging still rattling outside. Not the best of days out for everybody! The owner and his entourage were probably glad to return to London.

Marjie and I settled in to enjoy a few days in the lovely Georgian market town that lies on the west bank of the Lymington River in the New Forest National Park. It's always been a pleasure for me to visit Lymington, with its narrow streets lined with colourful period cottages and the cobbled hill leading down to the Town Quay. The weekly market dates back to the 13th century and there has been a connection with sailing since the Middle Ages. The town made its money from salt production, shipbuilding and smuggling with all three reaching their peak in the 18th century. It was also famous for its sailmaking up until the 19th century. We wasted no time exploring the town and restaurants and had an enjoyable few days before we took a taxi to the coastal town and seaport of Poole that is set in a large natural harbour. We located the schooner and set off for Lymington on a drizzly, windless, dull day. I arranged with the boatyard to haul the boat out of the water so that the necessary work could be carried out.

The Pirates' choice

I'd never sailed a schooner before and was looking forward to making the most of the opportunity. When I first began sailing in 1966, it was on a sloop. A sloop has a single mast with a boom to take the mainsail and a headsail attached to the forestay. The larger headsails are called genoas, the smaller ones jibs and the yacht would usually have a choice of different sizes of each. Sloops were around in the 17th century but became popular in the 20th century when sailing emerged as a recreational pursuit. They are the most cost-effective because they have a small sail area and less standing rigging, (shrouds and stays) so require less crew. They are good at sailing into the wind because of the tight sheeting angle but when they exceed a certain length the large sails become difficult to handle so two masts, called a split rig, is more effective.

My next sailing adventure had been on a cutter going from England to the Mediterranean and back again. Cutters are a popular choice for long-distance cruising. They still have a single mast with the mainsail but they have two headsails, a yankee or jib, which is the foremost sail and behind it a staysail. Traditionally, the yankee or jib would be attached to a bowsprit but these are less common on modern vessels. The combination of headsails on a cutter makes it easier to balance the yacht but they are less effective at tacking, (tacking is when the bow of a yacht is turned through the wind from one side to the other.)

The most popular rig for larger sailing vessels and motorsailers is the ketch. My first experience sailing a ketch was in 1970, sailing in the Western Mediterranean. A ketch is a split rig yacht with two masts, the mainmast and a smaller boomed mast to the stern called the mizzen. They carry a mainsail, a headsail and a mizzen sail attached to the mizzen mast, offering a variety of sail configurations to balance the yacht and allow a large sail area to be more manageable. Marjie and I were able to sail the Jongert under full sail without help and in a strong wind we'd maybe hoist just the mainsail and headsail or sometimes it was easier to sail with just the mizzen sail and headsail. I also found it useful to hoist the mizzen sail to keep the boat steady when we were at anchor. Ketches are good on a downwind run. Another twin-masted rig less popular than the ketch is the yawl, which has a smaller mizzen mast set behind the rudder post with the sail set over the stern. I've sailed many sloops and ketches but never a yawl, so cannot comment further on the benefits, if any.

And now for the romantic schooner. They first evolved in the 17th century and became the preferred vessel for pirates, slave traders and privateers in the 18th and 19th centuries because of their speed and versatility as opposed to the large, multi-decked galleons. A schooner is another split rig vessel like the ketch and the yawl but with an opposite mast arrangement that has the stern mast larger than the foremast. This allows for a large sail area and makes a good arrangement for running downwind. Traditionally, a schooner has two masts but three-masted schooners were introduced around 1800 and by the late 19th century, they were being built with as many as six masts. Schooners declined in popularity with the increased demand for the easier to handle sloops, yawls and ketches.

Our schooner, an Ocean 60, was built at Southern Ocean Shipyard in Poole. She had two boomed masts, was all fibreglass with a flush deck, deep cockpit, flat stern and a raked bow with a small bowsprit platform. She had a deep fin keel with an eight-foot draft and a spade rudder, (a spade rudder is self-standing with no skeg to protect it) She was a racer/cruiser and I was looking forward very much to setting sail in her. Two hatches on the foredeck gave access to the sail locker forward and the crew cabin aft of it. The cockpit was large with long benches either side of the steering pedestal and there was a hatch on the aft deck giving access to a storage area, called the lazarette. Below decks, the owner's stateroom was the foremost cabin, then there were two two-berth cabins on either side of the companionway which led to steps up into the spacious saloon. There was a settee either side of the central table, a good-sized navigation area on the starboard side and a well-equipped galley to port. The saloon deck was raised with doghouse windows providing good headroom and plenty of light. She was powered by a 6-cylinder Ford Sabre diesel engine beneath the saloon and had a Kohler generator, which had limited access because it was housed beneath the cockpit. As soon as she was put back in the water after the work, we set about stocking up for the trip. Throughout it all the weather was mediocre at best, in fact, it rarely seemed to stop raining and we couldn't wait to get back to the Mediterranean sunshine. It was to be a long wait and the weather was to get even worse once we'd set sail!

22. U.K. to the Med

CHAPTER 27
NEW PLACES

Water, water everywhere

Pat and Ian arrived a week before our expected departure date and helped us with the final arrangements. When I first met them in 1966, they were living on a 45ft motor yacht at Moody's boatyard in Swanwick. Ian had been in the merchant navy in his younger days before he started a plumbing business and was also a popular and talented Southampton musician. I knew from our sailing trips together that he was fearless, capable of tackling any problem that might arise without questioning and had complete confidence in me as I had in him. I had never sailed with Pat and didn't even know if she had ever sailed before so had no idea how she would be at sea but knew that she would be a bundle of fun. Shortly before we were due to leave we were informed by the owner that there had been a delay and that we would have to wait another week for cushions to arrive. It was disappointing but we made the most of the extra time in Lymington. When the cushions did arrive, Marjie and Pat went ashore together to buy enough provisions to last us for a couple of weeks whilst Ian and I checked everything above and below decks. I checked the engine and laid off a course to take us on the first leg of the journey, the 180 miles to the northwestern point of France and the dreaded Ushant, with the expectation and hope to arrive at the right state of tide to take us through the challenging Channel du Four. I estimated it would take us around 24 hours and I hoped the weather would be kind to us when we got there. The sky was overcast with a light drizzle but we were excited despite the dull, damp weather that hardly ever seemed to improve. The forecast wasn't as good as I'd hoped for but at least no gales were expected. With everything stowed in position, fuel tank and water tank filled to capacity and enough food and drink to last us, I started the Ford Sabre engine. It was a reassuring sound. The mooring ropes were hauled aboard and stowed, then the fenders were brought in and tied in position. I motored out of the harbour into the Solent. We were off!

I kept the engine running until we had cleared the Needles, a famous, much-photographed tourist attraction that lies at the southwestern extremity of the Isle of Wight. It is a row of three chalk stacks rising 30 metres out of the sea. There used to be a fourth, taller needle-shaped rock known as Lot's wife, which collapsed into the sea during a violent storm in 1764, leaving a noticeable gap. They are part of a chalk belt running through the centre of the Isle of Wight from Culver Cliff in the east, continuing undersea to the Isle of Purbeck in Dorset and forming Ballard Cliff near Swanage. The chalk ridge was connected to the Old Harry Rocks lying east of Studland until it was breached around 5000 BC, contributing to the formation of the Isle of Wight.

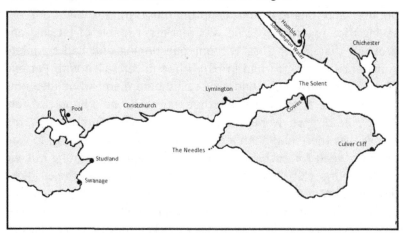

23. The Solent and the Isle of Wight

After exiting the Needles Channel, we felt the effects of a good breeze. I headed into it, slowed the engine and handed the wheel to Pat so that she could keep us steady into the wind whilst Marjie, Ian and I hoisted the sails. With all sails set, I took the wheel once more and swung it around to put us onto the compass heading for our destination. I cut the engine and we took off at a respectable rate of knots. The beautiful schooner sliced her way through the waves as we sat in the cockpit relishing the smell of the sea, the biting effect of the wind on our faces and the sound of the water swishing past the hull. Seagulls mewed overhead as we chatted and talked about what was to come, savouring the moment. The whole experience was exhilarating, as it often was at the beginning of a sea passage. We arranged four-hour watches, with Marjie and I being on watch together for four hours and then Pat and Ian taking over.

The schooner sailed like a dream and seemed to be enjoying it too, throwing up spray into our faces as she leapt over the waves, with masts creaking and sails humming. As we progressed and the day started to turn in to night, the wind decreased and the drizzle turned to rain. We switched on the navigation lights, lowered the sails and continued on our way using the engine. I switched on the radar and Marjie and I went to our cabin, leaving Pat and Ian to do their four-hour watch. I was grateful that I had Ian aboard, a reliable, conscientious, calm, knowledgeable crewman with a wonderful sense of humour. Nothing seemed to bother him and I was pleased to discover that Pat was equally fearless and eager to play her role as a competent deckhand. The darker it became, the heavier the rain fell. There were navigation lights all around us from a multitude of ships passing in both directions and Pat became alarmed when blips appeared and disappeared on the radar screen. Ian was in the cockpit steering. She called him to check the screen whilst she took the helm and held the course. He saw the same thing and called me to the cockpit.

When I got there bleary-eyed, I was soon brought to full awareness by the rain lashing down on my face, which made it difficult to see. There were so many lights, it was confusing. I wondered for a while if Pat and Ian had inadvertently steered too close to the shore. Confused, I stared at the array of lights trying to ascertain what was happening and then I saw two red lights, one above the other, which was the signal that a vessel was not under command. I assumed that the mass of other lights were tugs scrambling around to get control of the ship and claim salvage. Meanwhile, Ian had gone down below and scrutinised the chart to try to find an explanation. He saw that we were crossing a submarine exercise area so maybe there was an exercise taking place. Either way, once we'd realised what could be happening, I went back to my bunk, leaving Pat and Ian to competently carry on.

"Tony and Marjie," Ian called. It was to be a sound that we came to dislike. It was time for us to do our watch. We roused ourselves, put on our oilskins and went to the cockpit. It was miserable, pitch dark, with very heavy rain crashing down and without the steadying effect of the sails, we rolled more in the swell. It certainly shocked us into wakefulness after coming from our warm, cosy cabin.

"Everything been OK?" I asked Ian.

"Apart from the non-stop rain, everything's fine," he replied.

"The engine seems to be running nicely," I said.

"Yes, but I'll check it on the way down anyway."

"OK, thanks," I took the helm from him. He and Pat descended the ladder to the saloon. He lifted the hatch to the engine.

"There's a lot of water in the bilge," he called up to me. I handed the wheel to Marjie and went to look. We were both surprised that there was so much water. I switched on the bilge pump and emptied the bilge. It took longer than I'd expected and there shouldn't have been any water in the bilge anyway so where had it come from? Ian and I looked around in the bilges, we checked all the seacocks, the engine cooling system, the water inlets and filters, the freshwater pump and the stern bearing, but couldn't see any leaks.

"Let's leave it for a while and see what happens," I said, "You and Pat had better get some sleep, I'll keep my eye on it."

They went to their bunks and I went to the cockpit to join Marjie and the torrential rain. I checked the bilges from time to time and each time I did so, had to start the bilge pump to empty out the water. I crawled into the bilge with a torch but still couldn't see where or how the water was coming in. Something was wrong. I decided to wait until daylight, which was only a few hours away and by then Ian and Pat would be back on watch and Ian would be able to help try to solve the problem if necessary. Marjie and I had enough to do, watching the radar screen, looking for the lights of shipping and taking turns steering the course.

"Pat and Ian," Marjie called as she tapped on the door of their cabin and shortly afterwards they appeared, ready to face the elements once more. Marjie went to the galley and brewed up some tea for the four of us and we spent some time chatting and wondering about the water we were taking in. It wasn't disastrous but it was concerning. When daylight came, I stopped the engine for a while and we wallowed around in the swell whilst Ian and I again tried unsuccessfully to locate the source of the leak.

"I'm not happy about it, I can't understand where it's coming from - and supposing it gets worse," I said, "I think we'll call into Brest and stay there until we sort it out and if we can't then at least we'll have access to the facilities of the shipyards there." I'd been adjusting the engine speed in the hope of arriving at a favourable time to catch the tide through the Channel du Four and by a major stroke of luck, we were just about on schedule but had no time to spare.

24. Brest and Ushant

There were only four and a half hours of favourable tidal conditions to navigate the narrow channel and I didn't want to miss the opportunity. The alternative to taking the Channel du Four would be to go around Ushant, which would have added many extra hours to our journey.

Brest was 14 miles away from the course we would have taken across the Bay of Biscay to Spain, but we had no specific date to be in Antibes and besides I'd never been to Brest. When we'd navigated the Channel du Four, I laid off a northeasterly course into the totally landlocked Bay of Brest, which is entered through a 40 metres deep channel, 1.8 kilometres wide. The bay has a huge surface area of 180 km² with the town and port of Brest situated on its northern shore. In 1631, Cardinal Richelieu, the French clergyman, nobleman and statesman, recognised the importance of Brest's situation as a seaport. He constructed wooden wharves and it became a French naval base, second only to Toulon. The harbour was improved and masonry wharves replaced the wooden ones a short time later during the reign of Louis XIV, known as the 'Sun King'. Between 1680 and 1688, fortifications were added by the Marquis de Vauban who was also responsible for constructing the fort in Antibes. The town continued to develop throughout the 18th century. In 1917, during WWI, thousands of American forces disembarked there on their way to the front lines and in 1918, the United States Navy established a naval airbase there from which to operate seaplanes.

During WWII, Brest was a German naval base. They kept a large fleet of U-boats and surface ships there, providing them with direct access to the Atlantic Ocean. In 1944, the allied plan for the invasion of Europe called for the capture of port facilities to ensure the delivery of the enormous amount of materiel required to supply the invading forces. The port of Brest was a major target so that American ships could bypass England and offload supplies directly to the allied troops advancing towards Germany. After the Americans landed at Utah Beach in Normandy, they took Cherbourg but before surrendering, the German garrison destroyed the port facilities and the US VIII Corps was diverted into Brittany to take Brest. They arrived on 7th August 1944, surrounded the city and later stormed it. The Battle for Brest began. The Germans were well entrenched and the garrison contained elite German paratroopers who put up a strong defence against the intense American artillery bombardment, which was reinforced by the specialised British 79th armoured division. The battles raged from house to house until the Germans surrendered on 19th September 1944, after destroying the port facilities and leaving them unusable. The city of Brest had been razed to the ground. Unlike the port of Cherbourg, Brest was never repaired in time to be of any use in the war effort. After the war, the West German government paid reparations to the homeless and destitute civilians.

Unfortunately, the bay has suffered from a combination of factors. Although we weren't aware of it at the time, the enclosed nature of the bay, with rivers leading into it, has since led to a build-up of nutrients in the water making it an ideal breeding ground for toxic phytoplanktons which have had a serious effect on shellfish farms and fisheries. Another factor to the health of the bay is toxins from antifouling paints as well as toxic debris on the bottom left over from the war. Fortunately for lovers of shellfish, health dangers are minimized by extensive testing of shellfish for the presence of toxins as well as environmental phytoplankton monitoring of affected regions - all of which adds to production costs. Brest is now a university town and research centre with several distinguished educational establishments leading research into these problems and 60% of European research on the ocean is conducted from the harbour. Although very little of the town survived the last war, I was still looking forward to seeing what it was like.

Just before we arrived, I emptied the bilges completely so that a thorough inspection could be made starting with dry bilges. We moored alongside a quay, switched off the engine and in the good British tradition, put the kettle on to brew up some tea. The rain had stopped at just about the same time that we'd entered the Channel du Four but it was still overcast, cold and miserable so we relaxed with our tea in the saloon. As soon as we'd finished our short break, Ian and I searched for the cause of the leak and Marjie and Pat tidied up, laid out our wet clothes to dry and set about cooking a meal. The boat was inspected inside from stem to stern and no sign of a leak was found. We went on deck, lifted the lazarette hatch and were surprised to see it wet inside. Ian descended into the lazarette, passed me up the contents to spread on the deck to dry and looked around to see where the water was coming from. Once again we drew a blank. Then I noticed that the two drains situated in the recess where the hatch is seated when closed, were blocked.

"I think I might have found the problem," I said to Ian. He re-emerged from the lazarette. We closed the hatch, connected a hose to a tap on the quay and sprayed the area for a while then checked the bilges. Sure enough, they needed pumping out. We didn't have a leak at all, the blocked drains had allowed the torrential rain and the seas breaking over the deck to pour into the lazarette and into the bilges. I had worked on commercial and leisure craft for 23 years and had never known such a minor thing to cause the bilges to fill with water. I wasn't impressed! We took full advantage of the stopover and explored a little of Brest, bought some crabs and that evening had a scrumptious meal and a good night's sleep ready to cast off and cross the infamous Bay of Biscay the following day - but another shock was waiting.

CHAPTER 28
GALICIA

Eviva España

We woke early to another dull, cold, miserable day, had a leisurely breakfast, cleared away and started to prepare for sea. Pat and Ian went ashore to buy fresh bread and a few other bits and pieces whilst Marjie and I occupied ourselves with the preparations. The weather forecast wasn't good but not so bad that we couldn't leave. I set the courses to take us on the two days, 380 nautical miles run to clear Cape Finistère on the northwestern point of the Iberian Peninsular, via the Raz de Sein. From there we could then turn south to run down the coasts of Spain and Portugal and on to Gibraltar, a further 715 nautical miles and another four days sailing. Marjie and I had had enough of the dull, wet days and were desperate to reach the sun.

"Once we're clear of the Bay of Biscay, we should get better weather and then Gibraltar and sunshine. Just another couple of days to go," I said.

"Thank goodness for that," she replied.

It turns out I was being a trifle optimistic.

Before calling in at Brest, I'd called the owner on the radiotelephone to let him know of my intentions so that he would know where we were. Meanwhile, Ian's father had been trying to contact us. He'd called the coast guard to find out where we were and asked them to relay a message that Pat had to call home. Worried, they went ashore again to make the call. When they returned, Pat was looking upset and we could see that all was not well. They informed us that she'd just heard from her family that her father had died. She was in a predicament. She'd committed to help us take the schooner to Antibes and didn't want to renege on her word and let us down; on the other hand, she naturally wanted to attend her father's funeral and be with her family. Getting back home from Brest may not have been easy for her either - and if she went home would Ian go with her too? It was a complex situation for all of us and Marjie and I didn't want to interfere or influence her in any way, indeed, we had no right to. The usually ebullient, irrepressible Pat looked despondent and confused and we felt so sorry for her.

"Look, Pat, it will be OK with us whatever you decide to do, we'll understand," I told her. She and Ian went to their cabin to discuss what they should do. They emerged from their cabin half an hour later.

"I've decided to stay on with you and finish the trip," she said. We were fully aware of how harrowing it must have been for her to reach that conclusion and were grateful for her loyalty to us. Without further ado, I started the engine. The tide had fallen by a considerable amount and Ian had to climb the high metal ladder attached to the quay wall to let go of our mooring lines. When he was in position I called out to Pat and Marjie to let go their respective lines. Ian removed them from the bollards and climbed back down the cold, slimy ladder to jump on board. Unfortunately, we'd already drifted away so he was left clinging halfway down the ladder, a comical sight that we couldn't help but laugh at, in spite of the sadness of the occasion. I motored around in a complete circle to go back alongside for him and he jumped on board before we drifted away again. I spun the wheel around, increased the revs and headed back out to sea once more. It was always such a wonderful sensation to leave a harbour and head into the open sea, even if it was the notorious Bay of Biscay. We stood together in the open cockpit luxuriating in the freedom of being the only vessel in the vicinity at that moment, wondering if anything else would go wrong and where we would next finish up.

Heading in a southwesterly direction, we had the dramatic Brittany coast, the most popular coast in France after the Côte d'Azur, on our port side and away to starboard for as far as we could see, nothing but grey undulating water that merged into a similar coloured sky but for once it wasn't raining! There was very

260

little wind and we had just 18 miles to go before we went through the passage of the Raz de Sein so we motored along in a moderate sea, grateful that we would be able to pass through the difficult passage without risk. When we'd cleared the Raz de Sein, we left the coast behind and set our four-hour watches. That night the wind started to pick up whilst Marjie and I were on watch. We didn't want to wake Pat and Ian to help us hoist the sails so continued motoring. The next day, as each hour passed, the wind increased a little and the sea became more agitated until by late morning it was blowing quite hard; since all four of us were awake, I turned into the wind and throttled back. I handed the wheel to Pat to keep us into the wind, Marjie stood by on the sheets and Ian and I hoisted the sails. I switched off the engine and turned the wheel to put us back on course for Cape Finisterre. For the remainder of that day, we had a bracing sail in a worsening sea. We made good time, cracking along at an average speed of almost 10 knots.

By the next morning, the sea had become unpleasantly rough and the wind was forecast to reach gale force, so I decided to seek shelter in the busy port of A Coruña, a short distance away. I started the engine and swung around into the wind. With Marjie on the helm, Pat, Ian and I dropped and furled the sails and we altered course to take us into the Golfo Artabro and A Coruña in the Spanish region of Galicia. It was a rough ride without the sails to steady us and the sky was black and threatening but we were looking forward to visiting a new port and a new country. The closer we got to the Spanish mainland, the more spirited we became and Marjie and I started to sing "Eviva España," a pasodoble type song about looking forward to a holiday in Spain. It was written and first performed in Belgium but became popular in other European countries where it was performed by various artists between 1972 and 1977. It was so popular it is now considered part of the Spanish cultural heritage but it was manifestly unpopular with Ian.

"NO, NO!" he shouted, "STOP, STOP!" whilst we were mid-chorus.

"What's the matter?" we enquired. He explained how when he was playing in a band, they would get endless requests to play the tune, so much so that in the end it started to drive him crazy and he never, ever wanted to hear it again. So we sang it even louder.

Victories and defeats

A Coruña was and probably still is, a popular, well-known port of call for yachts heading to the Mediterranean. It is generally known as Corunna by the British but over time the Galician name, A Coruña has become more widely used. The origin of the name is unknown but may have been derived from the Spanish "Corona" or the French "Couronne," both meaning crown. A is Galician for "the". The Romans colonised the area in the 2nd century BC and A Coruña, which was then called Brigantium, became an important maritime port, which prospered during the 1st and 2nd centuries and then fell into decline after the 4th century AD until, by sometime after the 7th century, it was no more than a small village. It started to recover in the Middle Ages when it was known as Faro Bregancio. In the 8th, 9th and 10th centuries it was controlled by the Moors and then by the Portuguese in the 14th century. It was retaken by the Spanish in the 15th century and became a significant textile manufacturing centre as well as a major fishing port.

In 1588, the ill-fated Spanish Armada set sail from the city's Port Ferrol to conquer England and overthrow Queen Elizabeth I and her protestant establishment. The Armada, under the command of the Duke of Medina-Sidonia, consisted of 130 ships, of which 28 were warships, the rest were armed merchant traders. The English fleet consisted of about 100 ships at the time of the battle, 40 of which were warships. They were smaller, faster, more manoeuvrable and better armed than the heavy Spanish galleons. (The Spanish preferred to rely on their infantry boarding the English ships). The English, under the command of Francis Drake, navigated upwind of the Spanish fleet and staying out of range of the artillery, harassed them without causing serious damage. The Spanish fleet anchored off Calais to await the arrival of the Duke of Parma's army for the invasion of England. The English fleet anchored upwind, (to the west) of them. At midnight, they used the tide and wind to send fireships among the Armada. The Spanish cut away their anchor ropes and scattered. At dawn, at Gravelines, the English attacked the disorganised Armada causing serious damage and destroying four ships. The Spanish retreated to the north, being pursued by the English up the east coast of England as far as the Forth of Firth. They continued sailing around the north of Scotland and down past Ireland to return to Spain. The badly damaged ships were pounded by furious North Atlantic gales and in the absence of a means of discovering longitude, no charts and unable to seek shelter because they'd severed their anchor ropes, many of them were wrecked on the Scottish and Irish coasts or foundered at sea. Only 60 of them made it back to the safety of Spanish Atlantic ports for refitting.

The following year, Queen Elizabeth I took advantage of the successful crushing of the Armada and sent warships to destroy the Spanish fleet moored at A Coruña, San Sebastian and Santander. The attacking fleet of 150 ships was under the command of Admiral Francis Drake and General John Norris. Instead of focusing on Santander where the majority of the refitting was taking place, Drake headed for the largely defenceless A Coruña that harboured just a few ships. They took the lower town inflicting many casualties, destroyed the fishing fleet in the harbour and plundered where they could.

Whilst awaiting favourable weather conditions they decided to attack the fortified upper town and thus began the legend of Maria Mayor Fernandez de Camara y Pita, commonly referred to as simply Maria Pita. On 4th May 1589, the English breached the defences that Maria Pita was manning with her army Captain husband when he was killed by a crossbow bolt. She took up his spear and killed the flag bearer of the British forces who was making his way to the highest section of the defence wall. She took up a position there herself and shouted to the militia and other defenders, "Quen teña honra, que me siga!" ("Whoever has honour, follow me.") She rallied support from the defenders and they drove back the British who suffered severe losses and returned to their ships. They left fourteen days later when the weather became favourable and they'd received the news that Spanish reinforcements were approaching. Maria Pita was the Galician equivalent of Joan of Arc, and her heroism was rewarded by Philip II, who granted her the pension of a military officer and a statue was erected in her honour.

A Coruña was also the site for the Battle of Corunna on 16th January 1809. It took place during the Peninsular War, (1808 - 1814) when the Napoleonic forces were in conflict with the British, Spanish and Portuguese forces over control of the Iberian Peninsular. In October 1808, Napoleon attempted to place his brother Joseph on the throne of Spain by force and quite naturally was met with resistance by the Spanish armies. The British troops in Portugal, under the command of Lieutenant-General Sir John Moore, (also known as Moore of Corunna), were ordered to advance to Burgos to assist the Spanish. When they reached

Salamanca, 250 km away to the southwest, he learned that the Spanish had been defeated by Napoleon, who had taken Burgos and was concentrating on attacking the British who were outnumbered two to one. Moore decided to head northwest to Corunna, a distance of 500 km, where they would be evacuated by the Royal Navy. They set out on 25th December, pursued by French forces commanded by Marshal Jean de Dieu Sault. The long, arduous march across the Galician mountains through the harsh winter conditions of extreme cold and blizzards took its toll on both armies with the British losing 3,000 men. They arrived exhausted on 11 January only to discover that the naval transport vessels hadn't arrived from Vigo due to bad weather. The ships arrived four days later by which time Sault's troops had amassed and were approaching the port.

Moore moved his army a little to the south of Corunna between the village of Elvina and the shore. Sault attacked and took Elvina but was later repulsed by the 42nd Highlanders, (Black Watch), and the 50th Foot who retook the village. Sault counterattacked, forcing them to retreat. Under the command of Moore, the two regiments charged into Elvina again. The fighting was hand to hand and the French were driven out at the point of the bayonet. At the moment of victory, Moore was hit by a cannonball, which severed his left shoulder, leaving his arm hanging by the flesh above the armpit. He remained conscious for several hours before he finally succumbed and passed away. During that night and the following morning, when the fighting had ceased, the British boarded the transport ships and set sail for England. The Spanish Garrison held the city until the ships had safely departed and then surrendered to the French. Sir John Moore was buried on the city ramparts and his granite tomb overlooks the harbour. The British suffered around 800 - 900 casualties and the French around 1,400.

Various businesses were established in A Coruña during the 19th century with the principal activity centred around maritime trade. The economy suffered through the 1930s–1950s as a result of the Spanish civil war and didn't recover until the 1960s–1970s. These days, A Coruña is one of northern Spain's major ports. It is the second-largest fishing port in Spain, has oil refining, chemical, aluminium, textile, tobacco and machinery manufacturing industries. There are schools of navigation and agriculture and an army garrison is based there.

We lay at anchor in the bay waiting for an improvement in the weather forecast. It was a miserable day, cold, grey and extremely windy and we had little inclination to inflate the dinghy to go ashore. Its size meant it was a long job and it didn't seem worth it for a short trip, especially in bad weather so we saw nothing of the town. We relaxed and took the opportunity to catch up on some sleep. By early evening, although still windy, it looked as if the gales that had been forecast were not going to manifest into anything stronger than we already had. I contemplated the prudence of weighing anchor and setting sail once more. It was approximately 650 nautical miles to our next planned port of call, Gibraltar and it would take three days to get there. I preferred not to start out in a gale but since we were well protected in the bay it was difficult to assess accurately what the weather was like out at sea. There were plenty of other yachts anchored sheltering from the gale and I could see that other Skippers were wandering the decks, looking at the sky, wondering whether or not to set off. Whilst I was considering the options, one of the other yachts weighed anchor and sailed out of the harbour. About an hour later, a second yacht followed. I still had doubts and decided to wait until the next morning. My doubts were well-founded because as night fell, both yachts returned and dropped anchor once more, having concluded that the wind and sea were too violent and dangerous.

CHAPTER 29
PORTUGAL

The contrast of the Algarve

After a good, substantial meal and a few glasses of wine, we slept well that night. In the morning, we woke very early. It was misty and the weather seemed calm enough to hoist the anchor and head for Gibraltar. We were keen to be at sea and sailing again, unaware that we were about to suffer the worst part of the entire journey. There was not a breath of wind as we motored past the Tower of Hercules, the only Roman lighthouse still in use. Built in the 2nd century by the Roman emperor Trajan, it is thought to have been modelled on the Lighthouse of Alexandria and is considered to be the oldest lighthouse in existence. We headed west to pass by the steep-cliffed islands of Sisarga Grande, then southwest towards Cape Finisterre and the further we motored along, the foggier it became. I switched on the radar and under the guidance of Ian who had his eyes glued constantly on the screen, we continued on our way, seeing nothing at all, listening for the sound of other vessels that may have been in the vicinity - but we were all alone in the cold, damp, still air. Apart from the noise of the engine thumping away, there was complete, eery silence. It can be very unsettling in dense fog, especially if other ships are blasting their foghorns and can be heard but not seen. However, we heard and saw nothing at all for hour after hour as we peered into the thick blanket of nothingness, getting colder and damper. By late morning the fog began to clear and our mood lightened enough for Marjie and me to give Ian another rendition of Eviva Espagna to ease the tension.

His reaction got us back into the giggling mode but our merriment was short-lived. As the fog cleared, the wind came. It increased gradually until it became a howling gale directly on our stern. With the sails set, we would have had an outstanding run down the Portuguese coast but with the wind directly on the stern and the waves increasing in height, there was always the danger of gybing if a wave threw us off course. I'd already suffered the consequences of a gybe brought about by trusting others and still bore the scars and unpleasant memory. As much as I trusted Ian, I didn't think it fair to place such a responsibility on him and therefore took the decision to continue running under engine power. Besides, I knew we'd have ample opportunity for sailing once we'd begun our seasonal cruising in the Mediterranean.

25. Wrapped up against the cold

The north wind that roared down parallel to the coast was icy cold and whipped the sea into a frenzy. The waves lifted our stern high before sending us whooshing onwards and downwards into the troughs with the stern spinning sideways so that we had to fight with the steering wheel to keep on course. Then we were lifted up again on the wave before the next one came crashing onto our stern plunging us onwards and downwards once more. Ian struggled so much to hold the course that others had to light his cigarettes for him. When we were on watch in the open cockpit, we were concerned enough to put on our safety harnesses and shackle ourselves onto a secure anchoring point; I was pleased that I'd decided not to hoist the sails. Keeping warm was a challenge. We put on as many clothes as we comfortably could. We wore two pullovers and oilskins over everything else to protect us from the salt spray and the bitter cold and also hats and gloves. When we were off watch, the yacht was careering around so much that Marjie and I lay on our bunks fully clothed, complete with oilskins, ready for that knock on our cabin door and those dreaded words, "Tony and Marjie." It didn't ease for the next two days. We were tired from lack of sufficient sleep, constantly straining to maintain our balance and battling with the steering wheel to keep the yacht on course. At one time, a bird came and perched on the rope that went from Marjie's safety harness to its anchoring point. It was just a couple of feet away from her. We assumed that it must have been lost and exhausted and needed to recuperate. Those two days were harsh and exceptionally cold. The nights were crystal clear and we marvelled at the sight of the millions of stars.

It was reassuring when we saw Cape St Vincent looming into view in the distance. The cape, with its almost vertical, jagged cliffs rising to a height of 75 metres at the southwestern extremity of Portugal, is a conspicuous landmark for ships heading to and from the Mediterranean. We were thrilled to see it. The storm-blasted headland has been the site of numerous naval battles and is named after the Christian martyr, Vincent of Saragossa, whose remains were brought ashore there after he'd been killed by the Roman Emporer Diocletian, who persecuted many people over their religious beliefs, especially Christians. On its summit is Europe's second most powerful lighthouse that has a range of 60 miles. Once round Cape St Vincent we headed for the promontory of Sagres, a few kilometres to the southeast. On the eastern side of the promontory lies the small harbour of Balieera, which is where I hoped we'd get some respite from the brutal pounding we'd suffered but none of us could have envisaged the surprise that awaited us.

All four of us were in the cockpit together, still dressed in all our heavy weather gear when we reached Sagres Point. I swung around on a northeasterly course to head for Balieera port and it was suddenly completely calm. There was no wind at all, the sea was flat calm, the sun blazed down from a clear blue sky and there was a small boat lying at anchor with a single person in it. He was dressed in nothing but a pair of shorts, seated serenely, holding a fishing rod. I'd heard about the exceptional climate of the Algarve but the sudden, dramatic contrast was unbelievable and we felt and must have looked ridiculously overdressed. I motored in close to the harbour entrance where we dropped anchor and switched off the engine, thankful for the tranquillity. We were very soon too hot and shed our excess clothing in haste and stripped down to shorts.

Pat and Marjie prepared a meal, whilst Ian and I tidied up then opened a bottle of wine.

26. Pat, Ian and me

We sat in the cockpit having lunch, not quite accustomed to the fact that the yacht wasn't lurching around and we weren't being drenched by rain and saltwater. We luxuriated in the serenity, the heat and the beauty of that unspoilt western part of the Algarve and afterwards, we slept for a while. *H.G.Wells said of Portugal, "Wet or fine, the air of Portugal has a natural happiness in it and the people of the country should be as happy and prosperous as any people in the world."* Well, we were certainly happy to be there, even though our stay was short-lived.

Past the rock

When we woke, I informed everybody that I wanted to set sail for Gibraltar, a further 175 nautical miles away. I hoped that we had made it through the worst of the bad weather and that it would be kinder to us for the next 24 hours, by which time I expected to be in the Mediterranean Sea. It was disappointing to leave such an idyllic setting but we were refreshed and still had 1,000 miles to go before we reached our final destination, Antibes and at an average speed of 8 knots, we were still 5 days away. I started the engine, Pat took the wheel, Ian and I prepared the sails, Marjie hoisted the anchor and we set sail for Gibraltar. The wind had eased considerably, the sea was calmer and we had a cracking sail towards the southern tip of Spain. The closer we got to our destination, the less wind there was and the following morning we had to drop and stow the sails and start the engine. Just before lunchtime the next day, we arrived at Punta di Tarifa, the southernmost point of the Iberian Peninsula. The Point lies on Isla de las Palomas, a small island to the south of the town of Tarifa, to which it is connected by a causeway.

27. Approaching Gibralter

It is where the Mediterranean Sea and the Atlantic Ocean meet at the narrowest part of the strait of Gibraltar, 7.7 nautical miles from the African coast. The town and island are named after Tarif Ibn Malik, who began the Islamic conquest of Spain in 710; it was where I decided not to stop at Gibraltar after all but to continue sailing on our journey to the south of France.

If Pat and Ian were disappointed, they didn't show it. So, at Punta di Tarifa, I headed for Gibraltar and then on to Cabo de Gata, 130 nautical miles away, a wild, desolate area where Europe's only true hot desert exists, lying east of the town of Almeria, on the southeastern corner of Spain.

CHAPTER 30
THE LAST LEG

What, no Flamenco?

From Gibraltar, the journey was uneventful. The sparkling blue sea was calm, the sun blazed down from a cloudless blue sky and it felt so good to be sailing in the Mediterranean Sea once again. When the wind blew, we hoisted the sails, switched off the engine and used the wind to propel us effortlessly through the water. The silence was greatly appreciated and it felt good to feel the power through the steering wheel as the schooner glided smoothly through the waves. When the wind lessened or stopped altogether, we started the engine and motored on our way, occasionally stopping, switching off the engine and allowing the schooner to drift whilst we plunged into the sea and swam to cool off. One time, when Marjie and I were enjoying a nice relaxing swim in the warm water, it was payback time for Eviva Espagna. Ian replicated the sound of the threatening theme from Jaws, which evoked an automatic fear response. We laughed a little too loudly, pretending that we weren't concerned as we swam nonchalantly back to the yacht. The film, about a man-eating great white shark, had been released in 1975 and the award-winning music consisted of two ominous, alternating notes played on a tuba to signal impending danger. The film created a terror of sharks for many people and managed to take the shine off our sea-bathing for a while. Shark attacks in the Mediterranean are uncommon but not unknown; in fact, the first-ever recorded shark attack took place in the Mediterranean. It was mentioned by Greek historians many years before the birth of Christ. Of the 47 species of shark in the Mediterranean, 15 are considered a threat, including the great white, although most attacks by these fearsome creatures seem to have taken place around Italy. Nevertheless, we would have preferred not to have been reminded of the gory consequences of a great white straying from his usual hunting grounds.

From Cabo de Gata, I altered course to take us east of Cartagena to Cabo de Palo, which lies at the edge of a peninsula formed by a small range of volcanic mountains. From there, we headed towards Alicante. We had sailed approximately 500 nautical miles from southern Portugal and it had been more than a week since we had last set foot on dry land in Brest.

28. At anchor at Alicante

It was time to stretch our legs. I decided to stay the night at Alicante so that we could have a relaxing evening ashore. I'd been telling Ian and Pat how much I loved Flamenco and was looking forward to having a paella in a restaurant and watching a Flamenco show. I'd managed to get them and Marjie excited at the prospect. It was a hot, sunny day with not a breath of wind when we arrived at the port of Alicante. We dropped anchor in the harbour and set about the long process of inflating the large rubber dinghy and installing the outboard motor.

We got dressed and went ashore. It felt good to stand on a stable surface and to be able to wander through the streets and stop and drink a café con latte at one of the bars. After we'd had a look around the town, we went back to the boat for lunch and had a relaxing afternoon. In the evening, we spruced ourselves up for an entertaining night ashore, clambered into the dinghy once again and set off to look for a good restaurant and a Flamenco show. Alas, it was not meant to be; all we could find were mediocre restaurants serving horrible fast-food meals. As for Flamenco, it seems those days had gone. Discos were all that was on offer. The Spanish eat very late in the evening, generally not before 21h00 so most of the restaurants weren't open. That was partly responsible for the lack of choice but I felt sad that the Spain I knew from the 1960s was no more. I had wonderful memories of sitting in local bars where the proprietors and customers sang and danced Flamenco. At that time Spain was busy building hotels and apartments to satisfy the fast increasing influx of tourists and I remember that even the workmen during their lunch breaks would down tools and sing and dance Flamenco on the side of dusty, unmade up roads. My enthusiasm for Spain dissipated rapidly and I was pleased to leave the following day. I was disappointed too for Marjie, Pat and Ian who had been looking forward to the lively evening that might have been. It seems that I would have to go to Seville now to see Flamenco.

The next day, we set sail once more, taking our time to prepare at a leisurely pace after we'd finished breakfast. I planned to spend one more night in Spain at Palamos before we crossed the Golfe de Lyon for Antibes. It was 195 miles away so we only had one night of four-hour watches and expected to arrive there late afternoon the following day. Motoring along the Costa Blanca was disappointing; it was a mass of hideous highrise buildings that scarred what would once have been a beautiful coastline. All we saw for miles were huge white blocks of concrete along the length of the coast. I didn't like it one bit and ever since have avoided going anywhere near the Costa Blanca and Benidorm. The passage was calm and relaxing; sometimes we hoisted the sails and at others motored to keep a reasonable speed and we arrived at Palamos in the late afternoon as planned. It was a delightful place and unlike Alicante and Benidorm, had remained relatively unspoilt. It is situated at the northern end of a large bay on the Costa Brava and is well known for its locally caught prawns. It was there that I discovered how difficult the schooner was to handle when going astern to the quay. In every other case up until then, we'd moored alongside.

When a propeller rotates, the wash passes over the rudder and when the rudder is turned, the wash is diverted to one side, swinging the stern in the opposite direction, which is how a boat is steered. When going astern the wash doesn't pass over the rudder and instead is directed to one side or the other depending on whether the propellor is righthanded or lefthanded, which causes the stern to swing to the opposite side. This is referred to as prop walk and so steering is more difficult when going astern. It took me a while to get used to the surprising starboard prop wash of the schooner, which spun the stern around to port when I went astern. I had to go past where I needed to be and beam on to the quay so that when I went astern, the prop wash would swing the stern around to port in line with the mooring, which mostly was between two other boats. Marjie had to get a mooring line from our port bow to the next boat to prevent the bow swinging further to starboard. That worked well in calm conditions but not so easy in a strong wind. I'd become very experienced at handling single screw fin and skeg sailboats when I was working at the yacht agency and when Marjie and I were on the Dufour 35 sloop in Antibes. It was something I did almost daily and immodestly, I considered myself a proficient boat manoeuverer but I wasn't prepared for such a dramatic prop walk on the schooner and sometimes I had a difficult time.

Allo Allo

We had a relaxing afternoon in the sun with ample time to unwind and prepare for the final part of the voyage, the 250 mile stretch to Antibes and that night we slept well in the tranquil harbour in the knowledge that in another day and a half the long journey would be over. I'd occasionally called the owner of the yacht on the ship's radiotelephone to keep him informed of our progress and I knew that he would be arranging to meet us in a few days' time, that he would have booked the flights to the U.K. for Pat and Ian and that he would bring out their pay. We were jubilant when we cast off from Paloma to cross the Golfe de Lyon the next morning and thankfully it was a calm day with no prospect of the dreaded Mistral. We had a straight run of 187 miles to one of my favourite destinations, the island of Porquerolles. It was so calm that day that we had to use the engine most of the time but it was an easy journey with no real physical demands so we made the most of our time relaxing in the sun. Changing watch every four hours, we travelled on through the day and night and never saw another vessel, nothing was visible except the sea in every direction and the occasional pod of dolphins that swam around the yacht and put on a spectacular aquatic display for us. At night the sky was filled with millions of stars and the moon cast a silver glow on the calm sea. The morning was pure joy when the sun rose on the horizon and when we later sighted land my spirit sang as my beloved France beckoned me home.

I was elated when we passed between the Presqu'ile de Giens and Porquerolles knowing that in just seven hours or so we'd be at Antibes. Later in the day, as we approached Cap d'Antibes, I called the port office on the VHF set and arranged a mooring. I knew Antibes and the staff at the Captain of the port's office well so we

29. Sailing home

received a warm welcome and it really felt like home; well, it was home, the only one we had now that we'd sold our apartment. We had many friends in Antibes and we were looking forward to catching up on all the latest gossip and also looking forward to meeting up again with our friends in the village where we used to live and where we had our belongings stored. In the meantime, there was work to do on the boat. Small maintenance jobs as well as cleaning inside and out. All four of us started washing off the outside and as I was in a joyful and celebratory mood, I decided it was a good occasion to wet everybody with the nice cold water coming from the hose pipe. It had the desired effect. It was then that I realised I had made a big mistake. Three against one are not good odds when you are the one. I was later told that it was pathetic to start turning the hose on myself and shouting "Look, look. I'm wetting myself" whilst running around the deck in a panic.

After a few days, the owner arrived and treated us all to a meal in a restaurant and the next day Pat and Ian returned to the U.K.. The owner didn't stay for very long after that and as soon as he'd left we went to see our friends in the village and to collect some of our personal effects. We then returned to the yacht to spend the summer season in Antibes. Not a lot happened after that until we were forced into escaping France in July to save the owner money.

CHAPTER 31
TRUSTING DESTINY

The city of flowers

1981 was the year that François Mitterrand became the first socialist president of the Fifth Republic of France and introduced radical left-wing policies. Among other changes, he nationalised a number of industries, introduced a wealth tax, a 39 hour week, a yearly five-week holiday and increased the minimum wage, old age pensions and family and disability allowances. During his time in office, the franc was devalued three times. One of his socialist ideas resulted in us having to leave France. He saw the opportunity to increase government coffers by introducing VAT on charter yachts and like many socialist policies that target the wealthy in the expectation of getting them to contribute more to society, it backfired. Millionaires are no different to the rest of us – they don't like paying taxes; the difference is that they can afford to pay accountants and lawyers who can get them out of it. In this case, the consequence was a mass exodus of yachts from the French ports. They left for Malta, Spain, Italy, Greece and any other country where they could moor their yachts and continue to charter without paying taxes. I recommended to our boss that Marjie and I take the schooner to Italy as soon as possible. He agreed without hesitation. We said goodbye to our friends and cast off.

Sanremo is a tourist resort on the Italian Riviera in Liguria on Italy's northwestern coast. It is set in a bay with mountains to the north, which protect it from the harshest weather conditions so it has a mild Meditteranean climate all year round. The remains of a human settlement from the Paleolithic period have been discovered in the area but it was during the Roman period that the city developed, when it was known as Matutia. In the Middle Ages, the population expanded and moved to higher ground as a defence against repeated attacks by Saracen pirates and the walled village was called La Pigna. It is a maze of covered alleyways, small squares and terraced houses that twist and turn up around a hill, like scales on a pine cone, hence the name, La Pigna, meaning pine cone. It can only be accessed on foot and is separated from the new Sanremo by a gothic stone arch, the Porta di Santo Stefano. When the attacks came to an end, the population returned and the city was rebuilt along the coast. The name Sanremo or San Remo is derived from Sant'Eremo di San Romolo, (Roemu in Ligurian dialect), also known as Saint Romulus of Genoa. He was a ninth-century Genoan bishop who spent a large part of his life in the city and converted the population to Catholicism. Although it is still often referred to as San Remo, the municipality officially adopted the name Sanremo in 2002.

In 1543, having already captured the city of Nice that August, an Ottoman Admiral, who had previously been one of the most notorious pirates of the time, Hayreddin Barbarossa, (Italian for Redbeard), invaded and sacked Sanremo. This is the very same Barbarossa who later conquered Capri in 1553. In the spring of 1554, he returned to attack Sanremo once again and as if that wasn't enough, he attacked and ravaged the city a third time in the same year. In October 1745, the city was bombarded by a British naval formation under the command of Vice-Admiral William Rowley, who had been appointed Commander-in-Chief of the Mediterranean fleet tasked with keeping the French and Spanish fleets out of the Mediterranean during the War of the Austrian Succession. Around about the same time, when the city was facing severe economic hardship, it was in conflict with Genoa over the excessive taxes it was required to pay and in the end, in 1753, it rebelled. The uprising was brutally quashed by the Genoese who then built the fort of Santa Tecla in the port area. A widespread recession followed, which lasted for nearly half a century. Then, in 1794, Napoleon's troops took control of the city and eleven years later, the Italian Republic became the Kingdom of Italy with

Napoleon crowned as King, making his title, "Emperor of the French and King of Italy." Sanremo became the main town of the first French department of the Maritime Alps that was established in the same year. Napoleon was defeated in March 1814 and he abdicated that April. Sanremo became an annex of the Kingdom of Sardinia and power was returned to the House of Savoy. The city suffered squalor and atrocious hygiene conditions and in 1837, a cholera epidemic ravaged the population. A new cemetery and public washhouse were subsequently built to improve the situation.

Between the 19th and 20th centuries, Sanremo attracted writers, poets, scientists, monarchs, and society personalities, all drawn by the beauty of the landscapes and the healthy climate. The Tsarina Maria Alexandrovna visited and spent the winter there in 1864 and donated the palm trees that still decorate the long, impressive marble-tiled promenade today. The Empress Elizabeth of Austria also visited numerous times and as increasing members of the elite European noblesse arrived, palatial homes were built in the architectural style of the Belle Epoch. At the same time flower growing became an important activity whereas previously the surrounding hills had been used for the cultivation of oranges, mandarins and lemons.

Alfred Nobel, the creator of the Nobel Prizes, also chose to retire in Sanremo, to the villa that still carries his name. It is an elegant and impressive house in Moorish style which is now open to the public. He was born in Stockholm in 1833 and was a chemical engineer who, whilst working in Paris, had met a young Italian chemist who had invented nitroglycerine. At the time it was considered to be too highly explosive to have any practical uses. However, Alfred's father was an engineer and inventor; he built bridges and other buildings and was interested in finding different ways of blasting rocks. So father and son experimented with nitroglycerine, trying to make it more commercially useful and less dangerous. Alfred persisted even though there had been several accidents, including one which killed his younger brother. He continued trying out different additives to make it safer and found that adding a type of fine sand enabled him to produce a paste which could then be shaped into rods. He called this concoction, which could be inserted into drilling holes, Dynamite. He got a patent for it in 1867 and invented a detonator which worked from lighting a fuse. The inventions meant that the costs involved in construction work were greatly reduced and he eventually had factories in more than 20 countries. He also invented artificial rubber, leather and silk. For the last five years of his life, he lived in the Sanremo house and continued with his experiments. The neighbours weren't too pleased with all the bangs and he built a pier out from the beach to make blowing them up less likely. By the time of his death in 1896, he had taken out 355 patents and was a wealthy man. In his last will and testament, he wrote that much of his fortune was to be used to give prizes to those who have done their best for humanity in the field of physics, chemistry, physiology or medicine, literature and peace. The relatives, among others, were not very happy about this and it took four years for all parties to agree to his wishes. The first prizes were awarded in Stockholm and Oslo in 1901.

In the 20th century, the city prospered and grew and prestigious hotels, the casino, the golf course, the racetrack, the stadium and other structures were built, including the cable car to Mount Bignone, which at the time was the longest in the world. After the end of WWI, in April 1920, the Sanremo Conference was held by the allied powers in the Villa Devachan to decide the future of the former territories of the Ottoman Turkish Empire, one of the defeated powers in the war. It was attended by the Prime Ministers of Great Britain, France and Italy. It also established Germany's obligations under the Versailles Peace Treaty and the Allies position on Soviet Russia.

During the 1930s, tourism became a major contributor to the Sanremo economy and the flower-growing industry 'blossomed'. Fortunes declined with WWII, but after the end of the war, it flourished as tourists began to stay in the summer as well as the winter months. As demand grew, a new marina was built for leisure craft at the eastern end of the old port (Porto Vecchio). The construction of the marina, Portosole, (the port of the sun,) began in the late 60's and was finished in 1977. It has two shipyards, berths for over 800 yachts, chandleries and yacht agencies, as well as shops and professionals offering all manner of services for every size of yacht. It was to Portosole that we went to escape the money grab of Mitterrand's government.

Taking risks

Marjie and I thoroughly enjoyed our time in Sanremo. The yacht was not used at all by the owner but we did a two-week cruise with his former business partner and a one-week cruise with one of his business associates. We met many other yachts' crews; some that we already knew, who like ourselves, had left France to avoid the VAT imposed by Mitterrand and others who were cruising from various ports in the Mediterranean. In effect, it was a wonderful, lengthy paid holiday with nothing much to do other than soak up the sunshine and immerse ourselves in the Italian way of life and the joy of living in such a lively, colourful, splendid city. We got to know and like Sanremo so much that we still regularly make the one and a half-hour drive from our current home to visit the superb market, mostly spending a night in a hotel there beforehand to extend our stay and indulge ourselves sampling the delicious, mouth-watering Italian cuisine. Meanwhile, the disappearance of the yachts caused a recession in the South of France. The ports, as well as the associated industries of yachting and the suppliers, were all suffering economically. When President Mitterrand visited and saw for himself the deserted ports and the damage that his policy had caused, he reversed his decision and little by little yachts returned to secure a berth for the winter. Many of them, however, had already happily settled into new ports around the Mediterranean and chose to stay where they were. For us though, the stay at Portosole was over and we returned to Antibes at the end of the season.

We wasted no time; as soon as it was possible for us to leave the yacht we visited our ruin, bought professional-quality machinery, a chain saw, strimmer, motorised lawn mower, bill hooks etc. and began renovating it and clearing the overgrown three acres of land. We'd applied to the relevant authorities for permission to restore it and after a lengthy wait, permission was refused. We sought advice from various professionals and were recommended to employ an architect to submit plans and apply again to the authorities in Toulon, which we did and after another lengthy wait, were refused a second time. We were disappointed as we'd invested almost everything that we'd made on the sale of the village apartment and were stuck with a few useless stone walls on a plot of land. Returning to my theory that if you don't take risks, you don't get very far, we took the rather rash decision to rebuild the ruin anyway. It would have been a risky decision in any circumstances but to do so after we'd applied for permission and been refused twice was pushing the boundaries a bit but we'd spent our money and we had the building or what little there was of it so concluded that we had no other choice. We bought an old caravan in Nice and had it delivered and sited on our land so that we had somewhere to stay whilst we worked there. What happened next, however, is the subject for another book - the police arrived and whisked away the illegal workers who had been employed by our Spanish builder and we were forced to hide away for a while. We did eventually achieve our goal of self-sufficiency though.

The pool table purchase was concluded so we had plenty to occupy ourselves with. We spent time maintaining the schooner but as she was all fibreglass, there was really very little to do so we were able to concentrate our efforts on getting to know how the pool tables operated. I knew nothing whatsoever about pool, I'd never played and had no interest in playing, so I had to learn a few of the rules. The campsites closed down at the end of September and the pool tables had to be removed. The Australian worked with me for a few weeks whilst we moved the pool tables, re-covered them and looked for and found new sites for them. We bought a Citroën GS, had a tow bar fitted, hitched the trailer that came with the pool tables to my car and drove to the city of Alessandria in the region of Piedmont in Northwestern Italy, which is where the pool tables were manufactured. The Australian accompanied me and introduced me to the manufacturers. I bought two more pool tables, taking the total number to 26 and we drove back and sited them. I was satisfied then that I had sufficient of them sited to provide a reasonable income, yet not so many that Marjie and I couldn't manage them along with keeping our job on the schooner and developing the ruin. The winter passed, and by the spring of the following year, with the help of an experienced Morrocan mason called Mohammad, we had finished renovating the ruin to a good enough standard for us to move in. We'd built another room on top of the existing one, which was our one and only bedroom. We also added a room at ground level, which was to be our kitchen/dining room. The original ruined area had become our sitting room. We'd dug a trench and laid a water pipe and we had electricity. We were so happy with the result. We had a marvellous view and were within walking distance of an attractive medieval hill village. We were on our way to our goal of creating a self-sufficient smallholding.

Some things are meant to be

In 1982, the schooner was hardly used at all and we wondered why it was ever sailed to the Mediterranean. The owner seemed to be too busy expanding his business to have time for sailing. I find it difficult to understand why, when they already have more money than they could possibly spend, these tycoons don't spend more time enjoying themselves. I have only met one person, a self-made millionaire, who to my way of thinking, did what I like to think I would do or would have done had the opportunity presented itself. At the age of 45, he'd made enough money to live on comfortably for the rest of his life if he sold his business and he did just that. He built a house in a picturesque village in the hills behind Cannes, bought himself a 48ft motor yacht and cruised around the Mediterranean with his wife. When he was satisfied that he'd done all that he'd wanted to do, he sold the boat, bought a sailing vessel and set off across the Atlantic to cruise the Caribbean, eventually coming back to Cannes to settle down to a stress-free life. We became great friends and it is sad that he is no longer with us.

It was disappointing not to be sailing the schooner but fortunately, it gave us all the spare time we needed to finish restoring the house completely inside and outside. We had cleared most of the land and by the summer were able to accommodate guests in the caravan. Meanwhile, I was busy travelling the length and breadth of the Côte d'Azur and inland to search for new sites for the pool tables. I'd fitted a towing hitch to our old Renault 4 van and used that mostly for the pool table business so that Marjie had use of the Citroën whilst I was away. The pool tables weighed 500 kilos and the old van towed them without difficulty even when driving up into the mountains, where I had a few of them sited. Marjie, as usual, was indispensable. She travelled with me and helped whenever it was practical and convenient to do so and we soon developed a good system for lifting the thick, heavy slates. She also helped me re-cover them and became an expert at emptying the cash boxes and counting the money! For the summer season, we removed ones from the bars that weren't working well and sited them in numerous campsites where they made much more money, so we had to call at the campsites to empty the cashboxes every week. That presented difficulties if the owner or his guests were on the boat for a rare trip on the schooner. On those occasions, we had a trusted friend who occupied himself with our pool tables when we were unable to do so ourselves. We didn't go very far on the yacht and it was generally just for long weekends with friends of the owner and a two-week cruise with his ex-wife and her girlfriends; that was actually a riot and the best trip of all!

We had a verbal agreement to remain as professional crew on the schooner until such time as the owner had other ideas. In the early spring of 1983, I arranged to have the schooner hauled out of the water to be antifouled at the slipway on the Ile Sainte Marguerite. It was too good an opportunity not to sail there as we'd done so little sailing during the previous two seasons. As soon as we were clear of the port, we hoisted the sails and made our way to the slipway. The boat was hauled out of the water, chocked into position and we went home. We visited the island each day to supervise the outstanding jobs that had to be done and when everything had been completed, the boat was launched. Whilst still moored at the island, in the company of the yard employees, we checked all the seacocks and fittings to verify that nothing had happened to cause any problems. This is standard procedure; boats are designed to be afloat - hauling them out of the water and chocking them up ashore puts different stresses on the hull that could cause problems.

When we and the yard workmen were satisfied that the bilges were dry and everything was as it should be, we cast off for what was to be our final sail. With the sails set and the afternoon breeze already picking up, we had an invigorating sail back to Antibes. As it was late afternoon when we'd finished clearing up and washing off the boat, we treated ourselves to a meal in a restaurant that evening and slept on board. The next morning, we were anxious to get back to our new home in the hills so we showered, had breakfast and packed our bags with what little of our personal belongings remained aboard and loaded them into the Citroën. Before leaving and locking the boat, we thoroughly checked everything once more, secured the sails and put on the sail covers, checked the bilges, the seacocks and fittings and the mooring lines. When we'd convinced ourselves that there were no problems, we locked up and went home, secure in the knowledge that all was well. On the third day of being there, the telephone rang and it was the owner of the schooner. What he told me gave me an almighty shock.

"I've just had a call from the port office and they've told me my yacht has sunk." At first, I thought he was joking but soon realised he was deadly serious and with that realisation I told him we would go to Antibes immediately, which we did. When we got there, the yacht was above water but lower than usual. It had gone down until the keel sat on the bottom. I made all the necessary arrangements to have the water pumped out and have her refloated. When the boatyard employees searched for the reason why she sank, they discovered that a jubilee clip had sprung open on the prop shaft seal, which was almost inaccessible. I was horrified to learn that our lives had been dependant on a virtually inaccessible jubilee clip. It could have happened at any time whilst we were in the middle of the treacherous Bay of Biscay and we would have been no more. For this to have happened on a new, quality yacht, filled me with dread and I decided that I'd had enough of sailing on modern fibreglass yachts that weren't fitted with traditional stern glands and whose safety depended on crew crawling around in the bilges on a regular basis checking a multitude of jubilee clips. How fortunate that it happened whilst the yacht was moored up in a shallow harbour!

Not long after this, he told us that he wanted the yacht sailed back to the U.K., something which didn't appeal to us. We had our fabulous little house, the pool table business, lots of friends and were champing at the bit to start something new. I'd been sailing since 1966 and it was way past time for me to have a new goal. We were enjoying being in our new home, situated on a small hill with amazing views over the surrounding countryside and the nearby village. When the delivery crew arrived to sail the boat back to the U.K., I was more than happy to hand them the keys. We didn't hang around. We'd had enough of sailing. We wished them a safe passage, walked down the gangplank, climbed into our car and drove off into the hills to a new and completely different adventure.

How about a review?

This book has been a long time in the making and I've worked hard to get it to this point. It has been edited countless times so I'm really pleased that it's finally made it to the point that I no longer want to add or take anything away!

Like all authors in this digital age I need reviews. Without them a book will sit sadly in cyberspace and no one will read it!

So, if you could find the time to put a review on Amazon I would really be grateful. I look forward to reading it.

Unfortunately there is no way for authors to reply to reviews on Amazon, but if you would like a reply, I'd love to hear from you. Please go to my website and drop me a line.

The website address is:
www.happymariner.wordpress.com

OTHER BOOKS BY THE AUTHOR

PAID TO LIVE THE DREAM
If you like books about sailing adventures combined with an uplifting tale of achieving your dream, you will enjoy this compelling memoir.

A TUGMAN'S TALE
This book is extracted from part 1 of 'Paid to Live the Dream'. Anthony was born in the riverside town of Gravesend, which was a base for the steam tugs which operated from London docks to the mouth of the river Thames. A flash of inspiration had prompted him to apply for a job. Chance would have it that there was a vacancy on the very day that he plucked up the courage to walk down the Terrace Pier and timidly enquire.

VOYAGING TO THE SUN
This book is extracted from Part 2 of 'Paid to Live the Dream', and tells of Anthony's adventures after he left the Thames tugs (described in his book 'A Tugman's Tale'. After a gruelling six and a half years spent aboard the Thames steam tugs, Anthony was ready for a change.

YOU COULDN'T MAKE IT UP
This is a short book of amusing and inconceivable anecdotes from the author's experiences afloat.

THE CANCER COMPLEXITY
Anthony describes with his usual light touch his experiences of being diagnosed with prostate cancer, and then the double whammy of contracting Leukaemia as well. He also explores the research into causes and treatments – and the sense of humour is never far away.

THE AUTHOR

Anthony Edwards was born in Gravesend but since 1975 has lived mostly in Provence in the South of France with his wife, Marjie. Together they achieved their goal of establishing a self-sufficient, organic smallholding and later went on to study complementary medicine. He had a successful practice as a Kinesiologist, Hypnotist and Psychotherapist in Monaco before moving to York for nine years, where he continued his studies and founded a consultancy and teaching enterprise. He has made guest appearances on several radio programs in France and the U.K. He and Marjie returned to Provence in 2000, where they now live with Miss Daisy, their thoroughly spoilt, self-opinionated cat and persist in their never-ending studies.

Printed in Great Britain
by Amazon

24104202R00175